Dear Mama Williams

OTHER BOOKS BY
LYCRECIA WILLIAMS HOOVER
&
DALE VINICUR:

Still In Love With You (A Daughter's True Story)

Dear Mama Williams

Sympathy Cards & Letters
to the Hank Williams Family

FROM THE COLLECTION OF LYCRECIA WILLIAMS HOOVER

ARRANGED & EDITED BY DALE VINICUR

Audrey's Dream Inc
Nashville, Tennessee
a 501 (c) (3) organization
www.audreysdream.org

Proceeds from the sale of this book go to Audrey's Dream Inc and
The Hank & Audrey Williams Center of Nashville

Softcover jacket design by Gerri Winchell Findley of Go Design and Dale Vinicur

Audrey's Dream logo design by Gerri Winchell Findley of Go Design

Published by Audrey's Dream Inc, 206 Ocala Drive, Nashville, Tennessee

Library of Congress Cataloging-in-Publication Data

Hoover, Lycrecia Williams, 1941-
Vinicur, Dale 1945-
    Dear Mama Williams : Sympathy Cards & Letters to the Hank Williams Family / Lycrecia Williams Hoover & Dale Vinicur

    ISBN 0-9762137-0-2 softcover
    ISBN 0-9762137-1-0 hardcover

Printed in the United States of America

DEDICATION

I would like to dedicate this book to all Daddy's friends. By "friends" I mean his fans. I've had so many come up to me over the years and say, *"I never met Hank, but I feel like I knew him."*

This book is very special. All the letters and cards were written over 50 years ago and every one shows how much people young, old, and inbetween loved Daddy and his music. They thought of him as a member of their family or a close personal friend. There was no age boundary for his fans then and the same holds true today.

As I have matured, I understand more about my dad's talent and the influence he had on people – how he touched their lives – and it makes me want to cry.

I'm glad Mother thought of saving these cards and letters and I'm glad Dale and I were able to put them into a book. I hope they come to mean as much to you as they do to me.

May God Bless You All,

Lycrecia

Lycrecia Williams Hoover

JANUARY 1, 1953...

The sad news traveled quickly across this nation and around the world. Hank Williams, the greatest of all hillbilly singers, was dead. No one could believe it was really true. He was only 29 years old.

25,000 fans stood outside the Municipal Auditorium in Montgomery, Alabama where the funeral service was being held on a cold January 4th to pay their final respects. Thousands more waited at the cemetery. Tribute songs flooded the airwaves. Lights were dimmed on the stages of the Louisiana Hayride, the Grand Ole Opry, and in every little honky-tonk where country music was played.

Radio DJs told their listeners Hank's mama was lonesome and blue, and gave out her name and address for anyone wishing to send a card or note of sympathy to the family:

Lillian (Mrs. W.W.) Stone
(some still called her Mrs. Williams or "Mama" Williams)
318 N. McDonough Street
Montgomery, Alabama

Men and women, young and old, near and far, they wrote, not always knowing what to say, but wanting to at least let the Williams family know how they loved Hank and how they would miss him.

"I feel that Hank isn't really dead, not as long as people remember and sing his songs."

"Mama" Williams, who followed her son through life's gateway a little more than two years later

These cards and letters were preserved by Audrey Williams and passed on to her daughter Lycrecia Williams Hoover, sister of Hank Williams Jr. and beloved step-daughter of Hank Williams Sr.

FROM THE EDITOR

Recently, Lycrecia Williams Hoover, daughter of Hank & Audrey Williams, put some collectible items up for sale on eBay, including several packets of sympathy cards and letters sent to the family after Hank's sudden and untimely death New Year's Eve, 1952-53.

David Mitchell of Alexander City, Alabama purchased one of these packets and immediately called Lycrecia to suggest turning them into a book. (She and I previously wrote *Still In Love With You, A Daughter's True Story*, published in 1989.) A few weeks later David, Lycrecia, and I sat in a corner of the Hank Williams Museum in Montgomery and read the letters of a 14-year-old girl in New York who wrote *"Hank's loss was the angels' gain"* and a mother in Georgia who had lost a child of her own and addressed the envelope simply to: Mrs. Williams, Montgomery, Alabama.

After returning home, Lycrecia brought me the big plastic bin with the cards and letters Audrey had the foresight to preserve, and over the next two weekends I read every one.

I was deeply moved by these voices from the past which took me back in time to the America of January 1, 1953, when our boys were still fighting and dying in Korea, when young folks used words like "swell" and "tops," and when a great collective sadness was felt over the death of the much-loved, legendary singer/songwriter Hank Williams Sr.

We are proud to present these cards and letters in all their original simplicity and timeless beauty to *you* – the Hank Williams or Country Music fan, the nostalgia collector, or maybe one who has recently lost a loved one yourself. People care... often more than you know.

Dale Vinicur

Note: Some light editing of the cards & letters was done, such as brightening colors yellowed by age, correcting grammar/spelling in the typed letters for readability only, & excerpting to avoid repetition. dv

Dear Mama,

"While listening at the new song of Hank I thought of you, the one who loved him more than anyone on earth..."

Evelyn Hodges
Haynesville LA

Independence La.
April 24th 1953

Dear Mama williams

I heard Little Bill Stanby on the Happniss exchange talking about you and said you was blue. And he said for all the Fran's of Hank to write you. well Im a Hank williams Fan club member I hope you wasent be mad at me for Calling you mama williams but Little Bill Said we Could call you mama williams

I dont want you feeling blue we all love you. you are the mother of our Hank. And God knows we loved him, and still do. His records are still going strong, and will for years to come for we the club will see to that

I like his new record that has just came out. I think it will be a hit too. if I sound a little off dont think nothing, when it comes to talking about Hank Im just plain Nuts

well I guess I had better stop for now, I hope you feel better. I guess you will get plenty of letters I hope so. I know you Cant write to eur one but it would make me very Happy if you find time to write me. Im just a plain country Gal And Im proud of it. You will hear from me again I love you very much, Love always.

Dorothy Hand

January 12, 1953

Dear Mrs. Stone

While sitting here listening to your son singing I can barely write for the tears on my face. We sure are going to miss him. I want you to know from my whole family we send our deepest sympathy.

One day over a very weak station someone said on this program for all his friends to write to you. A person hardly knows what to write and to say in a time like this.

My little girl said she just couldn't understand why he had to die and I told her that God wanted him to go to Heaven, to help sing for the Angels up there, and she answered, *"Well, he could have taken someone else who couldn't sing, not one of our best singers."*

May God Bless and keep you in these dark days that are to come. Our church sent up a prayer for you and your family. I've prayed myself since he died for his soul, that God has taken him home forever to rest. A friend always and one we'll never forget.

Mrs. Campbell
Honea Path, South Carolina

My Dear Mother Williams

Thanks for the beautiful Christmas card. I'll treasure that because it has Hank's name written there. I cannot write down on paper how I feel about Our Hank. I usually let my heart run away when I talk about him.

I have one wish and dream. I'd love to come to your home and see Hank's room and feel his nearness everywhere. Do you think Hank would care? I seen the Opry once in '49. I saw Hank sing. He stole my heart. No other singer, and there is a lot of good ones, will ever be able to take Hank's place. My star has fallen.

But he'll never be forgotten. I'll help see to that. I have all of Hank's records and I request his records on my favorite show every day. I pray that God in Heaven will hold him close to his heart. I pray that Hank will be one of the first to meet Our Lord when He comes to collect His chosen few onto Himself.

May God Bless you, too, The Mother of Country Music.

> Sincerely with love
> Your gal,
> Dorothy Raschke
> Eau Claire, Wisconsin

January 13, 1953

Dear Mrs. Williams & Family

Truly my heart has been made heavy and sorrowful by the passing of your son and brother and our very favorite radio star singer and entertainer. I know this loss is Heaven's gain although we can't understand and with the many thousands you all have our sympathy. I lost my husband and was left with five boys to take both mother and father's place. While my sorrow and grief was heavy I depended on the Great God above. With the singers and players of WSM Nashville I have been able to keep going with the encouragement of the wonderful songs and the prayers of God's people. I have had a trial. I have a 19 year old boy with bad heart trouble that Drs say can't be cured so I just have to look for the best and trust the one who holds life in his hands. He knows what is best for us. As this son has to spend very much time in bed listening to the radio he is collecting pictures from cowboys and favorite singers. He would love to have one of Hank if possible. We was given an opportunity to visit WSM Grand Ole Opry Oct 11 last. Enjoyed it very much but was disappointed not getting a chance to see or meet Hank or Ernest Tubb after waiting so long...

My oldest son named Hank or Henry A. married a girl from Memphis Tennessee named Dorothy Williams. I guess that is why we loved Hank's singing and playing so well. You all seem very near to us. So if you all will please write to me I would appreciate it so very much. It sure would encourage my sons and I.

Mrs. Lester J. Becker
Alexandria, Virginia

"... America was built and is held together by guys like Hank Williams. Men who claim no glory or look for personal reward, but find reward in making others happy. Hank did all those things when he sang to people. Jesus knew that and that's why he took him home..."

Goodbye, *God Bless You*
Kenny Thomas
Montague, Michigan

Logansport Ind.
Dec. 13 54.

My Dear Mrs. Stone

Am almost ashamed to write as
its been so long since I got your lovely
letter and was more than happy to
recieve it. We've had so much bad
luck that is the reason for my not
writing. My husbands mother broke her
hip and I've had all the care of her.
She's 81 but, thank God we still have her.

We were to get our vocation in
September and we did so want to come to
Montgomery but, things did'nt turn out that
way. We were so thankful that some
one remembered and had that day in
September sit aside for that wonderful
boy of yours. No one in this world will
ever write the beautiful songs like he did

I try to listen to Ernest Tubbs show on
Saturday nite and some one generally says
they asked to gen or this or that

song is for you. Its sure nice that
people remember and I'm sure more
of them would if they meet you. We
think you are a wonderful lady no
more than eve talked to you in
Meridian that day.

        Well, will bring this to a close
and hope you'll forgive me for not
writing sooner hope you can find
time again some day to drop us a
few line til' then we wish you
and yours the best of every thing in
the coming new year.

                Love and best wishes.
                Mr. & Mrs. Russell Barney
                936 - 17th St.
                        Logansport Ind.

May God Bless him and keep
his soul in heaven and in every
heart of country music lovers.
  Yours truly,
  Joseph Profetto

January 8, 1953

Dear Mrs. Stone,

I don't know exactly what to say to you since I have never met you or have never met Hank either. But I will try to say something.

I was like many others very shocked at the report of Hank's death. I always listened to all of Hank's records. I like all of them. I thought that Hank had a wonderful voice & I loved to listen to him.

Mrs. Stone, I would like to have a copy of some of Hank's songs. And I would like to know where I can get a hold of some of them. You see the reason I would like to have them is that when my father comes out here from California I would like for him to sing them for me. He is a singer and plays the guitar with one hand. We were in a wreck when I was about a year old. He lost his arm in the wreck. Before that he was a very good guitar player. But after he lost his arm he had to learn to play all over again. My mother says that he can still play it well as before the accident. I haven't seen my father for 14 years, I am 16 going on 17. Mother and Dad were divorced.

I am very fond of western music since my Dad sings western music. I am in the mixed chorus and girl's chorus here in the Ashland High School. We have to try out for each of them.

Mrs. Stone, if it wouldn't be too much trouble I would like to have some pictures of Hank. I also would like to have some pictures of you.

Do you have any other children? If so I would like to have pictures of them also. And also what are their names, if I might ask.

Well as I can't think of any thing else to say I will close.

Your Friend,

Roberta Moore
Ashland, Kansas

Dear Mrs. Stone and Family,

I just want to tell you how deeply that my family and I regret that you have lost "Hank." It must be a comfort to you to know how deeply we and millions of others just like us mourn for him.

I am the mother of three boys, one 9, one 5, and one 3. Hank was a favorite of theirs and when the radio announcer interrupted the program to announce that he was dead – the 5-year-old came into the bedroom and grabbed me and with big tears streaming down his face said, *"Mother, he said Hank Williams was dead."* That afternoon Keith Ward – a disc jockey on KJBC Midland, Texas – played a 15 minute program of his records in memory of him – and when he played *Setting the Woods on Fire* which is Bobby's (the 3-year-old's) favorite, he jumped up and said, *"Listen, Mother, he ain't dead – he's singing 'Setting the Woods on Fire.'"*

So, Mrs. Stone, you see – when children can love a person as deeply as that and especially when they've never seem him just heard him sing, there should be no doubt in your mind that you have only lost his body. Our beloved Hank Williams will live in memory forever and ever.

I am going to close for now, and I hope that you can be brave and strong as he would want you to be.

We send our love and deepest sympathy to you.

Mr. & Mrs. Cecil Scarborough
James, Bobby and Terry

Goldsmith, Texas

"... And dear Lord as you're watching
From way up above,
Let Hank know how much
we cherished him
And how much he was loved.

Tell him we'll remember him
Till the day that we die.
Till the day we meet him
In your heaven in the sky."

From the poem
"Our Beloved Hank Williams"

by: Miss Jane Amodio
Albertson, New York

January 9, 1953

Dear Mrs. Williams,

I've never written a letter like this before and I don't think this one will be tops. But here goes anyway.

While I was listening to the Home Town Frolic I heard the most terrible news since my grandfather's death and that was quite a few years ago.

I still can't believe it and I want to share your sorrow. All of my friends and I feel the same way. Hank died on New Years Day and the next morning a very dear friend of mine walked 2 miles to my house and cried with me for 3 hours without stopping. Have no fear Mrs. Williams. Hank has millions of admirers that are sharing your grief now.

I'm from Texas really, but we came out to Long Island for my mother's health.

I'm crazy for cowboys, horses, and western songs and Hank was my favorite. We have a ranch in Texas and I'm homesick for it and then hearing Hank died, well, it doesn't make living so good. I am truly sorry Mrs. Williams.

But we can rest assured he is in good hands with our Lord and I know also Hank takes a peek down every day.

A Hank Williams Fan

Doris ("Tex")
East Marion, New York

Twas a lad who had singing as his fame,
Old ones loved him, the young ones the same.
He sang songs of love, also the blues,
We loved him, Hank Williams, we hated to lose.

Raised on a farm with lots of love not money.
To sing any song comes to him easy 'tis funny.
He sang them pretty and straight from the heart,
Hank Williams is in Heaven, from him we must part.

As a kid he sang for his own time and pleasure,
There in Montgomery, Alabama they found a treasure.
Then in Nashville he became loved by near and far.
Now in Heaven, Hank Williams is God's shining star.

Luke the Drifter he was known as, of him you all know,
He sang songs of weddings and God's path to you show.
He wrote many songs and sang them lovely, too,
Hank Williams is gone, we hope to meet him soon.

Good-bye dear loved one, from this earth you are missed,
In our hearts dear friend you'll never be replaced.
The records we have will never collect any dust.
If we ever get to meet above, I pray you will sing for us.

God Bless You, Hank

God Bless all of you

Mr. & Mrs. Ira Grafton
Tovey, Illinois

Jan. 10, 1953
Peekskill, New York

Dear Mrs. Stone,

I just heard Don Larkin of the Home Town Frolic, WAAT Newark, New Jersey announce about Hank Williams' funeral. I feel sorry about his death. When I think of him I just can't believe that he is dead and when I play his records it seems as if he is singing to me in person.

There are times when I look at his picture with a smile on his face as big as his heart.

May God Bless him and keep his soul in heaven and in every heart of country music lovers.

Yours truly,
Joseph Profetto

April 24, 1953

Dear Mama Williams,

Hope you don't mind me calling you Mama Williams. I listen to little Bill Stanley every morning. And on Hank's program this morning I heard him say that you were blue. He gave us your address and boy, does he get the mail for the Hank Williams program. Hank is my favorite singer. I'm really crazy about hillbilly music. I write to radio stations and ask them to play Hank's records. Will you send me a picture of you and Hank? Well I guess I'd better tell a little about myself. I am 5'5" tall I have black hair and dark brown eyes and I'm 16 years old. I will tell a little about my family. I have 2 sisters and 1 brother. My father raises strawberries and my mother works out. Do you like strawberries? I have one cowboy book and it's all about Hank and I have one 8x10 picture of Hank I have it in a frame. On March 31 when they had the Hank Williams program all over the country I had school but I didn't go I stood home and listened to the radio all that day. I am just crazy about hillbillies. I sing hillbilly music all the time. I wanted to get your address a long time ago but I didn't know how to get it. But now I have it I will write to you all the time if you want me to. Send me a picture of Hank and you. Hank's new record is going strong. Sure wish you could come to Hammond and get some strawberries.

Sincerely,

Mary Jane Calamia
Hammond, Louisiana

Allentown New Jersey.
Jaunry 19 53.

Mrs Stone this is to let you
no how sorry and heart we all
are to learn of your son hank
and one of our favorite singers
death- and you have our deepist
hart felt simpthy so we are
saying to you try to cheer up.
And just no that Earth has no
sorrys that heaven cant not
heal. now this letter is from
a group of colored listners
agian and agian we have your
   simpathy for the fine Boy thats
gone on.
   From Aleathia mae stephens
and others   Allen town YJ.

January 11, 1953

"...I became interested in his songs through my boy who has listened and learned those songs for the past 7 years since he was 8 years old, hoping some day he might play and sing as Hank did, who was his idol. You must be a very proud even though sad mother because he was such a wonderful artist. You shall meet again in the great beyond for life is just a struggle for us all to an everlasting eternity hereafter.

We all pray for you and for the repose of the dear boy's Soul."

God Bless you and yours
I am very sincerely,

Eileen Cremin (Mrs. Dennis)
Peapack, New Jersey

January 7, 1953

Dear Mrs. Stone,

I as well as thousands of others was so sorry to hear of Hank's death. He touched the hearts of thousands, especially the boys in Korea.

You see, I just returned from Korea myself and I should know how he was with the boys over there. He was wonderful and his name will never die.

I can truthfully say the world has lost something great in the Hillbilly field.

Sincerely,

SFC Don Hazelip
Livermore, Kentucky

February 4, 1953

"... Mrs. Stone, I'm just a country gal, and married have three children 2 boys and one little girl. My husband is a farmer and we are very poor people.

I guess you can tell the way I write I'm not well educated, but I wanted to write to you and tell you what's in my heart and how we feel about your Hank.

My little girl is 4 years. She cries every time they play on the radio one of the tunes about Hank's death. She says, *'Mommy, Hank's not dead, he's up in Heaven singing'* and that makes me cry also. She and I have a good cry nearly every day.

Mrs. Stone, I wish I could see and talk to you. You must be a wonderful person. It sure would be a great honor to meet you, but that probably won't ever happen.

Mrs. Stone, just one more word about your son before I finish. Your Hank must have been a swell guy and have a real likeable personality to have the whole United States to like him so much. I will say again he must have been a wonderful person.

I sure would love to hear from you so very much. I know you can't answer all the letters you receive every day. I must hush. Hope you won't think too bad about my letter to you.

Forgive all my mistakes and my stationery and this awful pencil, my boys have taken all the fountain pens to school.

Good-bye and *God Bless you and keep you.*"

Your friend,

Mrs. Jean Chastain
Alicia, Arkansas

Dear Mrs. Williams and sister,

We are sending a poem that was written by Joe Horoshak who was an ardent fan of Hank Williams. He thought very deeply of his songs and his singing. When he heard that he had passed away he wrote this poem. We hope you will appreciate it as much as we do.

Sincerely yours,
Mrs. Paul Horoshak
Eveleth, Minnesota

HANK WILLIAMS

Dear Hank Williams
You will never know
How much we listeners
Will miss you so.

I admired your singing
With all my heart
And such a disaster
Has driven us apart.

I'll always remember
Wherever you are
As America's most famous
Singing star.

Our Lord must have had
Some chores to do
He needed a good man
So he called on you.

You were so young
And so very great
That our Almighty
Couldn't even wait.

As I said before,
To us you meant a lot
And in our country
You'll never be forgot.

----Joe Horoshak

Eveleth, Minn.

Jan. 8, 1953
Munich, Ger.

Mrs. Williams,

I am a soldier over here in Ger.
and have listened to Hank Williams
sing, ever since he started singing
over the radio. And I have enjoyed
listening to him very much.

At this time I wish to express
my feelings for you and the
relatives.

I know it seems rather strange
for a soldier to be writing to
you personaly, but I thought if you
understood how much all the G.I.'s
worshiped him it might not be so
hard to take.
I certainly hope everything goes alright
from now on.

Sincerly

Cpl. Jane L. Snelling
"A." Bty. 20 6 F. A. Bn.
43rd. Inf. Div.
A.P.O. 112
% Postmaster
N.Y., N.Y.

"... When we think of Hank we think of the late Jimmie Rodgers who was a great favorite of ours and even though it will make 20 years that Jimmie died we often speak of him and still play his original records. I know that we'll be playing Hank's records years from now and we'll still think of him. When I think of Hank, it reminds me of the song that was made for Jimmie Rodgers but instead I see Hank's name in it. It goes:

Life is filled with sorrow
Each day demands a toll
We can not date tomorrow
For any living soul.
And so it was with Hank Williams
When angels called one day
They needed a songbird in Heaven
So they took Hank away."

Yours in deepest sympathy,

Orianna Bisson & Family
Worcester, Massachusetts

Creston Iowa
Jan 12 - 53.

Mrs Williams.
318. No. Madonna.
Montgomery Alabama,

Dear Mrs Williams,
I am writeing you to extend
to you and Family my most
Sincere Sympathy in the
Loss of your most Beloved Son
Hank, It was a severe blow to
the whole World but the greatest
Love of all of all is "Mothers Love"
I want to Congratulate you in
in haveing the most iloved
and Wunderful Son in the World
as you know now how many
loyal Friends he had. He will
live in the hearts of all forever
No one can ever take his
place in the music World.
No one could of been any more
shocked as I was siting at
the Radio when the Sad news
Came Hank Williams had
passed away so suddenly, I
never have heard what the
cause was Wont 4 in please

drop me a line tell me about
it. I set at the Radio and
heard his Pals and Buddys
at WSM Nashville Tennessee
sing his songs paid him so
many fine Compliments
I cried along with rest I
have been a Constant
Radio Fan of Hanks for over
3 years seem like I
realy did know him Every
one would Love him with
his most beautiful songs
I would love to have a
picture of him If you have
any. as I never saw any
pictures of him. It would be
so nice to have one Please
drop me a line. One of Hanks
Radio friends. Bernice Reed.

The Home Beyond

1229 Mason Street
San Antonio, Texas
January 1, 1953

Dear Mrs. Williams —

I was very sorry to hear about Hank's passing away. I, as I know many others will, want to extend my sincerest sympathies in this hour of grief.

Hank has been my husband's favorite, as well as mine. We shall never hear Jambalaya, You Win Again, I Saw the Light, Crazy Heart, and many, many others without thinking of Hank.

In fact, Jambalaya might be called my husband's and my love song. We danced it, my husband sang it and we listened to it during the time we went together prior to our marriage last August. The first gift I ever gave my husband was Hank's recording of Jambalaya.

My husband is going to Korea for the second time. He is on leave now before reporting to Seattle on the 15th.

We are but two of the many thousands who mourn Hank's passing.

So please accept our deepest sympathy and God Bless You and keep you.

Sincerely,
Barbara Smith

3516 East Clay St
Richmond 23, Va
January 3, 1953

Dear Mrs Williams,
    I would like
to express my
deepest and sincerest
sympathy to you
during your bereavement

My heart goes out to you in
sorrow at the loss of your son,
but to know the esteem and
admiration in which he was
held by the many millions
that knew and loved him and
his songs, will certainly be some
comfort to you. His name and
songs will last forever.
    I have many of his records
and his autograph which I value
a great deal. I had the pleasure
of meeting him when he made
a personal appearance here last
year. After meeting Hank I realize
that you must have been very

proud of your
famous son.
If any pictures
of Hank are avail-
able I would app-
reciate knowing
where I could get
one. I have a scrap
book on Hank Williams
and I don't think it would
be complete with out a picture
of him.
Sincerely,
Ann Burton
age 15

Thinking of
You

With
Best Wishes
as
Always

—so who his family is:

If there was ever a good singer and song writer, He was one. I just love that song "Jambulia." I was really surprised and kind of hurt when I heard of Hank's death, I sure you was too and probably more hurt than I was.

I would like to do something but I guess a card is all I can do.

Jane Kay Shilling
age 13
grade 8

P.S. If you possibly would have time write

He
Is Just
Away

Just a friend,
The Burrows

Levelland, Tex
Box 29.
Jan 10, 1953.

Dear mrs Stone.

If you ever git to read this - we no you will have thousands to read. we wont you to know this is from our hearts. we are so sad over. Hanks death. He has always been our favorite. when his records come out we couldn't hardly waite to git them. we seen Hank in Ft Smith Ark. & In Dallas.

The Station here in Lubbock. KSEL. had an hour program. for Hank. & we listened to it. & cried all the way through it. & our Station here in Levelland. KLVT. Had a 30 min program for him.

Just want you to know. we feel so sad for you - & if you ever can drop us a line - we would like to hear from you.

As Hank was our favorite & always will be. may God Bless you & help you through this trying time.

Sincerely
Mr & Mrs Henry McClesky
& Son. Henry allen.

Jan. 4-53.

Dear Mrs Williams,

Just a few lines to extend my heartfelt feelings and to tell you I had the pleasure and honor of knowing Hank and what a Wonderful person I thought he was.

I am a singer not famous, I do mostly charity work I had the honor of making the show in Biloxi, Miss Dec. 7th with Hank for the doll and Toy Fund and the pleasure of talking to him for several hours before the show and it's a memory I'll treasure for the rest of my life. You had a wonderful son. And a very kind one who was loved by millions. Sometime it is hard to take that God seen fit to take him but God's Will be done it seems hard to bear but may God take care of you and help you to bear it.

Mrs Williams I have some pictures takened of Hank the day we were with him if you would like to have them and will let me know your address I'll have some developed for you I think they are real good. I did and am really proud of them So let me know, I am taking a

chance you will get this as I don't know your address but I hope you do as I want you to know I considered Hank a friend and really thought the world of him.

May God Bless you & yours and take care of you always.

Lots of Love.

(Alice From Dallas)
Myrtilla Purcell.
La. Pres. of the Pinest
Hank Fan Club

Alice From Dallas is my professional name I use singing.

My address & name is.

Myrtilla Purcell.
New. Orl.
Arabi, La

Beyond
Life's Gateway

WITH *SYMPATHY* TO *You*

Sincerely,
Mrs. Daughdrill

MERRY Christmas

Mr. & Mrs. Russell Bailey

God's Love
Will Light
Your Way

We cannot know why tears must be,
Why sorrow comes to you and me,
But this we know - our Father shares
Our heartaches and our deepest cares,
That with a tender love divine
He's shaping both your life and mine,
And that His hand will lead us on
Until - through darkness -
BREAKS THE DAWN!

Jan. 14 - 53

Just to let you know my sympathy is with you in your great loss. Hank came to B.R. several times and I went to see him there, back stage, as my grand daughter got his autograph and she just had to talk to him, as he was her favorite singer, She adores all his songs and always will. There will never be another like him. God bless his memory.

Mrs. Julia Almand & Family. 959 Main.

Ferncliff Dr.
Cold Spring Hills
Huntington, L.I.

My Dear Mrs Stone:-
I want to express
my sincere sympathy to
you on the loss of your
son. The pleasure he gave
was immeasurable.
I have always had a
great fascination for the south
and especially for the hill
billy singers. His loss will
be greatly felt by hundreds.
I for one will miss his
records on the air. The
ones I have will be an

immortal monument to her memory.

You must have some wonderful memories to cherish.

My son is fourteen years old and my greatest wish would be to have him be half as wonderful as I know your Hank must have been.

I have been told that our children are only loaned to us, so have faith that someday you may be reunited with your wonderful son. God Bless you.

Sincerely

Mrs. E. M. Ritzmann

Dear Mrs. Stone,

"I received your very nice letter and want to thank you for writing.

From your letter I can easily see why Hank was such a wonderful person, with someone like you to guide and encourage him, he couldn't help but be.

I am sending you a poem taken from a booklet given to me by my mother several months before her death. Mom was a wonderful person, she died at the age of 44..."

Sincerely, Your Friend,

Jimmy Valentine
Richmond, Virginia

Roses Will Bloom Again
by Dr. L.M. Zimmerman

Time brings its varied hap'nings, and each must have a share
Whether of joy or sadness, for all we must prepare.
No one's exempt from trouble, some days we need for rain,
But tho' we have our troubles, Roses will bloom again.

Grain crushed by heavy rainfalls will oft again arise,
So help and do not hinder, others to win the prize.
Tho' crushed by some misfortunes, where sin has left a strain,
Yet by a loving Father, Roses will bloom again.

Morale may be deflated, with business dull and slow,
But do not be discouraged, take hold and make it go.
Look up, take heart, and hold on, until success is plain,
For when you least expect them, Roses will bloom again.

Someone may rouse your anger, but you will happier live,
If you can curb your temper, and then in love forgive.
Be patient in your actions, and tho' you suffer pain,
The pain defines the spirit, Roses will bloom again.

Has there been cold indifference, kind words heal many wounds,
Sad tears are dried with kisses, and joy and cheer abound.
Life is too short to quarrel, we must our vows maintain,
And love, tho' we may differ, Roses will bloom again.

Bright homes are often saddened, with loneliness and loss,
Death takes away a loved one, and leaves a heavy cross.
But from celestial mansions, there comes a sweet refrain,
That in the heavenly garden, Roses will bloom again.

Would you in all things triumph, win God's eternal praise
Then trust in Christ your Saviour, and serve him all your days.
Sometimes the way is weary, and tired hearts complain,
With Christ we shall be victors, Roses will bloom again.

Thus face to face with trials, be brave and do your best,
We are to plant and water, our God will do the rest.
Cheer up, dear one, be hopeful, Life will not be in vain,
After the storms of winter, Roses will bloom again.

"... I know Hank loved Audrey as long as he lived for most every song he sang was about her..."

Mrs. A.D. Pitchford
Willacoochee GA

Russell ark
1.13.53.

Dear mrs Hank williams.
I heard about Hanks death
I sure did hate to hear about
it he was my Best singer
on the air I seen Hank at
Indianapolis Ind.
I seen some more of the
stars I have one of his
song Books did hanks
have a heart atack I sure
did like to hear him sing
rite me a little about hank
if you dont mind you
sure have got my sympky
I lost my husband in
1938 I know how you feel
I was very poor I was left
with 5 children the oldest
one was 12 the Baby was
4 years I worked awfully
hard I hope you have
good luck I just thought
I would rite you I hope
you dont mind I feel
sorry for you and the
children I know good will
help you
          love
          ada Davis
          Russell ark
          P O Box 5-23.
my prayer is may god
Bless you and the children
I am wating for a ansver
rite soon.

January 7, 1953

Dear Mrs. Williams

I know just how you feel for I had to give up my baby boy in the war in Germany in 1944. He wasn't 21 years old at the time – it is sure hard to do. I never did ever have a chance to talk with your son Hank but have been places and saw him and heard him sing. He sure has put out some wonderful songs which will long be remembered everywhere. I liked his singing best of all. It is sure hard to have to go so young. I just feel like writing you and sending this card. Hope you don't mind.

A friend,

Mrs. Ola Pate
Houston, Texas

January 27, 1953

"... I'm sure I know how you feel for I've had a niece who passed away, not quite a year ago, on her 3rd birthday. But I'm sure they're much happier where they are. Her name was Betty Ann.

Enclosed is some pictures of me and my nephew and niece. I hope you will like them. I will close now and again you have my deepest sympathy. If you would care to write and send a picture of Hank I would enjoy it very much."

Yours truly,

Genevieve Garner

Jan 10

My Dear Mrs Williams
                    We loved So Very
Much to hear your late Son Hank
Sing we have So Many of his Records
and have traveled to Nashville to
hear and See him on Grand
"ole opry".
        It is With deep regret that we
learned of his Passing. But let us
think of him as Dwelling in that
Mansion that his Good friend Jimmy
Davis So often Sings for truly Im
Sure he Must be in that Mansion.
        Hank Was Indeed a dearly loved
Person by all Who heard him Sing.
        Surely God Needed a Song Bird
in Heaven, So He took our Hank
        I Can truly understand Your
Sorrow and your loss for I to
lost a Son Just 23 Killed in
Action - During World War two.
        We do not understand all, But,
we do know God does all things
Well.
        So My Dear May He Bless
Comfort. Guide and help you all
Way.
        The Songs Hank Wrote and
Sang Will live for ever in the
hearts of the entire Van family
        God Bless you
                May I Sign
                    as your Friends
                Mr and Mrs John Van

"... Mrs. Stone, our Master gathers choice flowers for his bouquet and he has plucked a beautiful bud. Hank is at rest now. In that great beyond. In that home not made with natural hands. But a perfect land where there will be no more sorrows and heartaches.

May God bless you, comfort you through these sad dark hours is my sincere prayer."

Someone in deep sympathy,

Mrs. M.L. Hollingsworth
Moselle, Mississippi

Dear Mrs. Stone.

I am writing to say I really do sympathize with you in the death of your Son Hank. I know how you feel for I have lost 4 sons. Also my companion, he was 72 and I am 60.

I never met Hank, though I knew him and loved him. My family and I had listened into all his programs while he was playing over the Montgomery station since he first started playing there. I have one of the first pictures of Hank that he had made when he first started playing. I sent him 25 cents for it. He could express my feelings in Song and we never tired of hearing him.

He will live on and on in his songs he left behind. Can you tell me where I can get one of his last songbooks? I have tried all the music stands here. I have several of his books but wish very much to get one of his last books.

Mrs. Stone, I am sending a song I wrote about Hank and his son. Please send it to Audrey and see if she can use it. We sing it to the tune of *Tell Me Why My Daddy Don't Come Home.* Tell her if she can use it and can put it on a record to let me know and I'll buy one. That is all I ask.

I have a son just one year younger than Hank, this boy knew Hank and thought he was tops. I have his life story and picture book and sure like it. You have all my heart-felt sympathy and love.

Sincerely,

Mrs. W. A. Graham
Phenix City, Alabama

Mommy Write My Daddy To Come Home

A lad of four was playing
One night upon the floor.
When all at once he bowed his head
And tears began to flow.
His Mommy clasped him to her breast
Saying, "Son, why do you cry?"
He turned his tear dimmed eyes to her
And with these words replied:

> *Mommy write my Daddy to come home.*
> *Tell him we're so lonesome here alone.*
> *Tell him that I miss him more each day.*
> *Oh Mommy why did Daddy go away.*

His Mommy told him that his Dad
Had joined the Heavenly band
To sing and play with the Angels fair
Over in another land.
The Angels came for him one night
To play around God's throne
Where there is joy and peace and love
In that Eternal home.

Hank Williams was his Daddy's name
Hank Jr. was this lad
He was left with many memories
Though most of them are sad.
His Mommy told him that one day
They'd meet with Dad on high.
It broke the Mother's heart to hear
The little lad reply:

> *Mommy write my Daddy to come home.*
> *Tell him we're so lonesome here alone.*
> *Tell him that I miss him more each day.*
> *Oh Mommy why did Daddy go away.*

MISS FELICE ITZKOFF
3482 FENTON AVE.
NEW YORK 69 N.Y.

Dec. 10, 1953

Dear Mrs. Stone,

I find it very difficult to find the words, that will express my sorrow over the passing on of your immortal son, and to tell of my deep sympathy for you and your family.

Hank's death was a great loss to all who loved him and his music.

But try to think of it this way. Your loss is the angels' gain. Think of how happy they will be when Hank starts pickin' and singin' for them.

I'm very much afraid that this isn't a very good letter, as I am 14 years old and not very much experienced at this sort of thing, but I know I express the sentiments of all who loved your son. I wish to express my sorrow and that of my father, formerly of Bay Minnette.

May the good Lord rest Hank's soul and may he bless you. Amen. Hank's memory will live forever in my heart.

All my sorrow,
Felice Itzkoff

"...No, you don't know me. I live down here in the heart of the last Texas oilfield. If ever you get a chance to come down in this part of the world we'd be glad if you would come to see us. We are just poor folks. We have a filling station here in Arp. I have 2 boys ages 9 and 5 and one girl age 13 and every time my baby boy hears Hank's songs he says *'Poor old Hank Williams.'* They love a guitar better than anything. If I had of been financially able I would have come all the way out there to Hank's funeral because I have just lived so in hopes of someday seeing him. He was the most beautiful singer I ever heard. I can't hardly bear to hear them play his records now. I'm so sorry for you Mrs. Stone. *May God bless you in every walk of life.* I'll always think of you and we all loved Hank's singing..."

Your true friend

Mrs. O.L. Calicutt
Arp, Texas

Jan the 8 1953

"... I am an old lady 75 years young but I
have always loved music. I have 4 sons,
my youngest son looks like he may be
about the same size of your Hank as I
have a very good picture of Hank. Well, I
just want you to know that we will all
miss Hank. I am a widow of 16 years.
Well, bye from a friend of Hank and I
hope a friend of yours.

May the Lord bless you in your sorrow."

from Mrs. G.A. Van Landingham
Grayson, Louisiana

"... But what everyone liked about him he sang from his heart. He would sing some sad song and then he would turn around and sing some song to cheer everyone up."

Mrs. Arthur Brooks
Hartselle AL

Sanctuary

I am a salesman for my Lord,
He has a home for you.
The deed is made - the title clear,
There is no mortgage due.

You sign no papers, pay no bills,
You ask no lawyers aid.
The land is bought; the house is built,
The price has all been paid.

The Master asks you to accept
This house not made with hands.
And with it goes eternal life,
Spent on its golden strands.

The place is Heaven where streets are gold,
The angel voices sing.
The most exclusive part of town –
You have to know the king!

And when you see the pearly gates
That stand beside the road.
I know you'll want to tarry there,
And throw aside your load.

For Christ has died for all your sins,
There is no trouble there.
The only law is God's Command,
The burdens he will bear.

This offer doesn't stand for long,
We know not when we go.
Don't take a chance, accept I pray,
You must let Jesus know.

                Love Always,

                  A Friend,
                  Janice Hollis
                  Hub, Mississippi

January 9, 1953

Dear Mrs. Stone:

In sympathy of your son Hank Williams. I'm not much on writing such letters like this but just want you to know how sorrowed I was about his death. I can say from the bottom of my heart he was my favorite singer. My little girl 8 years old really liked him. She set by the radio the day of his death and cried. As we know that is something we all have to do young or old. Mrs. Stone I wish there was something I could do, but am praying for you. So I will sign off now. If you ever have time write me and if you ever come to Nashville, Tennessee please drop around to see us. So good-bye.

With love & best wishes

Mrs. Allen J. Tate
Nashville, Tennessee

Atlanta, Georgia
February 28, 1953

Dearest Mrs. Stone:

Of course you don't know me, but I'm one of your wonderful Son's fans. I sent you a sympathy card, but at that time I didn't know your name and I addressed it to Mrs. Williams (Hank Williams Mother). Sure hope you received it, because it expressed so much just the way I felt. I also sent Audrey and Billie a sympathy card.

I know you and his family have all been in deep sorrow and grief over his death, and that is truly a matter to grieve over. I know what you must have gone through with losing such a Dear person and Dear and Wonderful Son. I'm not married, but during the other War in 1945 I lost my fiancé and I know how that hurt me because I loved him so much; so I know very well what this means to you, and his dear ones.

I have always loved the way Hank would sing and all of his songs have been so good. I thought too he was such a wonderful and gracious person, and he had such a nice way about his singing that people couldn't help but love to listen to him. I never saw him in person, but I have certainly always wanted to, and was hoping the next time he was in Atlanta that I would get to see and talk with him. I have numbers of his records and am still buying them and will always buy them as long as new ones come out. I have several pictures of him also. I sent for the souvenir booklet of Hank's life and have enjoyed it so much. You really wrote a good and enjoyable history on his life. I like all the pictures in the booklet so much.

I wrote to Montgomery and got several papers of the *Montgomery Advertiser* and *Alabama Journal* which carried pictures and stories about his death etc. Also got several copies of the Nashville paper. I'm keeping all of these along with his other pictures and booklet etc.

Mrs. Stone I do plan to be married soon. Am sending you a clipping of my picture and engagement which came out in the *Atlanta Journal* Feb. 18. Just thought maybe you might like to read it. We plan to be married on Wednesday night March 4 at 7:30. Gee, that's just next week, so you see I'm all excited and guess that's why I'm making so many mistakes typing your letter. We plan to go to New Orleans on our honeymoon. We will stop in Montgomery on the way down or back and I want so much to see you.

(continued from pg. 66)

Of course I just want to meet you since you are Hank's Mother. I don't know just when we will stop but either on Thursday March 5, or Saturday March 7 or Sunday March 8. So I hope it will be so I can meet and talk with you awhile. I was unable to attend his funeral, but I would like to pay my respects and love to Hank and You by coming to see you.

Guess this is all for now and I must close. So here is hoping you are well and enjoying the best of Health; and May God's Greatest Blessings be with you always.

Love,
Margaret Cleveland

MARGARET CLEVELAND

Miss Cleveland Engaged to Wed Frank Melton

Mr. and Mrs. W. A. Cleveland of Elberton announce the engagement of their daughter, Miss Georgia Margaret Cleveland of Atlanta, to Frank M. Melton of Atlanta. The wedding will take place March 4 at the Athens-Elberton District parsonage in Athens.

The bride-elect attended Atlanta School of Commerce and for several years has been employed by Militant Truth. She is a member of the Ruckersville Methodist Church.

Mr. Melton is the son of Mr. and Mrs. B. F. Mauldin of St. Petersburg, Fla. He has been employed by Sears, Roebuck & Co. for several years in Mobile, Ala., and was recently transferred to Atlanta, where he is a division manager. He is a member of the Peachtree Road Methodist Church.

Dear Friend -

Heard of your sorrow from Don Larkin on WAAJ station. Oh, I cannot explain how badly I feel my dear. God bless you and give you strength to carry your great burden. God will carry you through. I have seven children myself living and six gone to be with our Lord - thirteen in all. My seven are all married and doing very nicely, thank God. It truly is a sorrowful thing to lose them. But we have got to know God knows best and if you have noticed as I have, God always takes the best, giving others a chance to repent of their sins.

Now my dear, I do hope you are feeling well and you will have my most earnest prayers.

> Mrs. R. C. Frohm
> (Mrs. Rose Carolyn –
>   my name on radio)
>
> Metuchen, New Jersey

305 North Titus St
Gilmer, Texas.

Mrs. W.W. Stone.

Dear madam.

Words can't express
my deepest grief and
sorrow over the death
of your son. and my
good Buddy Hank.
All of his listners are
bowed down with grief
for him, but we know
God needed him to
bloom in his garden
up yonder. I will say
there never will be. there
just can never be anyone
that can fill his place
in the singing field.

Hank, made a personal

appearance in our city
one time and I met
him and we became fast
friends right away. he
was my favorite Singer
I have a large picture
of Hank in a frame
also one of his song
folios. and couldn't any
amount of money make
me part with either one
of them. I am sending you
a sympthy Card. so just
thought I'd drop you a
few lines. so just look
up to God. mother. we
can't Call Hank, back to
us but we can go to
him some of these
sweet days

3

I wont you to know I
loved Honk just like
a brother. and his
going has touched me
more then I can express
so God bless you in
your grief and Sorrow
I am

Verry Resp yours.
Jesse Keel.
30 S. North Titus St
Gilmer, Texas.

January 19, 1953

Dear Hank Williams Family,

My heart certainly was with you all during your great loss. But I thought maybe I could bring a little peace to you if I wrote and let you know how we all feel up here in this part of the country. Although I never have met Hank we all feel we knew him always and loved him.

He was so young to go – but just stop and think not another young man in this world will ever live a fuller life or be loved by the public as he has. So try and be happy to know he has done so well in such a short life – very few will ever do half as well in a full lifetime.

I hope this letter lets you know how I feel.

God Bless You

Mrs. Paul St. Long
Westminster, Maryland

May 1, 1953

Dear Mrs. Stone:

Thought I would write you a line or two to say hello for the first time and to say we all share with you in your sorrow of the loss of your son.

We all knew that Hank was a great singer and composer. And not just great in the music field. Hank was great in anybody's field.

In my opinion he was the greatest. He was a hunk of heart and a great friend.

I've adored Hank's singing and the feeling he had for others ever since I was a little girl and was greatly shocked to hear of his passing.

In the hearts of people he will never die. He will live forever. Without his songs the folk music field would be nothing.

Hank wrote what he felt, set it to music, and recorded it on record and left it all for us to enjoy.

No, Mrs. Stone, we'll never forget Hank. He will always be in our thoughts. His songs will be sung and played as long as people meet, fall in love, and have their joys and sorrows, and by that way his memory will always be with us. He will live forever with his songs.

And I, like so many other people, want to express my feelings regarding Hank's singing.

Saying so long and *may God bless and keep you throughout life.*

A Hank Williams Fan,
Betty Jean Sellers
Corinth, Mississippi

To Hank williams mother

Dear Friend Mrs williams
So sorrow about Hanks death
I wanted to send this card
sooner to you But my mother
has Been Bad sick and
it sure was a shock to us
about Hank I was going
to that show that day when
they announced Hank
death it sure was a shock
to me. I know Hank very well
he sure was a swell Guy and
he will surey be missed
By a lot of his friends
Bill monroe is a great
Friend of mine I come
to visit Bill at his home
a lot I hear that he got pretty
Bad hurt I sure hope he gets
well soon Well Mrs williams
I have Never met you But
meby some time when I come
down to Bill monroe home
again I can come and see
you my mother and I send
are sincere Sympathy to you
and the Family Hank Friends
Mr Harley Ambrose and mother
1278 alberta ave.
Barberton Ohio

January 6, 1953

Dear Mrs. Stone

I want you to know how shocked and grieved my daughter and I both were to learn of Hank's passing. I happen to be visiting with my daughter in Miami, Florida and whenever we turn the radio on it is always to search for a program of Hank's. We lost track of him and didn't know where he was located and had decided to write and ask Nelson King in Cincinnati when we heard his death announced.

We knew Hank personally and he always said my daughter looked like his sister, and he died very close to my home town of Huntington, West Virginia where he made personal appearances. He always sang my request for *Wedding Bells* a great favorite of mine. We never missed the Grand Ole Opry until Hank was on it no more.

I do hope you all read the wonderful editorial in the *Montgomery Advertiser* by Allen Rankin. It sure was a sincere tribute to Hank.

Had seats out of here been available by airplane we would have come to the funeral, but at this busy season they were impossible to purchase.

To us there will never be another Hank Williams and my daughter joins me in extending our sincere sympathy in your great loss.

Sincerely,

Mrs. Madalene Johnson
Huntington, West Virginia

January 12, 1953

Dear Mrs. Stone,

I loved Hank almost as much as you did and I will always love him, even though I have never seen him. I have sat and listened to him sing over the radio so many times. Am so sorry to hear of Hank's death. Although he has gone on to a greater world, his voice and memory of his great and truthful songs will live forever in our hearts.

Yours truly,

Billy Howard Eaton
Camp Hill, Alabama

P.S. I am only 11 years old and I love Hank very much. I am especially fond of the songs *I Saw The Light* and *I Dreamed About Mama Last Night* and also *Cold, Cold Heart.*

"... He made all of us happier here while on earth and he can do more in Heaven. My husand says God has a job for him and that's why he called him..."

Lois & Johnny Murphy
Jackson Heights,
Long Island (New York)

My Dear Mrs. Stone,

Please accept my heartfelt condolences upon the passing of your son Hank Williams. A greater singer and a truer philosopher of human nature through his songs cannot be found. Although we are hundreds of miles apart we are side by side in our thoughts. I would like to recall to you if I may the last few words of the "Lord is my Shepard" psalm:

"...and I shall dwell in the house of the Lord forever."

Amen. I myself know that up in Heaven Hank is serenading the angels with his heavenly music. *God Bless You* in your sympathy, for you are not alone when you have all of us with you.

Yours,

Jack Mendelsohn
Irvington, New Jersey

Dear Mrs. Stone.

Sorry to hear the sad news about poor Hank. I am a widow with 5 boys and we live out in the country on a farm and we always listen to Hank. He was our favorite singer. We have bought all of his records he has put out. One of each rather and the record of *Lovesick Blues* I bought 5 and they all got broken. You will never know how sorry we were to hear about Hank.

My boys were so crazy about him and his singing. We are still sad when we hear his records. We also have a book with Hank and his first wife and the two children. They were a sweet family.

But God knows best. He takened my husband, mother, and daddy, brother and one sister.

I would like to get a good picture of Hank for my boys if you have one. If you are ever down this way come by to see us. Would be glad for you and his sister, Audrey and the children to visit us.

With our Sincere Sympathy,

Mrs. John W Mizell Sr.
McLain, Mississippi

August 26, 1953

Dear Mrs. Stone:

In my first issue of *Hoedown* that I recently received was a feature called "Saddle Bag" where fans of the Hillbilly and Western Scrapbook had written in to the editor and there was a girl, Jessie MacWatt who told of "our" Hank's bedroom being repaired for the public to see. I am very anxious to see the room, and would like to know when it will be opened to the public. I have been saving as much money as I possibly can as I want to make a trip down there to Montgomery this fall after the potatoes are harvested.

I had to stop writing, but now I may be able to finish. Randy Blake over WJJD in Chicago has two or three of Hank's records in his Suppertime Frolic and when Hank sings I have to drop whatever I'm doing and just listen.

Just recently I purchased a whole lot of Hank's records from a store I had order them for me. I still have a few more coming, but I've got most of them and I wouldn't sell them for any price! I just love the Luke the Drifter ones. He puts so much feeling in them!

I have also heard that they are going to build a monument to Hank something like the Jimmie Rodgers monument and I've wondered if this is so. Could you tell me if we fans could contribute something on that order? I'd be willing to give my "last thin dime."

How are you feeling now? I had heard that you were ill, but hope you are feeling real well now.

one of Hank's many fans,
Bertha Manglas
Elmira, Michigan

January 8, 1953

Dear Mrs. Williams,

I'll try to tell you how sorrowed we was to hear of the death of your husband Hank. I have a son that's 18 years old and everybody that hears him says he sings just like Hank. He is on the radio now. He plays a guitar and sings Hank's songs. When he gets through they say, *"Well we have to admit we have a Hank Williams here in Flint."* Do you think there's a chance you could help him get started with his music and singing? He's a wonderful kid. Never drank a drop in his life, don't smoke or even have a bad word. Wish I could hear from you. His name is Charles Marchbanks.

> Yours truly,
>
> his Mother,
> Mrs. Alfred Marchbanks
> Flint, Michigan

HARPER W.VA.
JAN-10-53

To THE FAMILY OF HANK.

PLEASE EXCEPT OUR HEART-FELT
SYMPATHY IN THE LOSS OF YOUR
SON, BROTHER AND HUSBAND, WE —
ONLY KNEW HIM THROUGH HIS —
WONDERFUL RECORDINGS OF HILL
BILLY MUSIC + SONG.

WE SHARE YOUR TEARS AND —
SORROW ALONG WITH A MILLON
OTHERS.

SINCERILY WRITTEN
RAY AND FAYE LESTER + CHILDRE
A/3c BOB LESTER. — OKLA.
  BACIL   "
  DENNY   "
  JIMMY   "
  JUDY   "
  PEGGY LESTER.
ALL OF HARPER W.VA.

January 8, 1953

Kindly Mrs. Stone

"...This is rather odd, for me to be writing someone I never knew or seen. I might as well use this line to introduce myself Mrs. Stone. This is Charles McGuire of Route 3 Anderson South Carolina. I am 29 years old the same age of Hiram. I am married have a real nice wife and 4 children. I guess that is enough about myself.

Guess you wonder why I am really doing this writing. Well Mrs. Stone along with millions of people I did love your son and the songs he composed. One recitation especially *I Dreamed About Mama Last Night.* I come from a family of 12 children, so that recitation suited my own mother, she was just like that song but January 26, 1950 my mother passed away, so you can see why I treasure that one recitation so much...."

Very Kindly,

Charlie McGuire
Anderson, South Carolina

January 11, 1953

Dear Mrs. Williams:

I am very sad to hear about Mr. Williams. He was my favorite singer.

Now I will tell you who I am. I am Miss Patricia Black. I am twelve years old. I have five brothers and two sisters. My oldest sister is married.

You may wonder how I know your address. I was listening to the radio and they said Hank Williams died and was I ever startled. I just couldn't believe it because at supper my Mom said Hank Snow died so when I heard your Hank died I didn't know what to think. Then they said your address on the station so I thought I would write a letter to you.

Hope I'm not bothering you by writing this letter.

They just played one of Hank's songs. Well here's wishing you the deepest sympathy and may you find comfort in knowing that the sympathy of loving and lots of friends is with you.

I know it isn't going to seem like home with Hank gone.

If it is not too much trouble for you would you please write to me. I would be more than glad to hear from you. My address is:

Miss Patricia Black
Johannesburg, Michigan

Dear Mrs. Stone,

It is difficult to find words to express the sincere sympathy I feel in my heart due to the death of your son and my favorite singer. The suddenness of his death is unreal to everyone. His short life on earth is over and we are left with only memories and a deep loss as God calls him to his reward in Heaven.

My prayers are with you during this your time of sorrow. I trust that the burden will be lighter by the knowledge that God's judgment is for the best. You see, I know how hard it is to have to give up such a fine boy, as I lost a son last year with heart trouble.

He was 22 years old.

Our will must be the will of God and if we put our trust in him he will carry us through.

Sincerely,

Mrs. Dan Thompson
Ponchatoula, Louisiana

Jan. 13, 1953

Dear Mrs. Williams & Family,

Extending my deepest sympathy in lighting your sorrow, may God give you courage and grant you most tenderly straight from Heaven share his unfailing love.

I feel as thought I should write this letter as people here and everywhere feel as though your deceased has been taken into an unknown land, of which God is watching over him. I am just nineteen years of age and I lost my fiance 8 months ago. I couldn't understand then why he had been taken away although I know now God needed him in Heaven.

There is an open gate through which each of us must go when Our Father claims us for his own. Beyond this gate our loved ones have found happiness, rest and comfort and so will each of us in the thought that God Above knows best.

Mrs. Williams, your son was well thought of here in Roanoke Virginia as he appeared here several times. May God help you and guard you day by day, may the sunshine of His love soon drive the clouds away. *God bless you and his family.*

Sincerely,

Miss JoAnn Spraker
Roanoke, Virginia

Dear Mrs. Williams & daughter

My sympathy goes out to you all in your trouble. My family's favorite singer was Hank.

I have a son missing in Korea sice Nov. 2, 1950. May the Lord Bless you both.

Mrs. Robert Luckett

January 5, 1953

Dear Mrs. Williams

I would like to express my sympathy in the loss of your son Hank. This is such a small tribute compared to the others you have received I know. But none are more heartfelt or meant anymore than this. We (my family and I) wish to express deepest sympathy from the bottoms of our hearts. We wish there was something we could say or do to lighten your burden, but we know only God and time can do that.

It may seem odd that we should feel such a loss, not even knowing Hank personally. But we had listened to Hank for quite awhile. In fact I listened to him when he was at Shreveport, whenever I could get the program. That was before he had won his fame in life. You get to feel that you know someone like that. Hank was admired by many for remaining down to earth, even though fame and fortune had come his way. That endeared him to country folks.

Mr. Jimmy Rule paid his tribute in a great poem written about Hank. You have lost a beloved son, the Opry cast and folks of the entertainment field have lost a great songwriter and friend, and we the listeners have lost a great and wonderful entertainer. In my opinion and many others too, Hank was one of the greatest, if not <u>the</u> greatest. We are sorry we never had the pleasure of meeting or knowing him.

We know you are *So Lonesome You Could Cry*, but let's think that *Hank Saw the Light* and you rejoice that we will have the pleasure of meeting him *When the Book of Life is Read*. God rest his soul.

Bless you Mrs. Williams and if we ever have the pleasure of meeting you, may it be under brighter circumstances.

With our deepest sympathy to you and each member of Hank's family.

Sincerely,
Juanita & Skeet Arrowood
Waverly, Ohio

Montpelier, Ind.
Jan. 9, 1953

Dear Mrs. Stone:

Just a word to try to comfort you somewhat in your recent sorrow. It seems so unfair for one so young and so talented as Hank after he had reached the top to be called home so prematurely.

His songs sounded as if they were coming from a boy with a broken heart. I hope not. I even shed tears when I heard of his death because it will stop wonderful music. But we can here is immortal records for a long time.

I'm just a farmer here in Indiana, so may God help you and yours in your sorrow

David L. Hicks.

April 24, 1953

Dear Mrs. Stone,

I heard Little Bill over station WNOE this morning, and he said he had a nice talk with you over the phone yesterday. He said you were lonely. Well Mrs. Stone that just must not happen. There's too much to do to be lonesome. You know Hank wouldn't want you to be lonesome. He isn't, you know, so don't you be anymore. Just think of all the nice happy tunes Hank sang, and how many people listen to them, young and old, near and far, sick and well, bedridden and crippled, we all enjoy Hank's songs. So don't you feel bad, just have a happy thought each minute that somewhere, sometime some person is getting lots of enjoyment out of one of Hank's songs. Hank made lots of people happy by his hymns. You be happy by the thought that you had such a wonderful son. I'll tell you what Mrs. Stone, you need a hobby of some kind, growing flowers, raising chickens, sewing, quilting, writing letters, answering the many nice letters you receive, exchanging pictures with each one you receive a letter from. Oh I can think of a lot of things to cheer you up Mrs. Stone. I hope these few lines I've written will help you. I hope I get an answer from you real soon.

Just a Friend,
Mrs. Mable Ward
Molino, Florida

January 12, 1953

Dear Mrs. Stone,

I have heard about your son's death and my husband and I wish to send you our sincere sympathy. We also loved Hank very much. I have almost all of this records and love them very much.

My husband also plays a guitar and he was just wondering if it would be possible for you to send us a souvenir of Hank's like one of his guitar picks or a picture or any small object. We would appreciate it very much and we will always remember Hank as one of the best hillbilly singers we know. Again, we say we are very sorry Hank had to go at such a young age. We hope the Lord will bless him in Heaven for all that he has done on earth.

Thank you

Mr. & Mrs. Lawrence Malouin
Brooklyn, New York

P.S. *God Bless You*

January 6, 1953

Dearest Williams Family,

I am so very sorry about Hank. He was loved
not only for his wonderful voice and the songs that he
wrote, but also for the wonderful person he was.

You know people can really be wonderful. Here
in Michigan, neighborhood stations have a special
part in their show for Hank's recordings.

When we read about things like this we just
don't realize that it could come in to our own family.

It's kind hard to say the right things in a letter
like this, but I hope my letter will show my deep sympathy, for Hank was my favorite singer and he still is,
for here we will still request his songs as if he were
still with us.

I am only in the 8th grade, so I don't know
much about how to go about a letter like this to show
just how sorry I am.

My girlfriend's little sister got killed by a train
this summer. People wrote from all over the U.S. to
tell Mr. & Mrs. Sheffield how sorry they were. They
were so swell.

I am truly sorry about Hank. I hope my letter
will show just how much I liked Hank.

Yours very truly,

Kay Sweeney
L.H.S.
Lapeer, Michigan

3 CENTS
UNITED STATES POSTAGE

Hank was my best singer, and even he is gone he will still be the best for me — I never saw him, so if you have a snap shot send it so I can show it to my two kid. My mother passed away 3 years on Jan. 30 and I know what it is.

Mrs Percy F. Petie
Box 161 B.
cut off, La.

Lincoln Neb.
Jan - 4 - 5 3

Dear folks;
I am enclosing this
letter, along with a
sympathy card, I wanted
to do something to
let you know how
I always felt about
"Dank" Hjelle, he will
be missed forever by
me and millions of
other people. and let
me tell you "Dank"
has a place in the
hearts of hundreds of
boys, in "Korea."
I know because I
was over there.

and when someone
said Hank Williams
is singing, you
would see boys
gather around the
only radio around
for a few miles,
they would quite down
to a whisper while
Hank sang and played
one of his many,
wonderful songs.
well folks. accept.
our deepest sympathy.
          Yours. Truly.
 Mr. & Mrs.
 Ray Vanderlic Jr.
 1428 "Y" Street
 Lincoln Neb.

"… His songs will be sung and played as long as people meet, fall in love, and have their joys and sorrows, and by that way his memory will always be with us. He will live forever with his songs."

Betty Jean Sellers
Corinth MS

Dear Mrs Williams:

Thanksgiving was very great shock. My husband our children & I felt so much sorrow in our hearts to have to put it into words. Frank was in Toronto twice. He was welcomed by great crowds especially the second time as no one people new him.

We visited him in Rockville Aug 1951. Six months later when in Toronto, he remembered us. It is with a humble heart my husband and send this card.

There is a home not made by hands,
Beyond its golden door.
Awaits the one who's now away,
Not lost - just gone before.
And in that home not made by hands
The Master will prepare
A place for you, and when He calls
You'll meet the loved one there.

With most sincere sympathy
To the Williams Family

from
Mr & Mrs Wm. Wiebe
Lakeview P.O. Ont, Canada.

My dear New Friend; As I was listening over the radio whereit was told about your son, and asking folks write you because of him being killed. I heard your son Frank was 29 years old I heard our Minister at Church say, Was he in an auto accident on way to Kent Ohio. You surly have my deepest sympathy, I lost my dear Mother not long ago with a sudden heart attack and I can surly feel and pray for anyone who has heart aches and as I have a son in service who has served over country in this division over in Korea & Japan but I sure trusted God and he brought him back. Be encouraged (dear) what day was he buried and where I am sending you a card rather with this letter asking that others may gather

return it to me, Please do
just call on God dear Sister
and in his great love he
will look upon you in
your sorrow and comfort
you. Do you have any other
children? We have a daughter
here in town wet and not.
far from where our son is
Ally son is in Calif now at
a Base La Tora now. His
service History story was in
the air May of you heart if
he is T/Sgt Lorain J Mokey
you tell us you dear Sister
Please answer this letter (I'll be praying for you)

Because your loss
is shared by all
Who knew your loved one.

Sincere Sympathy is with you
in this hour.

May it help comfort and
sustain you.

Mr. Mrs. Ray Vandelicht
+ Teresa.
1428 "G" St.
Lincoln Neb.

Sincere
SYMPATHY

With Sympathy

May the sympathy
of understanding friends,
and the abiding Presence
of the Heavenly Father
sustain and comfort you
at this time.

Mr. & Mrs. Olin T. Mee
Frederica, Delaware.

"In my Father's house are many
mansions: if it were not so,
I would have told you. I go
to prepare a place for you."
JOHN 14:2

Mrs. Williams - was a dear
friend to us. Twice this summer
we went 150 miles
to see him in Pennsylvania. He
to Lunset Park in April &
to know in April his received almost
She was all of last ones. We will close
knew all of last ones. I will close
except them poem. I Rivino didn't
get staying. If the Lord is willing
by and see you.
By Bye
Mrs. Olin T. Mee
Frederica, Delaware

AIR MAIL 6¢ U.S. POSTAGE

ARMY-AIR FORCE POSTAL SERVICE
JAN 3 1953
A.P.O.

FEB 12 1953

Mr. Hank Williams
c/o Little Jimmey Dickens
Radio Station WSM
Nashville, Tenn.

A MESSAGE
TO
COMFORT YOU

It's very hard to bear the loss
When loved ones go away,
But may the thoughts of many friends,
In some way, help today;

And may your cherished memories
Bring comfort to you, too,
And help to make your loved one seem
Still very close to you.

Sgt Eugene A Hemlock and Buddies
7961 USAREUR Det APO 163
℅ Post Master
New York, N.Y.   PARIS FRANCE

John Kozaroski
Darwin E. Watson
Lewis J. Shattuck
Ralt D Darnell
Bob (Wahewa—), Hawaii
Jerry Briggs
John Brickley
Bud Schultz
Tito Goffman
Dick Rodriguez
David McEvoy
Joe Warski—
(—Alila), Philippines

With all good wishes
for Christmas
& the New Year
margaret griffin

May He who is
all tenderness,
All truth, all love,
all peace,
Grant you the
quietude of Heart
That bids your
sorrows cease!

Miss Reeta Paige
Pres. of Sr. Class
Edmonton, Ky.

Edmonton, Ky.
1-15-53

The Williams Family,

The Senior Class of Edmonton
High School wish to express their
deepest sympathy on the passing of
Frank. Our favorite entertainer, and
We admired him deeply.

Even though Frank is gone, he
will live forever in our hearts.
His death certainly made your
Frank.
God bless each of you.

Reeta Paige
Pres. of
Senior Class

In Sympathy

Dear Mrs. Williams,

We were all sorry here when we heard about Hank's death. He was just like one of the family. He was always our top hillbilly singer. "I think he was tops."

I know he will always be remembered by all his fans, especially by me. And I hope wherever he goes that he will make as many friends there as he has here. I never had the pleasure of meeting him but I know he was kind and

miss Mildred Crutley + Friends

Words alone can't comfort you

Nor ease the loss you bear,

But may the sympathetic thoughts

Of friends who deeply care

Help bring you comfort at this time

Until___ as it will do___

There dawns a brighter morrow

When the sun comes shining through.

A former Skinner fan club
member—

Flora Roma.

Dear Winnie,

May I send this little stanza
from a well-known poem; for me
and the ___ people from my home
town in Ky... They loved your
Dan and took them to their
hearts.

"To each man is given a marble
to carve for the wall
A stone that is needed to
heighten the beauty of all
And only the soul has the magic
to give it the grace
And only his hands beneath
running to put it in place."

We think he did his work well;
And the carving will stay on the wall
far us.

With Sympathy

Dear Mrs Williams Jan 5/53
When I heard about
Hank. I felt as if it was
some one I knew for as
many years and as if I
lost a very close friend.
I am a boy of 17 years
so am high school
singing to my brother
you have my sincere
Sympathy but as they
say the Lord knows best
he who knows best
Sincerely Albert

The Rose Still Grows Beyond the Wall

by A. L. FRINK

Near shady wall a rose once grew,
Budded and blossomed
    in God's free light,
Watered and fed by morning dew,
Shedding its sweetness day and night.

As it grew and blossomed fair and tall,
Slowly rising to loftier height,
It came to a crevice in the wall,
Through which there shone
    a beam of light.

Onward it crept with added strength,
With never a thought of fear or pride,
It followed the light
    through the crevice-length,
And unfolded itself on the other side.

The light, the dew, the broadening view,
Were found the same
    as they were before;
And it lost itself in beauties new,
Breathing its fragrance more and more.

Shall claim of death
    cause us to grieve,
And make our courage faint or fall?
Nay, let us faith and hope receive –
The rose still grows beyond the wall.

Scattering fragrance far and wide,
Just as it did in days of yore,
Just as it did
    on the other side.
Just as it will forevermore.

From
Mr & Mrs Harvey Elliott

33 Alfred St.
Brantford
    Ont.
    Can.

To express
deep and sincere
sympathy

type of music on Juke Boxes
or over Radios on our Rigs
We will miss a very great
liked hill billy entertainer
who we hope this recording
Will Remain on Disk Jockeys Program

From
Some of the Boys of Local
299 (TRUCK DRIVERS) Detroit
Mich
as most of the truckers
love Hanks the Road love Hanks

Sorrowing
With You

Skies are so dark and somber,
Beclouded with grief and despair,
When a loved one leaves us here
For the yonder realms so fair.

Sweet the hope of eternal life,
It breaks asunder clouds of gloom,
As we think of our loved one
Safe at Home in that Upper Room.

Mrs. Darrell Brooks
& family.

Words seem to fail
at times like these,

But still the heart extends

Unspoken thoughts and sympathy

From understanding friends.

Mrs. Mattie Joplling
Route 3
Harrison, Ark.

Ralph was my
favorite son and
I'll always miss him

GOD hath not promised
Skies always blue,
Flower-strewn pathways
All our lives through
God hath not promised
Sun without rain,
Joy without sorrow,
  Peace without pain.

But God hath promised
Strength for the day,
Rest for the laborer,
  Light on the way,
Grace for the trial,
  Help from above,
Unfailing sympathy,
  Undying love.

Dear Mrs. Stone;

We did enjoy being with you, for a short visit in Hanks room, but sorry to cause you more tears and sorrow, so I know you miss him each time you show his room and beloved belongings. I did not know you, personally would bow us the room. Thanks a million and I know Hank would not want to cause you worry or grief...
I am the woman who came in with daughter and her 2 adopted girls, with a friend, about 2 weeks ago. My daughter and family have gone on to Alaska for 2½ or more yrs. We all love
I bought more of Hanks recordings yesterday, when so young..
his music, but sorry he had to go.
I hope your cold is better and you will have a nice Xmas and a good new year through 1954..
Perhaps, sometime, you will come to Ft. Lauderdale, Florida and we can visit more. You are as I expected to find you, a wonderful woman. May God Bless you always.
These verses have given me much comfort, since loosing my parents and husband too. Read them often, and I hope you get the same comfort from them. Sincerely,

824 S.E. 6th. Ct. Ft. Lauderdale, Florida.   Lucy R. Kyle..
Dec 19-53..

January 10, 1953

Dear Mrs. Williams

You have my deepest sympathy in the death of Hank. I am eleven years old. He was my favorite singer as long as I can remember. I would like very much to have a picture of Hank. Please let me know what it would cost me.

Sincerely,

Junior Rucker
Crawfordsville IN

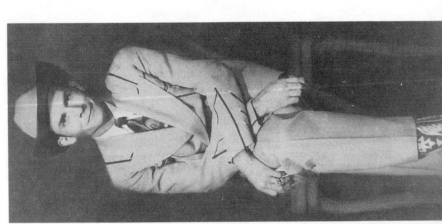

I cannot say, and I will not say
   That he is dead, — he is just away!
With a cheery smile, and a wave of the hand,
   He has wandered into an unknown land.
And left us dreaming how very fair
   It needs must be, since he lingers there,
And you, O you, who the wildest yearn
   For the old-time step and the glad return,
Think of him faring on, as dear
   In the love of there as the love of here;
Think of him still as the same, I say:
   He is not dead — he is just away!

—James Whitcomb Riley

One of Hank's Ardent Listeners

Joan Riley

Just these

little words of comfort

Like two friendly

outstretched hands

Come to let you know sincerely

That somebody understands!

from Mrs Louis Taylor

Goshen Ohio

Dear Mrs Williams

I know how you feel I lost a son in Korea Sept 17, 1951 I heard your name and address on radio this morning. I could not tell you how sorry I am but my heart is with you. your son was one of my favorite singers every one liked to hear him to I hope the good Lord will help you bear your burdens I'll be thinking of you altho I am a stranger to you.

yours. Mrs Louis Taylor

Goshen Ohio

January 17, 1953

Dear Mrs. Stone -

I know that you have received and will receive letters
and cards from millions of people who loved your son
even though they didn't know him personally. I am
only one of those millions and there isn't anything
that any of us can say to help you. Though I'm sure
we all want you to know we want to share in your sorrow. Your son will live on and never be forgotten.

I have 5 girls and we have a scrapbook that we have
kept about your son and we wonder if it would be
asking too much to ask for a picture of you and your
daughter to go in the book along with the rest we have
on your son. We know he must have had an awful
good mother to be the kind of young man he was.

A friend of ours, Nat Chambers, was in your son's
band at one time and he has told us a lot about him.

We hope that you'll answer our request in time so we
can complete our scrapbook. We have a dead baby
son named after your son and we have the clippings
about his death in the scrapbook also.

God be with you.

Sincerely,

Mrs. Evelyn W. Peters
Jonesville, Virginia

Mr. and Mrs. Louis Baker
313 W. Center St.
Albion, Mich.

Jan 15-19,53

Dear Mrs Williams

Oh how we miss your Love One. we know he gone to be With God. we have a little Daughter She is only 3 years old. She miss him on the Grand Ole Apry She hear him Singing ever Sat-nite so we hope to here from you some time.

From mrs Louis Baker,

Dear Friends.

"You have my sympathy from the bottom
of my heart. I know it is hard at this
time and will be in the time to come. But
just remember he is in a far better world
now and he done so much Good on earth
that he will always be remembered. He
was my idol of a singer. What I write is
from my heart for I lost my husband on
Sept 12, 1952, leaving two children, a girl
2 and a boy a year old Christmas. I
thought I couldn't go on but I have to for
my children and you can for Hank. He
has wrote some beautiful songs and you
can always play them and its so much
more than just a picture..."

Mrs. Elsie Lange
Blensoe, Iowa

Colquitt, Ga.
Jan. 10, 1953

Dear Mrs. Stone,

I would like to express my deepest sympathy in your hours of bereavement. I didn't know Hank Willams personally, But I knew him through radio and his recordings.

I have been without sight since I was a small boy, But I am not a shut-in, I am an ardent listener of the radio. And like millions of others made Hanks acquaintance that way. There are people all over America who may not write you, But still they share your sorrow.

Mrs. Stone, I am sure you are a wounderful person because you are Hank's mother. I hope you put your faith in the all-mighty god who, will see you and yours through your darkest hours.

I remain Sincerely,
Your friend
Angus Whitten
Colquitt Ga
R. F. D. # 5

January 8, 1953

Dear Mrs. Stone

Just a line to say how I can truly sympathize with you in the loss of your son Hank. Let us remember our loss is God's gain, which makes the way brighter since we will meet again. For 22 years I live on these hopes. I had a son 19 years of age to drop without a sign of warning and 3 1/2 years ago his father went the same, although he had been suffering for 4 years with heart attacks. Only experience can really make a person know how you feel. But their going helps to make the way easier since they are with our Lord and at rest in Heaven.

My husband now is a Bethlehem, Pennsylvania man. He had often heard the Louisiana Hayride and went several times. We enjoyed Hank over the radio, too, and will miss him as thousands of others.

My native state is Alabama – Anniston.

I have only been to Montgomery once about 11 years ago. It is a very pretty city. *May the Lord be with you is my prayer.*

Sincerely yours

Mrs. E.J. Bright
Ruston, Louisiana

January 6, 1953

Dear Mrs. Williams

I am writing to you to let you know how it hurt me when I heard that Hank was dead. I always liked his songs and the way he played his guitar and all the instruments. Mrs. Williams I always liked to play hillbilly music and if I had the things to get started I would like to play the way Hank did. You see of all the Hillbillys he was the one I liked the best of all. And if there is some little thing that you could send me to help me along in the way of my learning I would thank you very much. I have all of his songs. I know all of them too. The ones I like best are *Jambalaya* and *Window Shopping.* You see I am married and have five boys and I am 21 years old. Two of them are my stepsons and three are mine. My husband makes 100 dollars a month and it is hard to get time to learn how to play a guitar. I would get a guitar if I could but you see we are very poor and it is hard. Well, I will close this letter now. *And may God bless you forever.*

> Thank you,
> Mrs. Edna Brady
> Bowie, Maryland
> c/o Jim Daisey

Washington, D.C.
Jan. 10th 1953.

Dear Mrs. Williams –
    Due to illness I am late in
sending you this message but wish
to extend you my deepest sympathy on
the death of your wonderful husband,
my favorite of all hill billy artists and
surely hope his records will continue to
be carried on.
    I had the occasion to meet him
in person, also have his autograph but
sorry did not get his picture.
    Again my deepest sympathy to you.
            Sincerely,
        Mrs. Wm. R. Middleton
        7404 – Hovoford Street. S.E.
            Washington 28, D.C.

"... You have heard a lot of stories about the many wonderful things that Hank done. I would like to tell you a good deed he did that even he wasn't aware of.

When Hank first came to Shreveport I lived on a ranch outside of town. There were 14 boys and girls that ran around together all the time. We traveled in a jeep all the time. When Hank came to Shreveport he won all of our hearts. He became the one man that we wanted to be like. We never thought about going to a nightclub, we had much rather spend our time together singing Hank's songs. One day Hank told about going to church with you when he was a child. That made us like him more. We never missed a church service and they had 4 a week. One night part of our gang was going down the road singing and a man heard them as they passed. He got in his car and caught up with them and tried to hire them to sing the song again. We were never sure whether he liked the singing or was feeling sorry for Hank because his song was being ruined. When Hank left for Nashville it broke our hearts. But we knew it was best for him. We knew he would go over big.

After Hank left there were several changes that took place. I lost my Dad and we sold the ranch and moved to town. Out of the 14 who were together most of the time there are only 6 of us left in town. Some of the girls are married, some are working, others are still going to school. I am working as secretary to the owner of a record shop here in town. Most of the boys are in service, some are married, and one or two are going to school. But when we 6 get together or when the others come home and we have a get-together, we still have Hank's songs. We might not sing them as loud as we did, for we are supposed to act ladylike now, but we sing them and play his records anyway.

So you see Mrs. Stone, though Hank never knew us personally, we loved him. He will always live in our hearts."

Love,
Veona Jones
Longsview, Texas

January 9, 1953

Dear Mrs. Williams,

I know that you have never seen or heard of me, but to me you will always be one of my dearest friends, because you must be wonderful to have brought to this world a cowboy singer loved by everyone. My mom always told me that a child's upbringing reflects upon his or her mother. I can't find words enough to express my sympathy and the deep feeling I have for Hank. He was my favorite western singer and I still listen for his songs on the radio three times a day.

I am a high school girl, 16 years of age and a great lover of western music. My Dad likes Hank's songs and likes to listen to the western frolic songs while he works. Hank's one of his top singers.

I wish I could give you something to show my deep feeling for you and your son but I don't own too many things. When I do get something very pretty, I will send it to you.

You may throw this letter out after you have read it, but I wanted you to know you have many <u>true</u> friends here in New Jersey and I will now say: *"I love you."*

Sincerely,
Dorothy Bunce
Oakland, New Jersey

January 13, 1953
Imperial, Nebr.

Dear Mrs. Stone,

I would like to express my deepest sympathy for you over the loss of your son. He was a wonderful man. I did not know him personally but he was my favorite singer and many of the songs he recorded became my favorite songs also.

I always listened to his program on W. S. M. on Sat. nights and over Lexington, Nebr.

I am a 17 year old high-school girl and my ambition was to be as great a friend to everyone as Hank was. Many of my friends are as deeply regreted over his death as I am.

It seems as though God put us on this earth for a special

purpose and when that purpose
is completed he calls us home.
I guess he really never gives us
any one but just sort of loans
them to us for awhile. They give
us pleasure and joy, tears and
heartbreak, but above all this
is the glory of God who calls
us all home someday. God has
called your son home Mrs. Stone
and someday He'll call you home
to be with your son too.

Until then I hope his memory
will linger with you always and
I know that here on this earth
your son's songs will live eternally.
I know that your son was a great
man and I know to you he must
have meant the world.

Yours very truely,
Twilla Hiatt
Imperial. Neb.

January 13 '53

Dearest Mrs. Stone

It is a great pleasure to me to write to you. I understand you are our dear friend Hank Williams mother. I just wanted to write and tell you how much me and my family enjoyed Hank's songs – we really did love his voice and will on and on. Dear, I am the mother of 10 children. God called 2 of them away. I can understand how you feel about Hank. It hurt me so bad when I heard that Hank had passed away I could hardly believe that it was real. Dear, I just wanted you to know how much we loved your son. *God Bless you Mother* and bye bye for now.

Love, yours truly

Mrs. Emma Owens of
Elora, Tennessee

Dear Mrs. Williams

We are 2 old people who live on a farm of 110 acres. We own it. We get up every morning any time from 4 until 5 o'clock. I have a little radio I turn on while preparing breakfast and listened to WLWS this morning. Don Davis played one of your son's records, the one: *"Say a prayer for the soldiers over in Korea"* – it is a beautiful song, and told us Hank had passed on to that beautiful place where there are no more wars or sorrows. Don asked us all that was listening to send you a card so here is ours and our love and *God Bless You* and we will say a prayer for you, too. He not say what took Hank away, maybe he will tell more today.

Myrtle & Clyde McNeil
West Union, Ohio

Elliday Ga

Dearest mrs willims   Jan 9 1953
I will Drop you a few Lines to Let you
no as I am a mother my Self I no how
Troubled your heart is and to Let you
no That hank was my Fasorrite Singer
on The radio and we all That Lisen to him
miss him sery much But I no That you
his mother misses him The most But our
father in hesen nowlest The Best But
Some Times it Seemes we cant hardlie
Bear it But I pray That god well Ese your
heart as he Did mine when I Lost one of
my Little Twins you may Think hard of
me for riten But you Being hanks mother
I wonted you to no how much I endoyed his
program and how Sorry That he had to Lese
us hank neser came to our Town with a
Sho and I Dont hase a piecture of him my
Self But I Seen one of him one time That
my nabor had and It was a Food one as I
am not much of a riter I will Sine
off and may god Bless you all That Losed
hank   from one of hanks Listeners
mrs Bernice worley
R# 4 Box 26
Elliday Ga

March 1, 1953

Dearest Mrs. Stone,

"I'm writing this for my Grandma who is eighty-six years old, and I hope with all my heart that you will take time to answer it. When Hank died she felt just as bad as she did when one of her boys died. She sits in her rocking chair by the record player and plays his recordings over and over, and she never fails to say that she believes that he went to Heaven. Grandma feels just like she knew Hank, although she never met him. I know it's asking a lot to have you answer this but it means so much to her..."

Sincerely,

Betty Hawley
Swartz Creek, Michigan

Duffee, Mississippi
January 12, 1953

Dear Mrs. Stone:
 I was very sorry to here of Hank passing away as
he was one of my favorite Hill-Billy artist. He will never
be forgotten to those of us that listen to him, and liked
him so well.

 As I am a victum of Infantile Paralysas, I listen
to the radio alot. When I am home from school on Saturdays.
 I am in the nineth grade, .

 I would have liked very much to have attended Hank's
funeral. But was unable to go to Alabama.

                              Sincerely,
                              Tommy Hitt

April 11, 1953

"... Every time I heard Hank sing the songs went right to my heart. He was such a real person over the air and could make us patch up our spats with his songs. It just sounded as if he was trying to keep us going. Hank was a down to earth person and no fooling. We miss his music so much. And I know how you feel in the loss of your son for I too lost one of my baby sons. I have 4 children yet none can take the place of the boy I lost. *God bless you Mrs. Stone and little Hank and his mother too.*"

Yours sincerely,

Mrs. M.L. Curry
Catlett, Virginia

January 9, 1953

Dear Mrs. Williams

Just a few lines to let you know you have my sympathy in this sad hour. I know what you are going through to lose a loved one. I lost my Daddy last month Dec 5th. He was eating supper, started to drink some coffee and just died all at once. Never could say a word. He was dead before they could get him on the bed. He looked so pretty, look like he was asleep. He loved to hear Hank sing so good. I'm sure they are better off altho we can't see it. There will be times you will give anything to see him. I would give anything to see my Daddy and talk to him. They was a large family of us. That was the first death in the family. Mother hasn't been well since Daddy died. I'm afraid she won't be far behind him. I never seen Hank in person but we heard him sing so much seems we knowed him. We all loved him. I'm sure everybody that heard him sing loved him. Try to make the best of it you can and look to the Lord.

One who loves you,
Your Friend,

Mrs. W.H. Rodgers & Family
Wildersville, Tennessee

318 Woodfield Road
Toronto Ont.
Canada.

Dear Friend and Mother
of Hank. I am so pleased he
always had his Mother in all
his sorrows and his Joys.
He lived on earth about as
long as our dear Lord did.
all my friends felt so sorry
when the dear boy died.
he wont have any sorrow
where he is gone. it was
nice seeing your Pictures and
reading about Hank. E Quinn

Dear Mrs. Williams

I want you to know how great a sorrow it was to my
husband and I who had never met your son, but who
has enjoyed so much the wonderful music that he has
made. We have rocked our babies to sleep so many
times while singing his songs. Our oldest boy 4
(when a baby) would ask his Daddy to *"wear out
another trunk Daddy"* and I guess he wore out a thousand. My husband Bob and I heard the news about
our Hank and he had tears on his face when he
turned his head to me and said, *"You know that
hurts."* It's unusual for a man to have tears. Just
think of the thousands that felt the same way. I
know you will be forever proud of your son, and a
whole nation has loved him, and will never forget him.
I pray that he will be as loved in Heaven as on Earth.

God Bless You.

Helen Wardlow
Chicago, Illinois

January 4, 1953

Dear Mrs. Williams,

This is a great time of sorrow for you, but I would like for you to know that the hearts of the many people who loved him are heavy also.

Your "Hank" was a wonderful person. To me he's the greatest singer and composer ever. He done more for me than anyone else could. No, I never met him, but I'm probably one of his most devoted followers. You see his song *"Thy Burden Is Greater Than Mine"* gave my life more meaning than anything else could. He sounded sincere when he sang that and the rest of his songs. It gave my life a purpose when I was lonely and hurt and ready to throw that life away. Surely God looks after such as he. I believe he did "See the Light" as he closed his eyes and that his eternal sleep is in Heaven.

I know things pass, Mrs. Williams, and a sweet memory will remain, never to be forgotten. I wish there was more I could say to you to help. Try to be content with the knowledge that it is God's will and we'll all meet some day where there's no parting. There is a verse in the Bible I'd like for you to read: Rev.21:4:

> *"And God shall wipe away all tears*
> *from their eyes, and there shall be*
> *no more death, neither sorrow, nor*
> *crying; neither shall there be any*
> *more pain: for the former things are*
> *passed away."*

May God bless and keep you, Mrs. Williams, you done a marvelous job of raising a fine boy. We are all going to miss him and he'll never be forgotten. My prayers are with you.

Very Sincerely,

Miss Ann Evans
Winston-Salem, North Carolina

January 8, 1953

Dear Mrs. Stone:

"Your son's death comes a severe shock, and left grieved hearts of his millions of friends over radio-land. He sang his way into the hearts of millions, and throughout the coming years, his songs and personal appearances will be a lasting and cherished memory for all. Surely his life, fame and host of friends everywhere are a great consolation for you..."

> Deep Sympathy from
> A Lousiana Friend,
>
> Janice Callens
> Belmont, Louisiana

506 E. Buffalo St.
Polo, Illinois
Dec 12, 1953

To Hank Williams Family:

Its hard to forget a Great Entertainer like Hank Williams. I know It must be unbearble hard to forget. If he's a member of the family it must be miserable time. Forget you'll never will. The only thing a person can do is remember Hank's happy up above singing with the master's choir.

No matter how long I'll live, I'll hear (Cold Cold Heart), (May You Never bealone) and many many other great songs.

I remember him only as a entertainer who I saw and listen to only once, but never forgot him. You remember him as a loved one, may God keep you from heartaches and Sorrow.

A boy who can Never forget, Hank Williams
Marvin Barst
A loyal fan

ACKNOWLEDGEMENTS & THANKS

A Special Word of Appreciation to David Mitchell of Alexander City, Alabama: Your creative thinking inspired this book and we can't thank you enough!

Credits:

Itzkoff, Worley, and Ritzmann letters and photo of Audrey with letters courtesy of David Mitchell, Alexander City, Alabama

Photo of Lillie, Audrey, and Hank Jr. with letters courtesy of George Merritt, Huntsville, Alabama

Hornbeck sympathy card courtesy of Peter Trenholm, Pugwash, Nova Scotia

To all who donated their time, money, a pre-order for this book, or unfailing support, we thank you from our hearts. We greatly appreciate your patience and your trust.

Love & Thanks!   Dale & Lycrecia

Sam Vinicur
Norris Hoover
Kristi & John Grant
Merle Kilgore
Bernice Turner
Robert Ackerman
David Mitchell
Philip & Miriam Vinicur
Mark Benedetti
George Merritt
Peter Trenholm
Beth Birtley
Carolyn Halloran
Erin Burris
Anne Walker Blake
Simeon Smith

Gerald Swick
Richard Bonser
Ronny Elmore
Dennis Schut
Larry Crocker & Shasta Purple
April Adams
Brian Turpen
Judy & Danny Winchell
David & Gerri Findley,
   Nora & Suzanne of Go Design
John Webb
Eddie & Jenny Wilson
Jimmy Beall
George Merritt
Beth Birtley
Bill Lechler
Jack Waddey

Index of *Photos*, Cards & Letters

Thank you everyone for your beautiful cards and letters. People do not always take the time to sit down, write a note or card, and send it to a bereaved family, but comforting words and sentiments can mean a lot.

If your name or the name of your parent or grandparent is on this list, we would love to hear from you! Visit our website www.audreysdream.org for email and mailing address information and receive a special gift!

Dale & Lycrecia

"... Hank Williams wrote a great song when he wrote 'I Saw The Light' and we hope he saw the light before he left us."

Mrs. George Mitchell Jr
Meridian MS

SISTERS OF SEVERCY

'Go to the captain,' said Anne-Marie, seeing Charlotte's reluctance. 'Offer your lips and your breasts, thank him for his efforts. Go on all fours. Show him your behind. He will want to touch it and feel the weals as they rise.'

Charlotte did as she was bid, crawling on all fours like a supplicant to an eastern potentate. When she reached him, she turned around so that he could see the stripes across her buttocks and thighs. He touched her with the cigar still in his hand and she felt its heat against the already burning skin. His fingers found the wetness of her sex and immediately she began to groan. He had her twist around so that he could watch her face as the hand worked and she hurried towards orgasm. He let her climax, but took his hand away as soon as she began so that it was only a taste and she wanted more. When he had her kiss him afterwards, there was arousal and gratitude in the tongue that sought his with such great urgency.

A NEXUS CLASSIC

SISTERS OF
SEVERCY

Jean Aveline

Nexus

This book is a work of fiction.
In real life, make sure you practise safe sex.

First published in 1998 by
Nexus
Thames Wharf Studios
Rainville Road
London W6 9HA

This Nexus Classic edition 2001

Copyright © Jean Aveline 1998

www.nexus-books.co.uk

ISBN 0 352 33239 5

Typeset by TW Typesetting, Plymouth, Devon

Printed and bound by
Cox & Wyman Ltd, Reading, Berkshire

Contents

1

Severcy

Alain and Robert arrived in Severcy in early June, after a stay in Paris. The country was already dry and shimmering in a permanent heat haze. The two men crossed the bleached landscape of jagged chalk outcrops and precipitous valleys at a steady pace, resting the sweating horses regularly. The only shade came from the ancient cypress trees or when they passed through dusty olive groves.

Robert was aware of a change in his friend as soon as they entered the boundaries of the estate. Alain was a man who always impressed by his sheer physicality. Although not as tall as Robert, he was exceptionally broad and his chest was as deep as any two ordinary men. In this place, the land of his birth and the land of which he was master, Alain seemed to become even more substantial. His skin displayed evidence of smallpox as a child and the thousand tiny scars gave his broad, square face the appearance of one of the rough rock outcrops that they were so often forced to skirt on their journey. It was the blue of his eyes that saved him from being monstrous, the same distant blue that formed the dome of the sky.

Behind these two men trailed the tiny figure of Anna on a chestnut mare. She had been their only servant on the journey and it had been both practical and pleasing, to Alain at least, to dress her as a boy. Her hair had been cropped and she wore leather trousers and jerkin, clothes chosen to be bulky enough to conceal her fine figure, but warm, far too warm for the southern part of the journey. She wore a sulky expression as they journeyed on into the estate. Beads of sweat ran from her bronzed features, however much she fanned herself with the boys cap that she had been forced to wear.

As they drew nearer to the villa, the land flattened out and fields of sunflowers and maize replaced the dried grass and scrub land. Around the scattered cottages, fig and pomegranate trees clung precariously to life. Nothing could have been more different from the careful, green landscapes of Robert's native England. In these dry places, he sensed, new thirsts could develop and old restraints loosen.

Alain was watching the sun. It had already begun its descent to the horizon some hours ago.

'We won't be able to reach the villa tonight,' he said in his slow, heavy voice.

Robert shrugged. They had journeyed for three long weeks, one more night would not worry him.

As they reached the top of a ridge, the track they had been following was crossed by another, smaller path. Alain took them on to this, travelling east so that the sun was on their backs. After an hour or so they reached a clump of fig trees inside which nestled a long, low, whitewashed building. Once, it must have been a substantial house but now it was a ruin. Large cracks criss-crossed the mud brick walls and their substance was spilling back into the ground from which they were made. Part of the pan tile roof had collapsed and many of the windows had lost their shutters.

An old man, tall and lean, emerged from the shadow of the building as the riders approached. His face was deeply lined and his skin dark and leathery as if charred by the sun. He showed no surprise, greeting Alain as 'Maître', and when they had dismounted he gave a little bow and led the horses away.

'That is Bartelomie, he was my farrier for fifteen years,' said Alain.

Robert looked from the old man to the broken down building and wondered why Alain had brought them here.

2

'Let me show you something,' Alain said, as if to answer that unspoken question. He led them to the back of the house and across a paved courtyard. Where the ground began to dip they found a large pool of clear water surrounded by ancient straggling willows, trees quite different from the ones that Robert was familiar with in England, but still astonishing in such a place.

'It is the largest expanse of natural water on the estate,' Alain told them, 'spring fed, from those mountains probably.'

Alain pointed to the jagged outlines of rock on the horizon.

'It is so marvellous,' murmured Anna, who seemed almost faint with the heat. She sank to her knees at the edge of the pool and slipped her hand into the water. 'And cool.' She carried some to her face, splashing it on to her skin which was grimy with the dust of the road.

The old man reappeared and Alain called to him.

'Bartelomie, is the water still good for bathing?'

'I bathe every day, sir. They say it is good for the circulation.'

'Then help – help the boy take off his boots and undress, before he is overcome.'

Alain smiled a rare smile as the old man led Anna to a nearby rock. Anna sat and presented one of her legs. Bartelomie took the heel of her boot in one hand and the toe in the other. The boot was tight and the man stronger than his years suggested. Anna had to hang on to the rock tightly and dig the heel of her free foot into the sandy ground to steady herself. Gradually, Bartelomie eased the boot off. He smiled at her as it slipped from her foot.

'There lad, that must be better,' he said kindly, like an old uncle.

Anna nodded and smiled. The old mans eyes gleamed, still new in the used face. The second boot came off easily and Anna sighed her pleasure to be free of them.

'The jerkin next,' said the old man.

Anna stood and held out her arms. Bartelomie took the sleeves and Anna bent forward so that he could pull it over

3

her head. She would accept no help with the cotton undershirt, and, as used as she must have been to undressing before strangers, she turned her back on Bartelomie, facing her master, Alain, instead. As Anna eased the material from her torso, material that was sticky with sweat and clung to her, Bartelomie looked at her back with a measure of interest. Her dark, Mediterranean skin was fresh and tight with youth and her muscles, strong for a girl, flickered as she strained to remove the shirt. It was only when Anna began to remove her thick leather trousers that Bartolemie realised a joke was being played on him. He smiled to see the girl's behind emerge into the sunlight. His eyes opened wide as they swept across the slender hips and flanks and caught the exceptional narrowness of her waist. Anna raised her left foot to tug off the trouser leg, her body bending into an 'S', giving him a vision of one full breast. Between her legs he could glimpse dark hair, discretely trimmed and within it, the promise of pink.

'So what do you think?' asked Alain.

'A fine boy, sir, fit and healthy,' Bartolemie replied.

Alain smiled thinly. 'We give him good exercise.'

Anna finished undressing and collected her clothes into a pile.

'Is he too grubby for your pool, Bartolemie? Or will you permit him entry?'

'He is welcome, sir, to anything that is mine.'

Robert had already seated himself on a grassy ledge a few feet above the level of the water and Alain joined him. Together they watched Anna as she waded into the pool. It was genuinely cool, betraying its mountain origins, and the girl was tentative. When the water had reached the level of her knees she scooped up handfuls and splashed it across her arms. Robert heard her little gasp as she ran her wet hands across her breasts and belly and saw her shoulders hunch with the surprise. She waded out further and deeper then turned, twisting from the waist as the water lapped at her thighs. She smiled broadly and her teeth were very white in her tanned face. Robert smiled too. He smiled to see her calculation, the way that she knew how good she looked. The water just kissed her sex at that moment and her lips made a full circle, a pout of surprise for the benefit of the audience. Her coy exhibition had the desired effect, and Robert knew that he would have to have her as soon as she left the water. Turning he saw that Bartolemie was also watching the girl but the old man's eyes were sadder, as if he would never possess such youth and beauty again.

Apparently satisfied with her performance, Anna slipped into the water, sinking beneath the surface with the grace of a dolphin. She swam several metres, her body emblazoned with ribbons of sunlight, before emerging in the centre of the pool. Turning on to her back she floated, allowing the coolness of the water to penetrate and to soothe.

Robert closed his eyes and listened to the buzz of the cicadas. They reminded him of Honduras, where he and Alain had spent the last few years establishing a trade in coffee. In that distant place there were other sounds, the cries of monkeys and the shouts of men who laboured in hot fields. Here the cicadas seemed muted, and the gentle splashing as Anna swam slowly across the pool lulled him. He thought of Charlotte, who he had married just two months ago in London, after returning from Honduras; and he thought of the keys, the five keys he had had made which gave the holders access to her bedroom. At that moment, as Robert drowsed, his wife's sweet body might be heaving beneath the caress of a stranger or beneath whip or cane. He had left a journal for her to record such things and on his return he would have her read it to him. It stirred him to think of such things; it stirred him to remember the few brief weeks they had spent together before his journeying to France.

Robert's daydreaming was interrupted by the sound of water being disturbed by wading feet. Anna was emerging from the pool, shaking her dark, cropped hair so that plumes of water shot from it and gleamed in the golden light. She shivered, and since there was nothing that she could use to dry herself, she turned to the sun and held up her arms to capture its heat. She looked for all the world like a pagan worshipper.

Robert pulled his large frame upright and went over to her. As his hand trailed down her spine she turned to him. He could see the goose bumps on her flesh and he brushed his hands down her sides and across her breasts to drive away the clinging water. She shook her head again and sprayed him, smiling as he rubbed the droplets into the skin of his face. His fingers found her sex and he toyed with her until her face went slack and she was wet inside.

'On your knees,' he told her in a low voice.

She sank down and reached for his sex, looking up into his face as if to make sure that this was what he wanted. He was already hard. Her chilled fingers struggled to undo the buttons of his breeches, but finally she managed, pulling the tall column of flesh into daylight. It was hot, very hot, and she leant her wet cheek against it, cooling it, before taking it into her mouth. He heard her sigh of pleasure as she began to suck and his pelvis pushed forward, seeking velvet depths.

Bartolemie watched the girl as she worked. He watched her legs opening and closing and her hips pushing back and forth as her whole body seemed to pivot on the sex that speared her mouth. Robert pressed his hands to the girls head and began to fuck her. She made her mouth soft and laid open her jaws, encouraging him with little grunts at each of the thrusts. Her hands clawed at his thighs then sought out his sac where she used her fingernails in a light, scratching caress.

When he pulled himself clear of her mouth and took his sex in his hand, it seemed that he would climax, but somehow he stilled that impulse. The girl looked up at him, her mouth still open, offering itself for his seed if he should want to use it. Instead, he commanded her to present herself on all fours and, when she had done so, he knelt behind her. He chose to enter her wet sex, driving in without reservation in a way that made her cry out with pleasure. As he fucked her strong and deep, he cradled the side of her head in his hand so that he could watch her face; watch all of its transformations, watch as it moved from voluptuousness to frustration to frenzy. When she was close he told her to climax and she did, her cries breaking across the still water. Still Robert fucked her and she pressed herself lower, grinding her breasts into the sandy soil, clutching at the few dry grasses with her little hands as her face twisted and her breathing came in sharp gasps. Robert looked down on the split of her behind, a behind that she thrust even higher as he rested his thumb against the smaller opening and began to push. She edged her torso back, so that her belly was pushed further between her legs and so that the thumb, as it went into her, pierced the highest point of her body. He climaxed then, grunting and bucking into her as if possessed.

Robert finally withdrew from the girl and sank to the ground. She remained as she was for a while, her behind fully presented and rotating slowly. Then, rousing herself, she crawled over to him on all fours like a cat and licked his sex clean. Her face had the look of certain women confined to asylums; abandoned, forgetful, enraptured by forces others cannot see. Robert's hand went to her head and pressed down so that she licked underneath, deep between his legs.

When Robert was entirely clean, Anna carefully disengaged herself and went once more to the water's edge to clean herself. First she washed the dust from her body then, squatting and opening her legs, she washed her sex. She kept her back upright and her head high in this task, dignified and unselfconscious. Any man seeing her in that beautiful place so completely involved in such an intimate task would have wanted her. Alain, watching from the grassy ledge, called out her name and beckoned.

She padded over, water still running from her thighs, her features smooth and fresh after the catharsis of orgasm. Alain knew she would be expecting him to take her now, for that was the way that it went: one of them would use her and immediately the other would reach for her. But it was not for his own sake that Alain called her this time. As Anna stood before him, naked, waiting for him to begin, he indicated to the old man whose hungry eyes followed her every movement.

'Go to him,' said Alain, 'tell him that I recommend your mouth.'

The girl looked at the old man. The faintest frown betrayed her reluctance as she turned back to Alain.

'This is not a command,' he told her, 'I ask it as a favour for my old friend.'

Anna smiled and murmured her assent. She walked over to the old man slowly, halting in front of him, where he sat with his back against the rock. She stood quite still, parting her legs so that he could see her, allowing him to fill his memory with her. She gazed at him softly as his eyes fixed on to her breasts, then on to her thighs and the treasures that nestled between them.

The old man was shaking, visibly quivering from head to foot as she knelt between his outstretched legs. He allowed her to pull the cord that secured his trousers at the waist and to draw the fabric down. Beneath this he wore nothing. The flesh of his legs was much paler than his face and, though the skin was loose, it was unlined. Half standing, she pulled the trousers completely clear of his bare feet and knelt between his legs once more. His shirt still shielded his sex, but he was obviously erect.

'Monsieur Alain recommends my mouth,' she told him.

He nodded and his eyes examined the sweetness of her lips. 'I feel weak, my child, it would be a blessing.'

She leant forward, her breasts swaying, and lifted his shirt. If he was weak then all of his strength must have gone to his sex. It stood proudly from it's nest of greying hairs, as hard as wood. She bent forward and touched her lips to it's very tip. There was a smell of the pool, a clean smell but with a faint presence of algae and something sharper, something mineral. He shivered from head to foot at this first touch and, as if fearing that he would climax too soon, she transferred her lips to his thighs, kissing slowly along their insides. At the juncture of those thighs she found his sac and took it into her mouth. He murmured, 'beautiful so very beautiful', over and over again and when she raised her head he reached out his hand, thin and shaking, to caress her cheek.

'Has it been a long time?' she asked.

'Many years,' he replied, 'and many years more since a woman as fine as you.'

She smiled and dipped her head to his sex again, taking it deep into her throat this time, but not moving, simply allowing him to feel the whole of her soft mouth and the tongue that quivered involuntarily as it pressed against that most sensitive place, the place below the tiny opening that wept a milk of desire on to her palate.

'Please,' he groaned, unable to contain the feelings for another moment.

Instantly, she began to move strongly, sweeping her pursed lips up and down the hard rod. His belly began to spasm and a deep groan came from his throat. He climaxed, spraying his thick seed into her mouth, filling it completely.

He stroked her head over and over again, his belly continuing to spasm until she finally withdrew her mouth.

The three travellers spent the night in the ruined building, sleeping in beds that had not seen guests for many long years. The girl spent the night with Bartolemie as it was judged that he had the greatest need. She had little sleep, for the old man had regained his strength, and with so little time was determined to take full advantage of her. In the middle of the night she begged him to take her outside, 'into the desert', even though it was not a true desert and, seeing that it had some special significance for her, he agreed.

Beneath the stars she changed, becoming somehow shy and furtive, avoiding his eyes like a young girl. When he touched her, her arousal was immediately strong and when he lay her down on the dry ground and took her, she groaned continuously. Towards the end she murmured, 'Don Luis', over and over again. The old man took this to be the name of a former lover, but she would not speak of it, even afterwards when he took her back to his bed. In

9

the morning she had dark rings around her eyes and a fragile appearance as if her heart had been opened. The old man told of what had happened, and Alain treated the girl kindly for he knew of 'Don Luis' and the desert, the desert in Mexico where Anna had been born. She was allowed to wear a light summer dress for the remainder of the journey and they treated her as a lady of good birth. By evening the travellers had arrived at the villa.

2

The Villa

For the first few days Alain and Robert attended to the business of the estate. The steward, Remenie, showed them the accounts and offered grave descriptions of the recent poor harvests and severe weather. He told of how many tenants were behind in their rents, that storehouses were empty and water reserves in the cisterns low. On top of this wine prices had fallen and there was a surplus of olives across the whole country. Implicit in all that Remenie said was the criticism that Alain was taking too much from the estate to fund his lavish life style and leaving too little to invest in the land.

Together, Alain, Robert and the steward toured the estate on horseback, covering dusty, gruelling mile after mile. Alain said very little as Remenie pointed out the buildings in need of repair, the olive trees too old to produce fruit and the barns plagued by vermin.

At the end of three days, after pouring over the accounts and talking with many of the estate workers, Alain sacked the steward.

'You have been lax,' Alain told him, 'and you have probably stolen from me.'

The steward protested his innocence but left quickly when dismissed. In those remote hills and valleys the maître's word was the only law.

Robert, as part owner of the estate, had followed the course of these events with interest but without becoming actively involved. He didn't understand olive or wine production and contented himself with the pleasures of this new country, hunting in the rough scrub of the hills for boar or simply idling in the sun.

The villa itself had been built by Alain's father after a fire had destroyed the original. It was exceptional in its classical elegance and the surrounding gardens were large and well kept, despite the problems of the estate. The site had been chosen because of the abundance of water from an underground river. So whilst the outlying lands baked and cracked, the gardens of the villa were an oasis; the scent of rosemary bushes filled the air, verdant lawns were overshaded by majestic sweet chestnut trees, and everywhere there was the sound of running water, whether murmuring fountain or carefully constructed stream.

Alain's father had been an admirer of the architect Palladio and his passion for the antique villas of Rome. The villa was modelled on a palace that had once entertained emperors on the hills above the Tiber. Most of the building was only one storey high, spreading over a large area and enclosing gardens and terraces, baths and fountains. The brilliance of its terracotta rooves and the whiteness of its marble stood out in the landscape like a string of jewels. The large windows and doors of the many rooms were kept permanently open in the blazing heat and it was possible to walk through the building unimpeded, passing from drawing room to garden to bedroom to courtyard to gallery, in endless procession. It felt to Robert like an exotic emcampment, except that the tents were brick, stone and glass.

Having sacked the steward, Alain set about putting the affairs of the estate in order. He ordered repairs where necessary and the furnishing of new seed and stocks for the various crops. It became obvious that finding a new steward and attending to only the most pressing matters would take some time, far longer than they had first planned.

'I must stay for at least a month,' Alain told his friend. 'Perhaps two.'

'I can think of no better place to pass time,' Robert replied.

'And your wife?'

'Safe in Anne-Marie's hands, I'm sure. Improving with each day that passes.'

'Improving?'

'In the pleasure that she can give us.'

Alain smiled. 'If you are content in that regard, we should find some pleasures for ourselves here. There are certain privileges that fall to the maître of this estate. Ones that you should share in.'

Having said this, Alain refused to expand further, advising his friend to have patience.

The next morning, Alain and Robert rode out early before the sun could attain its full, blazing strength. They visited many of the tenanted farms and the cottages of the estate workers. At each, Alain would be greeted with great flurries of activity. He would be offered wine and food, the women would strip off their aprons and brush their hair, while the men would hurry in from the fields, if they were nearby, to be of service. Alain would be civil and inquire after their well-being, offering assurances that he would rectify the mistakes of the incompetent steward, Remenie. His main purpose, though, was to find the prettiest and most accommodating girls. These he would praise and flatter and offer employment at the villa. Some would refuse, others accept only to have their parents forbid them. It was well known what employment at the villa meant, some of the older women had experience of Alain's father and his unusual tastes. Even so, a number of the girls were persuaded, and a number more defied their parents injunctions, stealing away to the villa when they were not being observed, leaving behind the drudgery of the fields. In this way the two friends found many pleasures in the mouths, sexes and behinds of those simple girls.

3

Charlotte

Charlotte and Anne-Marie were sitting down to afternoon tea on the lawn at Fulstead when the note arrived. The maid presented it with a pretty curtsey and Charlotte took it from the silver tray, hoping that it might be a letter from Robert. She didn't hide her disappointment when she saw her name written in an unfamiliar, if elegant, hand.

'Who is it from?' asked Anne-Marie.

Charlotte turned the envelope over, examining it carefully. The wax seal was stamped with a key, a key that was familiar to her, and seeing this, her heart missed a beat. Charlotte showed it to the Frenchwoman.

'Open it,' she said, with a slow broad smile.

Charlotte hesitated and then took the knife from the tray to slit the black sealing wax.

The note was brief.

> *Madam,*
>   *Expect me at eight. Have Mademoiselle Belloque prepare you,*
>   *V.*

Charlotte dismissed the maid and passed the note to Anne-Marie.

'V,' said the Frenchwoman with a faint frown, as she tried to guess the identity of the note's sender. 'It may be that we are expecting a Russian gentleman.'

'A Russian!'

'He is very civilised, and very handsome. If it is the gentleman that I think it is, I shall envy you.'

Charlotte was not entirely reassured by this information. She brushed two tiny crumbs of wax from her lap before they softened in the afternoon sun and ruined the perfect whiteness of her silk dress. Looking across the carefully nurtured parkland that swept down to the valley below, Charlotte wondered if she had the resolve to keep her promise to Robert. On his last night in England she had promised to honour his friends, unnamed and unknown to her, as she honoured her husband. Each had been given a key to her bedroom and she was to offer them her body as freely as she might offer her hand to a stranger to be kissed. When she had made that promise it had excited her to give Robert that small gift. He had wanted to imagine her with others while he was away and so keep his desire for her fresh and keen. Now a promise given in the heat of passion was to be made good. She shivered, even though it was warm, and glanced at Anne-Marie.

'When his hands are on you, you will want it,' Anne-Marie said softly with a smile, 'I think that I know you a little now.'

Charlotte flushed and looked away. In the last few weeks the Frenchwoman had explored her body with all the insistence of a man, introducing her to pleasures that Charlotte could not have imagined, pleasures that Robert had wanted her to be acquainted with. At first, Charlotte had submitted to them for Robert's sake, but finally desired these pleasures in themselves.

'Look at me, my darling,' Anne-Marie told her.

Charlotte looked. Every aspect of Anne-Marie breathed the thick, sweet scent of sensuality. Her steady blue eyes always had that sense of knowingness, as if she understood another's desires better than they did themselves. There was a kindness there too, an allowingness that made any desire, any feeling, acceptable. Charlotte knew well that Anne-Marie was shocked by nothing and afraid of nothing. No avenues of pleasure were ever closed in her mind. She could be ruthless, as ruthless as any man, but

15

there was always that warmth, a warmth that enveloped her accomplices, or victims, in the pursuit of sensation. Part of the warmth came from her smile, part from her body, full and tall, which glowed with health and strength. Her breasts were sumptuous, perfect. Charlotte had lost her senses many times in the last few weeks with her head buried in their soft, protecting embrace. The Frenchwoman's hips too were ample, curving outwards like arms that sought to draw a person in, to draw them to a sex, hidden now, but overpowering in its richness when bared, like a full petalled rose. As Charlotte gazed at Anne-Marie she already felt herself becoming excited.

'Make me want him,' Charlotte breathed, 'for Robert's sake.'

Anne-Marie took the girl's hand and raised it to her lips, pressing her soft lips to the palm.

'I shall,' she replied, 'and I shall make him want you so much in return he will be like a wolf.'

That evening the two women ate early and lightly in honour of their visitor and then retired to Charlotte's large bedroom on the first floor. In the adjoining dressing room two baths had been set out side by side under Anne-Marie's instructions. The hot water they contained steamed in the light of the evening sun. The two women were attended by a young chambermaid as they prepared for the gentleman's visit. First, she helped her mistress to undress, and then Anne-Marie. Once they had taken their places in the high-backed baths, Anne-Marie and Charlotte faced each other. The Frenchwoman indicated that the maid should begin with Charlotte, and the girl began sponging her mistress nervously.

'There is no hurry, Sara,' Anne-Marie said when the girl had finished Charlotte's arms and chest, 'go back to the beginning and start again. Polish your mistress until she shines like marble.'

Charlotte smiled at this and held up her arm for the maid. The girl, Sara, also smiled, her fine, translucent skin flushing with pleasure. Anne-Marie had seen that the girl had a crush on Charlotte from the beginning and included her in these intimate tasks to tease her young heart. She had a good body and most especially, a beautiful, slender behind that, one day, Anne-Marie was determined to open with her tongue.

The girl started again with the hand that Charlotte held aloft, moving the sponge slowly and lightly, like a lover's caress, along the gleaming arm. From time to time she would pause to smooth fragrant oils into the skin. At her mistress's bosom the girl was especially attentive, circling the taut globes with the sponge and repeatedly applying oils and soaps with her small, nervous hands. When the breasts were completely hidden by a rich lather, Sara poured fresh water across them from urns beside the bath. Charlotte's skin turned to gold in the sun's fading light and the coral tips of her breasts stood fully alert, as tempting as fresh strawberries.

'Her legs, Sara.'

Charlotte raised her legs, opening them and allowing them to rest on the rounded walls of the tub. There was the sense of a ritual in all this. On many previous evenings Sara had performed these services and must have known her mistress's body as well as she knew her own. She used the oil to massage Charlotte, first kneading the flesh of calves and thighs with the heel of her hand and then using her knuckles and fingers, working until the muscles were loose and the legs heavy in her grip. All the time that this was done to her, Charlotte seemed to sink deeper and deeper into a sort of dream. Her eyes half closed and her head fell back against the enamel of the backrest to expose a sweet white throat. Charlotte would never know how it stirred her watchers, how it stirred Sara especially, to see her give herself over to these simple pleasures so unreservedly.

When the maid had finished her mistress's legs she stood back and waited.

Anne-Marie motioned to the girl and she washed the Frenchwoman. When the girl's hand ran along her shoulder, Anne-Marie bestowed the lightest of kisses on its

17

back and the girl jumped. Even Charlotte, as distracted as she appeared to be, smiled to see this. When the girl washed her breasts, Anne-Marie pressed her hand over the maid's hand and held it against the soft flesh for a moment before the girl pulled away. It was a delicious game but one that Anne-Marie would not force. Instead she wore at the girl with compliments and smiles. She told her how sweet were her eyes, how glowing her hair, how appealing her behind as she bent over her mistress, how pleasing it was to be touched by her. Anne-Marie reported the remarks that Robert had made before he had left, remarks on the maid's obliging nature and discretion, then asked her if she would wash her master as carefully as she washed her mistress, asking if she could be discrete if he grew hard as she washed his manhood. The girl was easily flustered by these questions and silence was her refuge. Even so, she didn't flee as other young girls might and Anne-Marie knew that there was a satisfaction for the maid in these attentions.

When, at length, Anne-Marie was as thoroughly washed as she could be whilst reclining, she stood and the girl used the sponge on her back and her behind.

'Look at me child,' Anne-Marie said as the girl worked the soap between her legs. The girl looked up, her eyes gleaming. Anne-Marie dipped her head and kissed the girl on her cheek. Sara accepted this with a blush, but when Anne-Marie tried to kiss her lips she turned her face away.

'Another time,' said Anne-Marie softly and turned her attention to Charlotte.

'Help her, Sara.'

The maid complied, and with her aid, Charlotte stood so that she too could feel the sponge between her legs. Anne-Marie stepped out of the bath and kissed her charge very fully while this very intimate task was undertaken. Sara used the same oils and soaps on Charlotte's sex as she had used on her legs and Charlotte was wet inside as well as outside by the time she was finally released.

It was well past seven o'clock before all these ministrations were completed. Anne-Marie had Sara light all the candles in the bedroom, not because they were

18

needed then, but because they would be needed later. As the maid carried a burning wax taper from candle to candle, Anne-Marie asked Charlotte to lie down on the bed. She arranged the girl in various positions, stepping back now and again to judge the effect. Charlotte was as pliant as a mannequin as her legs were drawn this way and that and as Anne-Marie made her lie first on her front and then on her back. It took a while to find the position that best displayed her rich charms. Finally, Anne-Marie settled for Charlotte lying on her side with one leg straight and the other, the upper leg, bent and pulled up. This displayed the swell of her behind very well and anyone coming through the door would immediately see the invitation of the twin openings between her legs. Since Anne-Marie had twisted Charlotte at the waist so that both shoulders were lying flat on the bed, her breasts were also offered sweetly.

When Anne-Marie was content with Charlotte's position, Sara applied light dabs of perfumes to her underarms and to the folds behind her knees and between her legs. The alcohol in the scents made the delicate membranes of Charlotte's sex sting. Anne-Marie had Sara part those membranes and touch a little to the pink bud that swelled at their apex. Charlotte writhed as if a bee had found her most sensitive place and stung her. Watching her behind clench and unclench, Anne-Marie knew that the visitor would want the girl and she was satisfied. Now there was only the matter of providing those small accessories the gentleman might need to get the most from the girl.

'Fetch the box,' Anne-Marie said.

Sara went to the linen chest at the foot of the bed. On top of the carefully folded sheets was a large rosewood box. Lifting it in two hands she carried it to the bedside table.

'Open it,' Anne-Marie told her.

Inside was a collection of whips and lengths of fabric that could be used to tie a girl. Moving over to the box, Anne-Marie selected a neatly coiled whip with a black ebony handle. She laid this on Charlotte's hip and the effect was dramatic.

19

'I want more light on her behind,' Anne-Marie told Sara.

The maid fetched two tall, silver candle sticks from the dressing room where the women had bathed and set them on the linen chest. As similar candles burnt on both bedside tables, Charlotte was now surrounded by a ring of fire. Anne-Marie sat at the head of the bed and stroked a few stray hairs from the girl's face.

'It is our visitor that I envy, not you,' she said.

Charlotte smiled. 'Will you stay with me?' she asked.

To Charlotte's evident disappointment, Anne-Marie shook her head.

'You are his alone tonight.'

After dismissing the maid and applying a final series of lingering kisses to the soft, glowing flesh laid out so temptingly, Anne-Marie retired to her bedroom.

A little before eight o'clock two riders appeared in the driveway. They paused to look up at the old stone house. The warm glow of the lights in Charlotte's bedroom were clearly visible in the gathering gloom. The younger man set off at pace and the other, his servant, hurried to keep up. At the large, oaken entrance door the younger man quickly dismounted from his horse and handed the reins to his companion. He didn't trouble to knock and the door was not locked when he pushed. In the hall he found a maid dusting a painting of a man standing with his hand on a globe as if he owned the whole world. The girl was startled by the stranger and took a pace backwards.

'I want your mistress's bedroom,' the man said. He had a faint foreign accent that the girl couldn't place and there was something about his manner, his rapaciousness, that seemed to unnerve her even more than his abrupt and unannounced entrance. She pointed to the stairs without speaking. The man strode past the maid and took the stairs two at a time.

Anne-Marie had left the door to Charlotte's bedroom slightly ajar and when the man came upon it, he paused only momentarily before opening it. The sight that met his

20

eyes froze him in his tracks and his face turned almost purple. His desire was immediate, like a charge of lightning and Charlotte, looking at him with half closed eyes, shook as if swept by a hot wind. He closed the door quickly and taking the key from his pocket, locked it. Many sounds came from the room that evening; cries, sobs, shouts of exultation, and climactic screams from mouths whose sex could not have been identified.

Two hours later, the man unlocked the bedroom door and shouted for a servant. It was the same girl that the stranger had startled on his arrival who answered the call. She stood back from the door nervously as the man demanded to know if there was vodka in the house. When she shook her head the stranger sent her for brandy. It was a very nervous maid indeed who knocked at the bedroom door five minutes later with decanter and glasses on a silver tray. The man called for her to enter, and against her better judgement the girl did. Her mistress was lying in the gentleman's arms, her back against his chest as he propped himself against the head board. There were angry red marks on Charlotte's behind and she had been crying. What the girl would not forget though, was the look of abandonment on her mistress's face. The man's hand was between her legs and his fingers were buried deep in her sex. Charlotte writhed against this hand as if it and the pleasure that it gave her, were the only fact of her existence. It frightened the girl to see such absence of shame and she hurriedly placed the tray on the bedside table nearest the door. As she turned to leave, Charlotte raised her behind a fraction and the girl saw something that made her heart miss several beats. The man's sex was erect and buried in her mistress's behind. Its size chilled her and so did the groan that Charlotte gave, a groan of the deepest longing as she drove down on that member. The maid fled and the man laughed, reaching for the brandy.

As she hurried away down the corridor, the maid ran straight into the arms of Anne-Marie.

'Sara! What is the matter?' she asked softly.

The girl burst into tears and Anne-Marie took her into her arms.

'The mistress . . .' sobbed Sara.

'You love her, don't you?'

'Yes.'

'And the man? Is he frightening?'

'Yes,' she said, grateful that Anne-Marie understood these things.

Anne-Marie kissed her full on the lips and Sara opened her mouth, sagging into Anne-Marie's all-enfolding arms.

'You are mine,' said the Frenchwoman, 'and I will not give you to men until you are ready.'

Sara made a feeble effort to escape but Anne-Marie stilled her with a hand pressed to her sex.

'You want this don't you?' Anne-Marie asked, pressing into the young girl harder and taking the whole mound into her hand.

'Yes, mistress,' she whispered.

They walked to the bedroom as Charlotte cried out one more time.

4

The Belloques

It was only in the second month of his stay at Severcy that Robert found a woman who genuinely interested him. He and Alain were riding back from a hunting expedition when, on impulse, Alain decided to call at a large, handsome house on a hill covered with fig trees. Robert had never been in that area before and was surprised when Alain told him that it was the house of Madame Belloque, Anne-Marie's mother.

'Why haven't you visited before?' Robert asked.

'It is a delicate matter,' was all that Alain would say.

Madame Belloque was a tall, striking woman in her late thirties with a fine figure and the quick, graceful movements of Anne-Marie. After her initial surprise she greeted Alain warmly, extending the same friendliness to Robert whom she addressed in fluent English despite his own excellent French.

The late Monsieur Belloque had been steward to Alain's father and he had left the family well provided for. The house was comfortably furnished and rich in the gifts of civilised living. Through an open door from the hall, Robert saw a library and from another room came the sound of a piano being played.

Madame Belloque led them out to a courtyard at the side of the house which was cool and shaded by a particularly large fig tree. At an ancient, weathered, oak table she asked them to sit and called for her maid.

'You must allow me to offer you refreshments,' she said graciously.

Both men accepted her offer with gratitude after their long day in the dust and sun. The maid brought pitchers of cold wine and fresh water from the well.

As Alain and Madame Belloque chatted politely about old times, Robert settled into his chair and listened to the piano. The player was clearly practised and surprisingly expressive in the execution of the music. It was almost the last sound that Robert would have expected in such a remote place. Finally, he could contain his curiosity no longer and asked Madame Belloque who was playing.

'That is my daughter, Isabelle,' she exclaimed proudly. 'She practises for at least an hour every day, sometimes she will do nothing else.'

Again, Robert was surprised. He had not known that Anne-Marie had a sister.

'She is a talented pianist,' Robert allowed.

Almost as he spoke, the playing stopped and a few moments later a young woman appeared in the courtyard. Clearly surprised by the guests, she froze as soon as she saw them.

'Isabelle,' her mother called.

The girl still hesitated, half hidden in the shadow of the house.

'She is not used to strangers,' her mother explained to the two men. 'Isabelle, come,' she called again.

Isabelle crossed the courtyard rather timidly, blinking in the bright sunshine. Robert was taken with her immediately. She was quite different from Anne-Marie; slighter in build, dark haired and less sure of herself. Her face showed a sensitive intelligence and her eyes were bright with curiosity. The sudden appearance of the two men, while catching her off her guard, seemed not to be unwelcome.

'Mademoiselle Isabelle,' Alain said with measured surprise.

The girl smiled uncertainly.

'How different you are after only two years.'

'She is a woman now,' her mother interjected.

'Indeed,' Alain agreed.

'And she has attracted a good offer of marriage from a

24

merchant in Arronville. She will be married in the cathedral there in November.'

Madame Belloque seemed to be offering this as a warning to the two men.

Isabelle, clearly taken aback by all of the attention, blushed deeply. When Alain rose and took her hand to kiss it, Isabelle took a step backwards. Her hand in his was tiny and she was unable to meet his eyes, as intense and unblinking as they always were. Robert also rose. He took her hand firmly, almost insolently, as if it were rightfully his, but she seemed to find his smile attractive and returned it without reservation. When Robert's lips brushed the back of her hand the girl coloured again. He saw this and felt a current of interest pass between them.

After all the introductions had been completed, Isabelle sat with them quietly. While Alain and Madame Belloque talked, Robert studied the girl. She said very little, but when she did speak it was clear that she was both thoughtful and passionate. There was a quality of sadness around her eyes, a solitariness perhaps, that he found appealing and he wondered what such a girl could find to do in so remote a place. He imagined the pleasures and practices that he might introduce her to. Her body, ripening with each day, would bruise or blossom at the lightest touch.

During the ride home, Robert expressed his interest in Isabelle and was surprised by Alain's coolness. While Alain did not dismiss his friend's desire, he did not offer any help in procuring the girl. Neither would he offer any explanation for refusing to use his influence with Madame Belloque when Robert requested it.

'She is to be married in six months time,' Alain exclaimed when he was pressed.

'Then now is the time to enjoy her,' replied Robert, surprised by Alain's reservations.

The next day, after a night of thinking of the girl with increasing desire, Robert went to Alain and demanded an explanation of the mysteries surrounding the Belloque family. Alain refused to satisfy the other man's curiosity

25

and it was only after a furious argument and many threats that Alain agreed to return to Madame Belloque and discuss the matter with her. He would promise nothing more than to arrange a meeting with the girl.

Isabelle heard that she was to visit the villa with surprise and excitement. Alain had arrived early one morning a few days after the first visit and, happening on her outside the house, he had asked her if she would accept an invitation. She agreed immediately almost out of politeness, believing her mother would refuse to allow it. Over two hours later, Alain emerged from a meeting with Madame Belloque which had clearly been a trial for both of them. Whatever they had discussed, it had been decided that Isabelle should visit the villa if she wished.

Madame Belloque obviously still had grave misgivings but something had persuaded her to put them aside. Later, when Alain had gone, she spoke very carefully to her daughter.

'Isabelle, you are very young, and when one is young –' she halted, perhaps concerned that she might say more than she should. Then in a stronger and more direct voice she declared, 'You must promise me that you will be on your guard at the villa as a young woman should.'

'On my guard?' asked Isabelle, affecting not to understand her mother's concern.

'I think you follow me.'

'Might I be attacked?'

Madame Belloque was clearly determined not to be deflected by her daughter's teasing.

'You must promise me that you will still be a virgin in six months' time when you walk down the aisle at Arronville with Monsieur Chabard.'

'Please, mother!' replied Isabelle, affronted.

'I have assured that gentleman of your purity. It is a good match and he would expect nothing else. Now promise me!'

Her mother was so insistent that Isabelle, still surprised by her mother's bluntness, was finally forced to swear that nothing would compromise her virginity.

'Monsieur Alain has also sworn,' murmured Madame Belloque.

'Mother! You have discussed my virginity with Monsieur Alain. He is a stranger!'

'There are reasons.'

'Then you should explain them.'

'I am your mother. That is enough!'

Isabelle was momentarily silenced by the sharpness of her mother's tone. She suspected that much of what had happened between Alain and her mother had to do with Anne-Marie. The circumstances surrounding her sister's departure from the estate were never discussed.

'I'm sorry,' said the girl. 'I will trust your judgement if you will trust mine.'

With these words the subject was closed. Isabelle spent the remainder of the day choosing her clothes and preparing for her visit. She carefully hid her excitement so as not to worry her mother further. She knew far more of what happened at the villa than her mother suspected. She also knew that Anne-Marie was more than the simple housekeeper that she described herself as in her regular letters.

As she laid out her finest dresses, Isabelle thought of the look of desire in the Englishman's eyes as he had studied her during the visit. She compared him in her mind with Monsieur Chabard, the merchant she was to marry. Chabard was coarse and dull in comparison and the proposed marriage seemed less attractive the more that she thought of it.

From beneath her bed, Isabelle recovered Anne-Marie's many letters and read through them for the fiftieth time. Her sister's descriptions of the world beyond the estate thrilled her. Isabelle too, wanted to ride down the Champs Élysées in a gleaming landau. She wanted to cross the Mediterranean to Morocco in a fast sailing ship. There was a richness in Anne-Marie's life that made her own seem pale.

5

The Second Key

One afternoon, Charlotte was walking in the grounds at Fulstead when a maid surprised her. The servant was completely unfamiliar and for a moment Charlotte thought that Anne-Marie had engaged a new girl.

'My master is waiting for you, madam,' said the girl, 'I am to show you this.'

The girl held out her hand, opening it to reveal a key.

'And where is your master?' asked Charlotte.

The maid looked back to the house. Seated at the table where she and Anne-Marie regularly took tea, Charlotte could make out the figure of a man.

She started out in that direction but the maid halted her with a hand on the arm.

'He wants you to be naked, madam.'

Charlotte looked at the maid for a moment, taken aback. The maid's eyes slid downwards, deferentially.

'Very well,' said Charlotte finally.

The maid helped Charlotte to undress, taking the garments as they were removed and folding them over her arm until there was nothing more to take. The grass was moist under Charlotte's feet as she walked up the slight incline to the veranda. As she drew nearer, Charlotte could see a very finely dressed man, quite immaculate in black frock coat and flesh coloured trousers. He was as handsome as a Greek statue and wore a white cravat in the Byronic style, loose and rather dashing. The man took his hat from his head as Charlotte approached, and laid it on the table. His long slender hands rested on a silver-topped cane as he surveyed the naked woman before him. His hair was strikingly fair and his eyes were cool, insolent as only a young man's can be.

'The girl has shown you the key?' he asked.

Charlotte nodded.

'So I may be free with you?'

'Yes, sir.'

'Good. I understand that you keep a journal?'

Charlotte nodded reluctantly.

'Then kindly fetch it.'

The maid laid out the clothes on a chair while Charlotte fetched the journal. It seemed shocking to her that it should be read anywhere but the bedroom and that it should be read at all in daylight. When she had returned to the veranda she held out the red, leather-bound book and the man took it. Glancing down, Charlotte realised that the man, or perhaps the maid, had undone the buttons of his trousers and that his sex was now exposed. It nestled on its bed of blond hair as if sleeping, indifferent to the two women. As the man began to read though, so it rose, and he looked at Charlotte as if to assess her, as if trying to read in her face the woman that she was. Perhaps he was wondering if she could truly be the same woman described in the journal.

'Kneel, if you please,' he said, and she knelt before him. 'Take it in your mouth.'

Charlotte bent forward and took the half erect sex as he had directed. She did not know if she was to suck or move at all as he hardened and lengthened in her throat. He said nothing as he read more of the journal. After a few minutes she felt a hand on her cheek. It coaxed her into a slow up and down motion. Soon he was very hard and it was only with difficulty that she could take all of him into her mouth as he seemed to want.

'Jane,' he called.

The maid came over to him and he handed her the journal.

'Read,' he said, 'start anywhere.'

29

The girl read well for a servant and in a voice far calmer than Charlotte felt to hear the words.

'Anne-Marie came for me in the middle of the night again. She is different at night, more intense. Usually she blindfolds me on these nocturnal visits but this time she didn't. She used the strap. I lay across her lap as she sat on the edge of the bed. The strokes weren't especially hard but went on for a long time. It was only when I started crying that she stopped. She had me kneel between her knees and kissed me. I was wet when her hand went to my sex. It is delicious to be touched by her after she has beaten me; she is all softness and care, as if it were someone else, some cruel stranger who had hurt me and not her at all. It is one of her games.'

The maid paused to clear her throat and Charlotte glanced at her. The maid avoided her eye and Charlotte saw that the girl was flushed. She was not as calm as her voice suggested.

'Carry on girl,' the man said. The arousal in his voice was obvious.

'Anne-Marie had me use my tongue on her sex and behind. I could hear her breathing getting faster and faster and thought that she would climax, but she pushed me away and took up the strap again. This time I lay with the small of my back across her lap. I was afraid that she would use it to my breasts but the blows fell only on my thighs. She reduced me to tears again. When I struggled, she said that she would have to tie me and that if she did, she would use the cane. I managed to still myself long enough for her to strap me as she wished. She told me how much she loved my tears, how she loved to have me so soft afterwards, how if she could have me so soft without using the strap she would throw it away tomorrow. She started to speak only in French, whispering, *"ma petite, ma belle soeur, ma chère,"* over and over again.'

The maid cut her words short as her master climaxed into Charlotte's mouth.

Afterwards, after he had been washed by the maid, he stood and went through the double doors into the library.

Through these doors, Charlotte heard the maid reading out the remainder of the journal and it made her feel bereft, as if part of her were being stolen. When the maid had finished, there was silence for a while, punctuated finally by a series of little cries, the pleasure cries of a woman. All of the time that the stranger used her home, Charlotte waited naked in the garden, kneeling before the chair where she had given him her mouth.

After an hour or so, the gentleman emerged from the library and handed her the journal. He gave a little bow and thanked her for her hospitality, then turned and strode away, the maid behind him, hurrying to keep up. There was the sound of a carriage in the drive and then Charlotte was quite alone.

That evening, when Charlotte opened the journal to record the gentleman's visit she found the first blank page to be damp and realised from the faint scent that it was his semen.

6

The Visit

The day after Alain had called, a carriage arrived for Isabelle, as arranged. Her mother fussed anxiously as Isabelle made the final adjustments to her hair and dress.

'I can manage, mother.'

'That ribbon is too fine, it will break.'

'Mother, please!'

'At least let me re-tie it.'

Madame Belloque tried to adjust the red satin ribbon that held Isabelle's hair from her face.

'Mother!'

Isabelle pushed her mother's hand away sharply, more sharply than she'd intended and apologised with a sigh. They were silent for a moment, then Madame Belloque laid her hand on her daughter's arm and smiled.

'Remember your promise,' she said softly.

'I shall,' replied the girl, avoiding her mother's eyes. 'Please say no more about that.'

'And be home before dark.'

Isabelle nodded and embraced her mother, holding on tightly. She too was nervous. Her quiet world was being shaken. The image of the Englishman had hardly left her mind since she had first seen him.

Robert was engaged in writing a letter to Charlotte in one of the many courtyards at the villa when Isabelle arrived. Alain had left to supervise repairs to an olive press in a distant corner of the estate. Before leaving, he had extracted promises from Robert that mirrored those that Madame Belloque had forced from Isabelle. Robert had been obliged, under pain of expulsion from the estate, to respect Isabelle's virginity and to refrain from force of any kind in her regard. Alain was so determined in these matters that Robert was obliged to agree.

The young footman who had conducted Isabelle through the labyrinth of the building announced her and bowed. Robert rose immediately, tucking his letter into the leather portmanteau beside the desk.

'Mademoiselle Belloque! It is so pleasant to have the company of such a charming and accomplished young woman,' he said.

This was the first of many flattering remarks as Robert showed Isabelle around the villa. Perhaps the finest room was the banqueting hall. This was at least as large as the whole of Isabelle's home. The walls were of polished travertine marble and the ceiling, high and domed, was ornamented by friezes of laurel garlands and bunches of grapes. Around the long, porphyry table, stood life-size marble statues, one for every seat. Each figure was beautifully carved and represented either a god, nymph or mythical animal. As Isabelle admired these, Robert asked if she would like to touch them. Her slender fingers grazed the back of a youth twisting as he swung a sword high over his head.

'They only come alive if you touch them,' Robert declared.

In the gardens Isabelle wished to visit the lake. She had seen this from the carriage as it approached the villa. It was not strictly a lake but a large circular pond with a fountain in the middle. Such was the power of the jets that long plumes of mist floated over the water and across the gardens, cooling them as they walked. She took his arm when he offered it and as soon as he felt her body next to his he was hard for her.

'I haven't inquired after your mother as yet, mademoiselle,' said Robert as they paused to admire a fine view.

'She is well, monsieur.'

33

'Is she still concerned that her little girl should visit this wicked place?'

Isabelle smiled. 'She does worry, monsieur, but I am not so little.'

'Perhaps not,' replied Robert and, holding her at arms length, examined her with undisguised admiration from head to toe, his eyes lingering particularly on her breasts and hips.

Isabelle reddened.

'Your blush is charming,' he told her with a teasing smile.

'You are embarrassing me deliberately,' she chided.

'Perhaps,' he agreed with a smile, watching as her breast rose and fell in agitation. 'And after your time here, do you think that your virginity is safe?'

'Monsieur!' cried Isabelle. 'You are indelicate!'

She pulled away from him angrily and he apologised in an amused tone.

'Very indelicate,' she said more quietly.

'I apologise doubly.'

There was a trace of genuine contrition in his expression and finally she accepted his apologies, allowing him to take her arm again so that they could walk on.

'Are you in love with Monsieur Chabard?' asked Robert, this time speaking more seriously.

'No, monsieur,' she answered with her usual honesty.

'But he is a worthy man?'

'My mother thinks so.'

'Well, he has a fine prize waiting for him.'

Isabelle smiled. 'You are trying to make me blush again,' she complained, and he laughed.

They talked together for most of the afternoon with Robert employing all of his charm and the girl responding with an easy pleasure. When it grew too warm in the sun they went inside and Robert continued with the tour of the villa.

The picture gallery had a small collection of Italian masters, including sketches and drawings by Raphael. Isabelle was especially taken by these and carried the yellowing sheaves of paper over to the windows to study them. In the slanting light and with her face open to those of the glowing Madonna and handsome children of Raphael, she seemed especially desirable to Robert. He was forced to crush his desire to take her there and then.

At one end of the gallery were the family portraits. Robert had barely glanced at them in his short stay but Isabelle seemed as fascinated by these paintings as she was by every other facet of the villa. Alain's family were not of ancient lineage and the portraits only went back three generations. It was Alain's grandfather who had acquired the estate after playing a successful part in the Moroccan wars. This remote estate was both reward and exile for a man grown too powerful with money and prestige. He was shown in full military glory, sword in hand. Alain's father was portrayed on horseback, also in magnificent dress, overlooking his beloved villa. In contrast, Alain had chosen to be painted plainly, at work in his study. He was seated at a desk with a pen in one hand and his other reaching for a document held by a standing woman.

'That is my sister,' said Isabelle in surprise.

Robert looked more closely. The woman was richly dressed but her clothes were ruffled and her blonde hair was a little out of place. The painter had made Alain the focus of attention by painting him in full light and face on. The woman was shown in part shadow and from an oblique angle so that most of her face was obscured.

'It is impossible to say,' concluded Robert, although his curiosity was aroused.

'I'm sure of it.'

'It was painted many years ago, I think. Alain is very young. Your sister would have been a child.'

Isabelle stepped closer to the painting. Her finger traced the outline of the well-rounded body of the woman, as if it was very familiar.

'Painters sometimes make their subjects seem younger to flatter them.' she said.

'Perhaps,' he agreed.

'Have you met Anne-Marie?' she asked.

This was a subject he would have preferred to avoid but it would have been foolish to lie.

'Yes. She keeps house for Alain in London.'

Isabelle smiled. 'I think she does more than that.' There was a mischievousness in her expression as she said this.

'What else do you think she does?'

'She is a ... companion to Alain,' Isabelle said delicately.

'Companion?'

'Or courtesan.'

Robert laughed. 'I imagined that you were a simple country girl,' he told her. 'Educated and cultivated yes, but innocent of the vices of civilisation. Where did you learn such a word?'

Isabelle's jaw set. 'We spend at least two months of every year in Paris, Monsieur! I am not an entirely foolish country girl.'

'Forgive me, mademoiselle,' Robert said with a smile.

'As it happens, my aunt was a courtesan to an Italian duke. It was an honourable arrangement. She bore him three children and they were together until his death. Only her humble birth prevented them from marrying.'

'So, a family of courtesans?' teased Robert.

'That is unfair.'

'But you say it is an honourable estate?'

'It is for women of humble station.'

'Humble station and high expectation?'

'My aunt was in love.'

Robert nodded. 'And you, mademoiselle? Have you met any eligible young noblemen in Paris?'

Isabelle flushed. 'I have not met any young noblemen. My mother and aunt protect me from the contagion of love. They are determined that I shall be a virtuous woman. It is only through the indiscretions of my cousins and my sister that I know anything of the world.'

Robert looked at her steadily, displaying in his gaze a pleasure that seemed to puzzle her.

'Do you think that I am an entirely foolish country girl after all?' she asked.

'Quite the reverse.'

Still she looked at him as if wondering if these words too were just a tease.

He took her arm and squeezed it. 'Absolutely the reverse,' he assured her.

That evening, they dined in the banqueting hall. Isabelle chose the nymph Zephyr as her marble companion while Robert sat before Mercury, the quickest of the gods. The silver plate they ate from and the crystal they drank from gleamed in the light of the two vast chandeliers. It was a heady mix for the young woman. With all of the excitements of the day combining with the wine that she drank, Isabelle felt her head swimming.

'I should return home,' she said. 'I promised my mother that I would be home by nightfall.'

'Please, stay a while longer. Play the piano for me'

'I must go,' she said with a sadness that surprised her.

Robert ordered a carriage and when it was ready, escorted her to the drive. She thanked him over and over again for his kindness. As they stood beside the carriage, the dusk gathering around them, he reached out and took her hand.

'Come again tomorrow.'

'May I?' she breathed.

'There are conditions,' he said with a smile and moved closer to her.

She looked down modestly. 'Conditions?' she asked.

'A kiss.'

'My mother . . .' she began nervously, but then looked into his eyes with a sudden desire. 'Yes, a kiss.'

He leant forward and brushed the corner of her mouth with his lips. Her eyes closed and a tremor passed through her. She wanted this so much, yet when his tongue tried to part her lips she pulled her head away. He took hold of her shoulders firmly, lifting her on to tiptoe.

'Be still,' he said, and when he kissed her again she parted her lips and allowed him into her mouth. She sagged against him and it was only his hands that held her upright. When he had finished with her she was breathing heavily.

'Tomorrow, if you come, you will not be allowed to refuse me a kiss. I shall not ask, I will simply take.'

He still held her shoulders and, looking into his eyes, she saw how fierce desire made him.

'I won't refuse you,' she said.

Robert relaxed at this and releasing her shoulders, he smiled. As he withdrew his hand he allowed his fingers to trail down her breast, momentarily brushing one of her nipples. She stepped back and looked at him with surprise.

'Until tomorrow,' he said with a bow, and turned and went back into the house.

All the way home in the carriage, as night fell, Isabelle shook. Everything she had experienced that day had been extraordinary; the villa, the kiss, the promise that she'd made. It seemed as if a giant hand had reached into the dolls' house of her familiar life and shaken her. Where his fingers had brushed her breast a fire burnt. Within her stomach, fear and excitement churned together and made her heart race. By the time the carriage reached her home she had calmed enough to answer some of her mother's anxious questions, but at the first opportunity Isabelle excused herself and went to her room. Her mind was still feverish when sleep finally claimed her. She dreamt of fierce wolves dining from silver plates.

Isabelle visited the villa three times that week. Robert took her riding, he listened as she played the grand piano in the music room, they walked and picnicked in the surrounding hills. She allowed him to kiss her as he wished and gradually, innocently, she was drawn into an erotic web spun from his careful attentions and also, somehow it seemed, from the essence of the villa and its gardens. It soon became natural for her to accept intimate caresses and to reveal her most private thoughts. Even so, he treated her with great respect, almost formally, so that a distance remained between them. Robert's intuition, divining what she most desired and what she would allow,

38

gave him a mastery of her feelings. This did not surprise him, he had seduced many young women. The careful distance that he created was for his own protection. He could not allow her to possess him in return.

7

The Caves at Marabar

At the end of that first week, Robert suggested a trip to the Marabar caves. Isabelle had mentioned them herself and her description had intrigued him. They lay about fifteen kilometres to the west of the villa in the foothills of the Albac Mountains. It wasn't easy to persuade her to go to such a remote place, as they would be alone together for the whole day and far from home. In the end she submitted, partly because he wore at her and partly because the caves had excited her ever since her father had taken her as a child.

They set out in the cool of the morning, Robert on his black Arab, Isabelle on an even-tempered grey mare. She wore a wide, loose skirt of the kind that certain Spanish women favoured, allowing her to ride astride her horse like a man. In the rough country beyond the edge of the estate this would be essential. For protection from the sun, Isabelle carried a parasol, while Robert preferred a wide-brimmed peasant hat borrowed from Alain's farrier.

They travelled slowly, partly to save the horses and partly for the pleasure of it. There was little cultivated land beyond the gardens on this side of the estate; it was the domain of fox and hare, lizard and scorpion. The sun-bleached grasses and tough little bushes blended into a plain of burning ochre. Excepting the occasional cypress tree, this plain was flat and uninterrupted as far as the mountains. The thirsty sharpness of the landscape, its wildness, was a liberation after the careful artifice of the villa.

They paused for refreshments only once, at the spring-fed pool surrounded by ancient straggling willows that Robert had visited with Alain and Anna. Bartolemie greeted them with the usual deference and if he was surprised to see the daughter of Madame Belloque, a woman he had once known, he did not show it.

Here the gathering heat of the day compelled Isabelle to remove her waist-length, satin riding jacket. For the remainder of the journey she would wear only a cool white blouse over her Spanish skirt. The blouse was prettily embroidered with tiny, pale flowers which Robert examined with his fingers before Isabelle was allowed to mount her horse and ride on. These fragile feminine things fascinated him. He could see whole worlds of care in their minute constructions, worlds so alien to the landscape they found themselves in.

From time to time Robert would rein in his horse and simply watch the girl. It pleased him to see her ride in such a place. Her narrow waist swayed with the movements of the horse and her breasts moved against the silk that covered them with a fullness and resilience. The circle of the soft white parasol formed a frame for her proud but slight shoulders. Her long neck was still so youthful that not one line flawed its elegance. Isabelle had grown used to being watched like this, used to having his eyes on her body. She had confessed once that his gaze was like a caress, a subtle hand that raised the hairs on her skin. When she smiled at him, her eyes gleamed from the parasol's shadow like those of a fox in moonlight. Yet there was nothing harsh in them, nothing predatory. They were both brilliant and soft like the finest clear honey.

As they rode on, the mountains grew, changing colour from a hazy blue to harsh sienna. Even before the land began to rise, the caves became visible as dark mouths in the cliffs. Isabelle pointed them out and Robert stopped to follow her finger.

'Everything that we can see belongs to Alain,' she said, 'except for the caves and those hills that surround them. Once they belonged to the Franciscans. They had olive

41

groves from that ridge to that.' Isabelle pointed to the bony spines of rock that capped the hills around the cliffs. 'The ruins of the monastery are over to the west, you can still see the outlines of the chapel and the dormitories if you climb high enough. The monks used the caves as storehouses for olives and they had presses there. Then there was a drought that lasted for ten years and all the olive trees died. That was a hundred years ago and the monks moved away. Now the caves and the hills belong to nobody.'

They continued on their way. The land began to rise and became stonier. Isabelle led the way through winding canyons of reddish stone. Lizards, disturbed on their basking rocks, scampered away from them. There was the occasional stunted, leafless bush but nothing, not even these, seemed to be growing.

After climbing for an hour or more they emerged from the tortuous system of canyons on to more even ground. The caves were suddenly much closer. They had to leave the horses and clamber the last hundred metres to the first of the cave entrances. The ground was steep and slipped under their feet in miniature avalanches. Robert, who carried food and torches, almost fell more than once; Isabelle caught her dress on a jagged rock outcrop tearing it at the hip.

Yet, if it was a struggle to reach the entrance there was great reward. The space inside was immense, many times larger than the interior of the largest cathedral. Half a dozen openings gave on to the single vast chamber leaving huge pillars of rock between them to support the distant roof. Robert laid down his burdens and together they gazed into the immense darkness in silence until he took Isabelle in his arms and kissed her. It was the first time that they had been together outside of Alain's domain; it was the first time that she had been so completely in Robert's power. By consenting to come to such a remote area she had placed herself in his hands, trusting herself entirely to his protection. Robert took her mouth in this knowledge and felt how much the kiss excited her. Between her legs, he knew that she would already be slippery with arousal.

When they separated Robert smiled to see a special vulnerability in her eyes and a special looseness in her body, but first he wanted to explore the caves, and then to explore the girl. Taking the torches from the ground he began to walk into the darkness. Isabelle hurried after him. The ground quickly became damp underfoot and the air humid. There were animal tracks in the red earth, belonging to goats and foxes. At one point they saw the remains of a copper-lined mudbrick tank, but neither could guess what purpose it might have served. Soon they could not manage without lighting one of the torches. The pitch burnt fiercely with an acrid smoke and a hint of sulphur. The light that it cast as Robert held it high above his head danced on the rocks, creating grotesque, unsettling shadows.

Gradually, as they advanced further, the cave narrowed so that first one wall was visible, then the other. On the wall to the left, a row of iron stanchions had been hammered into the rock and a rope looped its way between them at the height of a handrail. This was a legacy of Alain's father who had explored the caves and who liked to bring his guests.

'We must follow the rope,' warned Isabelle, 'there are so many passages and branches . . .'

Her voice echoed oddly and she cut herself short.

'How deep does it go?' Robert asked as they went on.

'They say that no one has ever gone far enough to find where it stops.'

At that moment the torch stuttered fitfully. Isabelle looked at Robert as if expecting him to light another but he didn't. Quite deliberately he allowed the torch to fail so that complete darkness and complete silence engulfed them.

'Robert,' she called, her voice small in that great black space.

'Hush,' he told her.

A hand brushed her arm and then seized it, startling her.

'You will do exactly as I tell you. Do you understand?'

His voice was not harsh as he said this, but it was

insistent. She struggled for a moment but he held her firmly.

'Exactly as I tell you!' he repeated.

Finally, she mumbled a yes. His hands felt their way around her body as if orientating themselves. When he found her breasts, he caressed them, taking the tips between his fingers and stretching them. He felt her body relax and knew that she was his to do with as he chose.

'Undo the blouse,' he told her.

At first she hesitated and he sensed her reluctance.

'It would give me pleasure to tear it from your back and have you ride home naked,' he told her.

Apparently believing him, and right to do so, she quickly undid the buttons. His fingers followed hers, shadowing them in the darkness, stroking them gently. When the blouse was completely undone he reached inside. She wore a fine silk chemise and he ran his hand across it bunching it up in his fist and pulling it from her skirt. A moment later she jumped as cold steel, a knife, was pressed against her stomach. He let it rest there for a moment so that she could feel it, then began to cut the silk. Sensing that she might struggle, he seized her waist with his free hand. When she was secured, he cut through the fabric completely and tried to pull it free. The shoulder straps still held and it was a moment before he understood the problem. When he did, he cut these too, and the chemise came away.

Now Isabelle's breasts were completely bare in the damp air and he kissed them, applying quick, sucking kisses across the whole expanse of bared skin. She groaned with the pleasure of it. His lips caught her nipples briefly, tantalisingly, then skimmed underneath and across her belly. At her navel he slipped out his tongue and delved wetly into the whorled depression as if it were her sex. Finally, he returned to her nipples sucking hard and deep on each in turn until they ached, ached to be left in peace and ached to be sucked harder and longer.

'Put your arms down,' he told her, for her hands had gone to his head as he suckled.

44

She lowered them obediently and he pulled the sleeves of her blouse down to her elbows. Her arms were partially restrained in this way so that she was dissuaded from resisting when he raised her skirt. His hand sought out her petticoats and pulled the material out at the waist. Again he let her feel the knife, this time against the bare skin of her hip. It slid downwards parting the fabric easily. She held absolutely still, apparently realising without being told just how sharp the blade was, and how easily it could cut her to the bone. Soon she was divested of all her under garments and the cool damp air of the cave licked across her unprotected skin making her shiver. Before replacing the knife in its sheath, Robert pressed it to her sex so that the flat of it cooled the tender membranes. It was the first time that he had touched her sex and he wanted her to remember it.

After a while, he let her go and a moment later she saw the spark of a tinder box and a little flame. Isabelle buttoned her blouse, a gesture that seemed absurdly modest after what she had just allowed. When the torch was lit and burning bright she had all the appearance of a well dressed lady on a Sunday outing. Robert smiled at her and making no reference to the preceding events led the way to the rope handrail. They followed it as the ground dipped into a narrow passageway. This wound its way downwards, steeply in places, before giving on to a large chamber with broad pools of standing water. In the distance they could hear the sound of a stream or river rushing over a rocky bed.

Robert wedged the torch into a cleft in the rock and beckoned to her. She approached him timidly, but with a smile on her face. When he reached for her she stepped back and then circled, staying just out of his reach. She teased him, allowing him to just catch at her with his fingertips before darting back. When he did catch her, he knew that she wanted him to.

'Remember you are a gentleman, sir,' she said, knowing surely, that he would not.

He pulled her into his arms and his hands took her

45

behind, drawing her pelvis forward and pressing it into his own. He was erect and he wanted her to feel it. She flushed, as if no man had held her so before.

'Why did you button your blouse?' he asked.

'It wasn't decent.'

'Do you want to be decent?'

'Not always. Not always with you.'

'I should have tied your wrists.'

She looked at him sharply and gasped.

'Where did you feel that? Where did you feel what I said?'

'In my stomach, low down, like fireworks . . .'

He touched her stomach, low down and she sighed again. Her eyes gleamed and held his until the hand went to her behind again. He began moving her, pulling on her buttocks and rubbing her sex into his. It affected her immediately. Her breathing became erratic and it seemed that she might faint.

'Put your hands in mine,' he told her.

Isabelle reached back and he took her hands, pressing them, one to each of the cheeks. The flesh was as pliable as dough after so much touching.

He kept moving her hands, working them into her behind for the pleasure of seeing her in that position. Her back was arched and her pelvis pushed out, pushed into his, into the hardness at his groin. Her shoulders, drawn back as they were, presented her breasts very fully and her nipples, large after his earlier attentions, blushed against the taut fabric of her blouse. He kissed the whiteness of her neck, vulnerable in such a position and then took her nipples into his mouth, wetting the fabric that protected them until it was quite transparent at those two points. She looked like a gypsy girl in the light of the torch, engaged in an obscene, camp fire dance. Her eyes narrowed and her mouth opened as his hands kept working her.

'Let me see your tongue,' he told her.

Tentatively the pink tip emerged from her mouth and ran its way across her lips. He watched her, appraising every movement. It was a test; he was testing her for her willingness to please, for her obedience, for her arousal. The hands that covered hers pushed inwards, invading the valley of her behind. He opened and closed her cheeks rhythmically, pushing all the time so her fingers pressed against the mouth of her behind and the beginning of her sex. There was a claustrophobic feeling. He felt it in his chest and saw in her eyes that she felt it too. There was an awareness of the mass of rock above them, pressing down, of their sexes grinding together, of fingers that strove and probed, of locked eyes, of excitement that flooded and drowned with heat and moisture and unreason.

Robert pushed her away for a few moments, while he regained his composure. He knew that she gave herself easily to these games, so easily that he wondered if she had played them with another.

'No man has touched you like this before?' he asked.

She shook her head with such obvious truthfulness that he pushed the suspicion from his mind. He pulled her on to his sex again and moved her slowly, sensuously, seeking the points of contact and the rhythm that most stirred her.

'The next time that I undo any of your clothing you won't refasten it unless I tell you to,' he said.

She agreed with her eyes.

He moved her body against his until she groaned unreservedly. When he stopped moving his hands she continued to move on her own for a moment before becoming embarrassed and halting.

Robert looked at her for a long time. She fired such a hunger in him; a hunger that he savoured for its own sake.

'You stir me so, sir,' she breathed, 'even as I know that I should run from you, I feel myself edging closer . . .'

Her voice trailed away and she lowered her eyes, waiting mutely until the intensity finally slipped from him and he released her hands. He picked up the torch and, without a word, led her deeper into the caves.

They spent the remainder of the afternoon exploring the various chambers of the caves. Robert was fascinated by the accounts she gave of her father's explorations, both inside the caves and on the surrounding hills. Often

Monsieur Belloque had accompanied Alain's father on expeditions to investigate the archaeology of the monks' former dwellings. On those hills, they had unearthed pewter drinking vessels in the ruined refectory and leather bound books of obscure learning in what they took to be a library.

When they grew hungry, Robert and Isabelle returned to the mouth of the cave and made themselves comfortable in the shade of one of the great pillars that supported the roof. From their vantage point they could look out on to the country that they had crossed on their way. It was possible to just make out a smudge of green where Bartolemie lived, but the villa was too far away to be visible. They dined on cold roast pheasants and hard corn bread baked that morning by Maria in the local fashion. They soaked the bread in olive oil flavoured with rosemary, to soften it as peasants did, and satisfied their thirst with wine cooled in water brought from the underground stream. Isabelle was suddenly tired after such a day and when they had finished eating she dozed in Robert's arms until the sun began to sink and he knew that they must return.

The journey down to the plain below the caves was more difficult than the journey up. The horses were afraid of slipping and needed to be carefully controlled. When they were clear of the canyons and the going was easy they paused to look back. The sun was setting and the rocks looked fiery in the reddening light. The mouths of the caves seemed almost alive, as if preparing to devour a passing crow.

Robert walked his horse over to Isabelle so that they were side by side.

'Stand up,' he told her.

She raised herself so that she stood in the stirrups. He pulled her skirt from under her so that when she sat down again her thighs, sex and behind pressed directly on to the slick leather of the saddle.

'Your blouse,' he said, and she knew that he wanted her to open it again.

When the buttons were undone, he pulled the fabric clear of her waist band and it fluttered a little in the faint breeze. From a bag slung over his saddle he took a length of leather thong. Isabelle seemed to know immediately what he intended to do but made no move to escape.

'Put your hands together behind your back,' he told her.

She complied and he looped the leather around her wrists several times, finishing in a knot that she couldn't see. Satisfied, he took the reins of her horse and led her on, into the scrubland.

From time to time he would stop and look at her. Her exposed breasts moved with the motion of the horse. Her expression was dreamy. He knew that she was aroused and he knew that he could do as he liked with her. Once, he came along side her and rested his hand on her belly, low down where the pubic bone starts. He pressed down hard and her sex opened, spreading out on the leather between her legs, making her quiver. Pulling aside the blouse he flicked her nipples with his fingernails until they were hard. Then, without a word he took up the reins of her horse and set off again. Another time he pulled her blouse off her shoulders and down her arms as far as her tied wrists would allow, so she was naked to the waist. Placing both hands around her neck he kissed her deeply. Always, he was conscious of the plain that surrounded them, of its vastness and stillness.

When they came across a dead cypress tree, half fallen and wedged between jagged rocks, Robert halted. Slipping from his horse he lifted Isabelle from hers. She followed him into the shade of the dead tree and he untied her, only to refasten her hands to a branch above her head. She was thirsty and he gave her water, kissing her between each mouthful, sharing it. He aroused her with a hand pressed between her legs until the moisture of her sex soaked through her dress and was visible as a darkening of the fabric. He poured water over her breasts until they were cool and then heated them with his tongue. Fetching more thongs from his bag, he tied her ankles, one to the shattered stump of the tree, the other to a rock, so that they were drawn wide apart. Sitting on a fallen branch, he looked at her while she gazed across the plain as if he weren't there. He untied the ribbon from her hair and drew it across her face so that she could see nothing. He found the tear in her dress and enlarged it with his hands so that her hip was visible, but he did not touch her. Picking up a twig he drew it across her nipples, pressing into her flesh until it snapped, startling her and leaving a mark. He kissed the indentation and sucked until the mark disappeared. Smoothing her hair back from her face, he kissed her and raised his leg until his knee pushed against her sex. This seemed to excite her especially and she groaned. Dropping to a crouch he began to raise her skirt but then halted. He contented himself with running his hands over her legs, feeling her through her dress, pulling it tight around her thighs so he could see their shape. He pressed the material into the valley of her behind and drew it tight between her legs pulling upwards so it buried itself in her groin. She endured all this patiently and she groaned with excitement. His hands were everywhere, hot and restless. Even though she was absolutely still and absolutely silent she appeared feverish as if she had been in the sun for too long. Her eyes had a deep hollow appearance and she shivered repeatedly, even as the sweat poured from her forehead and ran down her face. He fed her the last of the cold meat from his own mouth and gave her a little wine.

Allowing her no pause, he took her hair in his hand and pulled it tight against her scalp, then bent her head back. He kissed and bit her throat and pressed his free hand into the pit of her belly again. He let her head come back to level so that he could kiss her. His lips formed a seal around the outside of hers so that she could hardly breath. She fainted, and he cut her down. Isabelle lay in the dry grass as if dead, and still he touched her. He arranged her arms and legs in the way he wanted them, and in the way that made the touching easiest. When she began to stir again he threw water on her face and she gasped. After this he let her rest for a while before putting her back on her horse. She pressed her hands together behind her back and he tied her again. They hadn't spoken since they had left the caves.

It was dark as they passed the villa and still darker before they reached the Belloque household. Isabelle was untied and allowed to button her blouse only as they reached the stables. She would never know if any of the servants had seen her do this. Neither would she know if anyone watched as Robert kissed her and slipped his hand into the tear of her dress to touch the opening of her behind with his fingertips. For the first time she realised that he might want to penetrate her there and it shocked her. Later that night she thought how it would be to have a man's sex in that way and she touched herself, wetting her fingers and stroking the tight mouth nervously.

8

The Dress

On the Tuesday of the second week, Robert met Isabelle on the drive as her carriage arrived. He instructed the driver to stable the horses then kissed her in a perfunctory way and led her towards the villa. Once they were inside the entrance hall he stopped and turned to face her. She saw his intensity immediately and her arms fell to her sides knowing that he would want to touch her. His hand went to her breast without any preliminaries and moved in a steady circling motion. The simple fact that he could do this, without asking her, without even imagining a refusal, excited her.

'I need to ask you some questions,' he said.

She nodded.

'You've been kissed by boys?'

'Yes,' she murmured, remembering the peasant boys who had both excited and repelled her.

'You allowed them to touch you like this?'

His hand continued its steady work.

'Yes.'

'And between your legs?'

She looked at him sharply.

'Tell me,' he said.

'I didn't allow that,' she said finally, a tiny groan escaping her throat as the arousal built.

'Do you ever play with your sex?'

His hand moved to the other breast and she groaned again, loudly this time, knowing that she could not escape either his desire or her own.

'Please,' she protested.

He stroked her face gently.

'I need to know about you.'

'I touch myself sometimes, at night.'

'Did you last night?'

'Yes.'

'Did you climax?'

'I can't –'

'Tell me,' he insisted.

'Yes.'

'Strongly?'

'Yes.'

'What did you think of as you played with yourself?'

Isabelle felt as if she were drowning. At Marabar he had touched her as he wished and it was easy to allow that because nothing was asked of her. But these questions! She shook her head as if to shake them free of her mind.

'What did you think of? Or who?' he asked again.

She calmed herself for a few moments before replying. 'I thought of you, of Anne-Marie, of Monsieur Alain.'

'Of Anne-Marie and Alain together?'

'Yes.'

He nodded with interest.

'What did I do to you?'

'You kissed me and touched me. I thought of the Marabar Caves. You picked me up, stripped me . . .' her voice trailed away.

His hand reached for Isabelle's sex but the fabric of her dress impeded his access.

'Lift it,' he said.

Isabelle glanced around the grand entrance hall, with its mosaic floor, its pediments and pillars. The high domed ceiling reminded her of a church she'd once visited. In the distance she could hear servants talking softly as they worked. Some of those people she knew from the estate. At any moment one of them might walk across the hall. A sudden surge of shame and anxiety seized her and she tore herself from his grasp.

'Not here,' she said, backing away.

53

'You will be punished for that,' he said in an even tone.

She turned away from him, miserably.

Robert walked over to a bell pull near the door and rang. A few moments later a maid appeared, her quick steps echoing across the hard stone surfaces. Robert spoke to her quietly and Isabelle was unable to hear what passed between them.

'Isabelle,' Robert called finally.

She composed herself and turned to face him.

'Maria will show you some clothes that I'd like you to wear.'

The maid curtseyed and began to walk away. Isabelle hesitated, not wanting to leave while Robert was still angry with her.

'Isabelle,' he said with an edge in his voice.

Resigned, she followed the maid, hurrying to keep up. Maria wended her way through the various rooms without a backward glance or word of acknowledgement to the other girl. When they reached one of the large bedrooms on the south side of the villa the maid halted and turned to Isabelle.

'If you would take off your clothes, mademoiselle, I will find the dress that Monsieur Robert wishes you to wear.'

As soon as Isabelle saw the maid clearly she recognised her as the daughter of one of her mother's acquaintances. Maria's father sometimes supplied cheeses to the Belloque household. Isabelle froze. She knew too well how gossip travelled across the estate.

'Please, mademoiselle,' persisted Maria.

The maid waited impassively and Isabelle knew that there was to be no escape. With a sigh she began to unbutton her dress. As she slipped it down her body, Isabelle realised that her fine silk underwear, her very finest underwear, was stained dark between her legs. Robert's insistent attention to her breasts and his relentless questions had made her sex flood over. Isabelle flushed scarlet and twisted her body away from the other woman, sure that she would notice.

Maria, apparently oblivious to Isabelle's embarrassment, took the dress and went over to one of the many wardrobes in the room. As the maid opened the door, Isabelle was surprised to see how many beautiful dresses there were. Maria hung Isabelle's garment with great care, smoothing out the creases with quick, deft movements of her hands. Isabelle expected the maid to bring back whatever it was that Robert wished her to wear. Instead she returned empty handed.

'Monsieur Robert wishes you take off all of your own clothes, mademoiselle,' Maria said in a neutral voice, as if she were carrying out any ordinary task in the running of the villa.

'Surely not –' Isabelle began.

'His instructions were very clear.'

With a sinking feeling, Isabelle removed her shoes, bodice and chemise, finally standing naked and defenceless in the huge room. The maid glanced at her body momentarily and for the first time Isabelle detected a personal interest from the otherwise inscrutable girl. Maria took her shoes and tucked them into the bottom of the wardrobe. The underclothes she carried to the bed, laying them out on the counterpane. The dark stain was unmistakable but Maria said nothing as she folded them and carried them to a chest of drawers. When she returned, however, she glanced at Isabelle's sex and, with a faint smile, asked if she wished to wash.

It required all of Isabelle's composure to prevent herself from rushing from the room. Her throat had frozen but she managed to nod. The maid led her to a small adjoining room where, on a pine table, stood a ewer, bowl and soap.

'Will mademoiselle wash herself?' Maria asked.

'Of course!' replied Isabelle, incredulously.

The maid curtseyed and left.

Isabelle took her time, washing all over. Between her legs her sex was inflamed and sensitive to the touch. She had been aroused, almost without relief, since the day of her first visit to the villa. Not even the coldest water could have taken this away. Thinking of what had happened in the entrance hall, she regretted intensely that she had not

55

raised her dress when Robert had asked her to. The image of his hand cupping her sex burned into her mind as she soaped her thighs and a shiver of excitement passed through her.

When she was finished, Isabelle returned to the bedroom where Maria waited dress in hand. She held up the garment as Isabelle approached. It was a foam of pure white gauze and even at first glance, Isabelle knew that it was finer and more elegant than any dress she had ever worn.

'Are there no underclothes?' Isabelle asked, as the maid began to help her into it.

'Monsieur Robert says no.'

The fabric was so sheer that it turned pink against her skin. Standing before the mirror, Isabelle saw that though the dress was long and modestly cut, its transparency offered no protection to even the most casual glance. Where it gathered softly around her breasts the skin showed pink and the nipples rouge. Between her legs the fleece of pubic hair formed a clearly defined, dark triangle. In strong sunlight Isabelle knew that the dress would simply melt away.

'I can't wear this,' she said quietly.

'Monsieur Robert says that I am to order your carriage if you do not wish to wear it.'

Isabelle turned around and looked at her back view in the mirror. The divide of her buttocks was clearly visible as was the swell of her thighs as they met at her sex. She realised that these were the very parts of herself that she'd refused to expose in the entrance hall and that this dress was to be her punishment.

'There is no need for a carriage,' she said.

The maid nodded and finished dressing her. Once this task was done she led Isabelle back through the tangle of rooms and out into the courtyard where Robert had first received her. He was sitting at his table sorting through a collection of gleaming, leather-bound books. He smiled brilliantly as she emerged into the morning sun.

'You are dazzling,' he told her.

She returned his smile, grateful that he was no longer angry with her.

'Thank you, monsieur.'

'Turn around, please.'

She turned, rather self-consciously.

'It is yours to keep,' he said.

'I cannot,' she protested.

'Of course you must, and whenever you come in future I shall find something for you.'

It was clear that she wouldn't be allowed to refuse. Accepting this, she thanked him and sat at his invitation. For long moments he simply gazed at her.

'You shouldn't cross your legs,' he told her. 'Open them and allow the fabric to fall into the hollow of your legs.'

She did as he asked. The dress clung to the curves of her belly and thighs.

'Yes, that is the way to sit in such a dress. And always stand with your legs slightly parted. Will you do that for me?'

Isabelle, having refused him once that day, could not refuse him again. She nodded her assent.

'I feel as if I'm wearing nothing.'

'Does that excite you?' he asked.

'When you look at me,' she said quietly. 'But I'm embarrassed with Maria.'

He laughed. 'There is no need. You will see.'

Shortly, a young, rather pale maid brought out coffee and croissants on a large tray. Robert pushed aside the books to allow the girl to set down the cups and plates.

'Helene,' Robert said, as the girl turned to leave. 'Do you like Mademoiselle Isabelle's dress?'

The girl looked at Isabelle with large luminous eyes, eyes that made her seem like some exotic night animal.

'Yes, monsieur,' she said nervously.

'Would you be embarrassed to wear it?'

The girl looked at Isabelle's breasts, so clearly visible through the white fabric.

'In my father's house I would, monsieur,' she answered honestly.

Robert smiled.

'But this is not your father's house.'

'No, monsieur.'

'Perhaps Mademoiselle Isabelle would feel easier if you were a little less thoroughly clothed.'

The girl looked at him shyly and Isabelle saw with a shock the complicity that existed between them.

'Just remove the skirt, please.'

In an unhurried manner, and as if not at all surprised by this request, Helene complied. Underneath her skirt the girl was naked. Her hips were larger and her belly fuller and more womanly than might have been guessed from the thinness of her face.

'I would like you to continue your work for the rest of the day dressed as you are,' Robert told her.

The girl looked alarmed. Her eyes darted anxiously from Robert to Isabelle and back again.

'Monsieur Alain would wish it,' he said.

Helene curtseyed awkwardly with no skirt to hold on to.

'As you wish, monsieur.'

Isabelle watched as the maid walked away, carrying her skirt with her. The sun reflected from the two rounds of her buttocks as they rose and fell with her unhurried tread. As she entered the shadow of the building her dark clad torso disappeared and only the pale lower parts could be seen, ghostly sexual.

Isabelle was so taken aback that for a while she couldn't speak.

'She is so young,' Isabelle said finally.

'Hardly two years younger than you,' he replied.

'I wish you hadn't humiliated her for my sake.'

Robert smiled.

'It wasn't for your sake.'

'She must spend the whole day like that?' Isabelle asked.

'She agreed to. I wouldn't have forced her.'

Isabelle was still concerned for the girl.

'She must work with the other servants. There are valets, gardeners, grooms . . .' Isabelle's voice trailed away as she realised that her own predicament was little better.

'They will tease her, but she has a fine body. The men will desire her and the women will envy her.'

'Have you ever –' Isabelle could not quite ask Robert if he had slept with the girl. 'Is she in love with you?'

'Good heavens, no!' said Robert.

'Then why did she agree, willingly, to do such a thing?'

'It is for Alain's sake. She wishes to please him.'

Isabelle shook her head. There were so many things that she did not understand.

'Alain asks far more difficult things of her than I asked then.'

'As you ask difficult things of me?'

'Are they so difficult?'

'Yes,' she murmured.

'But they excite you?'

Isabelle looked at him sharply. 'Of course they do.'

'And I don't bring your excitement to completion?'

Isabelle lowered her eyes, suddenly ashamed, for he had read her thoughts.

'I will,' he told her.

With this he reached for the bowls of steaming coffee and offered one to her. Her hand was shaking as she took it. Robert searched through his collection of books and selected one on falconry. Isabelle refused a book for herself and settled back in her chair, watching him as he read. From time to time he would smile at her and occasionally read a passage from the book aloud. She enjoyed his enthusiasm even though the contents of the book held little interest for her. It had come to seem natural that she should wait patiently for him like this and there was a certain pleasure in it.

At the end of an hour or so, Robert put his book down, stretched his arms and rose.

'Shall we walk?' he asked.

Isabelle nodded, and Robert took her hand, drawing her to her feet. Her face was so open with affection that he was unable to stop himself from kissing her and pressing her body to his. She felt his erection hard against her belly as his tongue explored her mouth. It was clear to her at that moment that he wanted her as much as she wanted him.

They walked arm in arm through the gardens and down

59

to the lake. Isabelle was sharply aware of her near
nakedness as they walked. She was aware of the eyes of the
gardeners as they passed by, but oddly, felt no shame.
With Robert so close to her she felt both protected and
exposed, but her physical exposure was only a token of the
openness that she always felt with him. She would allow no
one to condemn her or make her feel shame for that.

Beside the lake Robert sat down on the soft,
well-watered grass with his back against the thick bole of
a sweet chestnut tree. She stood before him, awaiting his
pleasure.

'Raise your dress,' he told her.

This time she didn't hesitate, didn't even glance around
to see if she was being observed. The material slid across
her skin smoothly, like water over marble.

It was the first time that he had seen her belly and thighs
and the strength of his arousal shocked him. For Isabelle,
it seemed to her that her sex opened under the gaze of his
eyes, opened and folded out over her whole body. The
faint breaths of wind that sighed through the gardens felt
like tongues of fire as they curled around her belly. He told
her to turn around in a thick, hardly recognisable voice.
She did so, offering her flawless, virgin buttocks to his
gaze. He had her part her thighs widely so that he could
see her sex from behind. A tremor passed through her as
the lips parted to reveal their soft, salmon interior.

'Do you like me?' she asked, her back still towards him.

'There are so many things that I want to do to you,' he
growled.

She looked over her shoulder, her face drawn.

'I want you to do them,' she said.

Robert patted the ground between his legs and she sat
with her behind against his groin and her back against his
chest. She became aware that his heart was beating as fast
as hers and it was a while before either could breathe
easily.

Robert stroked her hair gently as a calmer mood
returned. He slipped his thumb into her mouth and
instinctively she began to suck like an infant.

'You are so greedy,' he said gently. 'Like a hungry bear cub.'

His free hand came to her belly and rested there. Isabelle closed her eyes and lost herself in this intimacy. It was an effort not to bite; the needs that were stirred as she sucked were dark and strong and primitive. Gradually these feelings exhausted her and she became drowsy. Finally she slept.

It was much later when Isabelle awoke. The sun had moved across the sky and the tree cast a long shadow. Robert must also have slept for his head lay heavily on her shoulder. She ran her fingers through his hair until he woke. Rising unsteadily, they walked slowly back to the villa.

'I have a few small tasks to attend to on Alain's behalf,' Robert announced, as they arrived at the building. 'Perhaps you would like to bathe?'

The idea of cool water appealed to her after the heat of the day. Robert summoned Maria who fetched towels and soaps and led Isabelle to the sunken baths in the courtyard between the bedrooms. These baths were partly overhung by a stone cupola ornamented with cupids and nymphs. Water issued from the carved horns and goblets held by these figures, and fell in soft soothing gurgles into the clear water.

Isabelle undressed without any self-consciousness and walked down the sloping floor of the baths until the cool water engulfed her. She floated on her back and looked up into the high blue of the sky. Maria fetched out some chairs and left the towels and soaps within her reach before departing.

It was perhaps an hour before Robert returned. He found Isabelle sitting in the shallow part of the baths gently moving her feet from side to side in the water.

'You look very contented,' he said.

'I am,' she replied.

Robert sat in one of the chairs and watched as she turned on to her back and swam into the shadow of the cupola.

After a time, Maria reappeared but seeing that Isabelle still wasn't finished with the towels she turned to leave.

Robert called after her.

'Send Helene, if you please, Maria.'

When Helene arrived she was still naked from the waist down. Isabelle watched from the water as the girl took up a position beside Robert's chair.

'You must be careful that your skin doesn't burn,' Robert told her, and Helene stepped into the shade. Framed against the elaborate ornamentation of the cupola and dressed as she was, the simple girl suddenly became extraordinary. The two figures looked at each other, apparently unaware that Isabelle was watching them as she swam slowly down the baths.

'I will come for you tonight,' Robert told the girl in a low voice, but not so low that Isabelle couldn't hear. She saw Helene start and look at him in surprise. There seemed to be an element of fear in Helene's response that puzzled Isabelle. She swam on, into the shaded part of the baths, thinking about what she had heard and trying to master the pangs of jealousy that stabbed at her heart.

At the end of the next length, Isabelle turned over and swam breast stroke back to the sloping, shallow end. Robert beckoned to her and she emerged, dripping, into the heat of the sun. At the top of the incline she paused and her hand went to her breasts, momentarily shy about being seen naked by the couple who watched her.

'Help her, Helene,' instructed Robert.

The maid gathered up the towels and hurried over to the dripping figure. She opened out the largest towel and enveloped Isabelle in its soft folds, rubbing the water softened skin gently. When every corner of Isabelle's body was dry she went over to Robert with the towel tied beneath her arms. She stood for a moment while he looked at her, aware all the time of Helene and the promise that Robert had made to her. She wanted to ask what he would do to her. She wanted to know why Helene had seemed frightened.

'Kiss me,' Robert said.

Isabelle ducked her head and found his lips. Her wet hair surprised the skin of his face and he flinched away, with a mock grimace. She swept her hair back, holding it in both hands and kissed him again to make amends. When she pulled away he indicated the chair opposite and she sat gracefully, tucking the towel beneath her.

Robert motioned to Helene to stand beside him. The girls eyes were cast demurely downwards and she clasped her hands together so that her sex was partially covered.

'Have you been teased, Helene?' asked Robert. 'Have the men looked at you with desire as you worked with your behind bared?'

'Yes, monsieur,' the girl said with a sigh.

'I have also been teased. Mademoiselle Isabelle has made me hard all morning.'

Helene looked immediately at his breeches and coloured. Isabelle's heart missed a beat and she went rigid in her seat.

'Yes, monsieur,' said Helene.

'My problem is that Mademoiselle Isabelle is a virgin and I have sworn that she will remain one.'

There was a momentary silence.

'You are not a virgin, Helene,' continued Robert.

'No, monsieur.'

Robert ran his hand up the inside of the girl's thighs. She made no move to resist him, even as his hand slipped into the crease of her buttocks.

'Part your legs a little,' he told her.

Helene complied and this allowed Robert access to her sex. With mounting distress, Isabelle watched as Robert toyed with the maid. She saw his fingers slip into the other girl to emerge coated in shining mucous. She saw the same fingers rubbing from the apex of the girl's sex to the narrower opening of her behind and back again, relentlessly stirring and probing.

Robert's eyes never left Isabelle as he did these things to Helene.

'Undo your towel,' he told her.

Isabelle glared at him. Part of her wanted to run as far as possible from the hateful sight of another woman

63

receiving what she herself wanted so badly but was denied. Another part was held enthralled as she watched Helene's pleasure mount. That part, to her surprise, wished it were her own fingers inside the girl compelling her to arch her neck and make fists of her tiny, pale hands.

'Open the towel,' Robert said again, that dangerous edge creeping into his voice.

Isabelle finally consented and once the towel had fallen open, leaving her naked, the anger subsided. All that remained was desire and jealousy. Even her jealousy faded as she saw how hungrily Robert's eyes fastened on to her breasts. It was clearly not Helene that Robert wanted, but her.

'Your mouth Helene. Quickly.'

The maid bent down and undid the buttons of his breeches, pulling forth his thickly engorged erection. Isabelle watched with both alarm and fascination as the girl took it into her mouth and sucked. Isabelle had only once before seen a tumescent male sex, and that had been a boy's. A number of years ago, one of the farm hands, whom she occasionally allowed a kiss, had surprised her in the kitchen while her mother was out. Seizing her waist he had rubbed himself against her behind saying that he wanted to show her something. Turning around, she had seen his erect penis and laughed. Not realising that her laughter was a nervous reaction, the boy had pushed her hard against the wall and left, angrily. He never tried to kiss her again and Isabelle never had the courage to ask him to.

Now, Isabelle was able to see a man's erection in all of its strength, and she envied the girl who worked her lips up and down its length, her cheeks domed and her eyes opening and closing in what seemed a kind of rapture.

It was only a matter of minutes before Helene brought Robert to a peak and during that time his eyes never left Isabelle. She felt that climax with him, squirming in her chair as he deluged Helene's mouth with his seed.

When the maid made a movement to rise, Robert rested a hand on her neck holding her to his groin. The other hand he used between the girls legs to bring on her own climax. Isabelle's envy deepened as the girl grunted her pleasure into the lap of the man that she loved.

'Clean me now, Helene,' said Robert gently.

The girl fetched a cloth and delicately washed his softening member with maternal care. Finally she eased it back into his breeches and redid the buttons. Robert thanked her and she left with her customary steady tread.

'It should have been my mouth,' said Isabelle as soon as the maid was out of earshot.

'Don't you think that I wanted that?' replied Robert sharply.

'Then why?'

'It would have been against the spirit of what I swore.'

'Does that mean you will never touch me as you touched her?'

Such was the intensity in Isabelle's voice that Robert looked away.

'I could talk to Alain.'

'Why Alain!'

'He gave his word to your mother that you would not be spoilt.'

Isabelle shook her head in disbelief. She had seen very little of Alain during her time at the villa. Mostly he was away on the business of the estate. When she did encounter him, he would bow courteously and perhaps ask after her health before moving on.

'Will Alain go to my mother and ask her permission for you to climax in my mouth?' she asked, with an irony he had not heard from her before.

'That is enough,' he said sharply.

Seeing his anger, she calmed herself. 'What you do to me is unfair. You make me want you, then . . .' She silenced herself.

Robert softened and knelt before her.

'There is no need for these,' he said, and kissed away a tear that had escaped her eye. She rested her head on his chest.

'I want you so much,' she whispered.

Robert pushed her gently back into the seat.

'Open your legs.'

Shyly, she did so and he began to caress the inside of her thighs. With a sudden surge of feeling she kissed him hard. He took hold of her hand and carried it to her sex. Pressing the fingers to her clitoris he moved them in a slow, circling motion. When she began to move her fingers of her own volition he released his grip and leant back. She stopped immediately.

'I can't,' she groaned.

He took her fingers and placed them on her sex again.

'Let me see you do this,' he said softly.

She reached out her free hand and he took it.

'Don't move away,' she told him.

'I won't.'

Isabelle began steadily masturbating, her eyes fixed on his. Gradually her self-consciousness eased and the pleasure came in waves. Robert watched as her breathing deepened and the muscles of her belly rippled. Her hand tightened on his and she began to make tiny mewling noises. Whenever she closed her eyes Robert told her to open them again.

'Are you close?' he asked, stroking her breasts.

She nodded.

He began to squeeze the muscles on the inside of her thighs hard, concentrating on those that joined to her groin. Her cries became louder and finally she gave a cry that echoed around the courtyard.

She wanted to be held afterwards and Robert picked her up and carried her to the bedroom where Maria had dressed her. He lay her down on the bed and held her from behind.

'That was so good,' she murmured.

'You were very beautiful when you climaxed,' he told her.

She kissed his arm where it wrapped around her breasts, showering many slow, sucking kisses, messy, wet · and childlike. His erection returned and feeling it she turned to him.

'Take me to London with you when you go,' she said.

He raised himself on one elbow and looked at her carefully.

'There are many things about me that you don't know.'

'I want to know.'

'The bruises that you will have on your thighs tomorrow are only the smallest of the injuries that I would cause you.'

Her eyes moistened.

'I can bear a few bruises,' she told him. 'I don't think that I could bear to lose you.'

He took her breast in his hand, cupping it, weighing its beauty, feeling the smooth, rich skin. Then like a falcon falling on its prey, Robert fixed his mouth to the soft flesh below the nipple. He sucked hard and bit. Isabelle gave a cry of pain and twisted to escape him. Opening his jaws, he released her and her hand flew to the injured flesh.

'Why?' she asked.

He shrugged his shoulders and looked away.

'It is the way that I am. It can only be real for me if I bite and bruise,' he said.

Isabelle became very still as she absorbed this information. She remembered how she'd felt by the lake as she sucked his thumb.

'I want to be real for you,' she told him softly, and lay back on the bed.

With a smile she took the injured breast in her own hand and lifted it to him. Robert saw the circle of reddened flesh and within this the white, indented teeth marks.

'I love you,' she said.

Robert took what was offered and bit into that tender, already bruised area. Isabelle stifled the groans of pain and stroked his hair as he fed on her. When his mouth moved to her nipple she stiffened, wondering if she could bear to be bitten there. This time though, it was the lips and tongue that worked and her groans were groans of pleasure. He alternated between these two places and between giving pain and pleasure for a long while. When he'd had enough, Robert lifted himself on to his arms and looked down on the girl. His face was flushed and beads of sweat as fine as dew clung to his skin.

'Do you still want to come to London?' he asked.

'If you will have me.' Her voice was strangely low, and it felt as if something were strangling her.

Reaching between her legs he pressed the heel of his hand into her pubic bone. She began to move, straining against him and gripping and ungripping her fingers in the bedclothes. Her climax came immediately but no words and no sound came from her mouth, neither was there any interruption in her movements until he took his hand away. They lay together in silence for a long time afterwards. When the light began to fade, Robert stirred himself and dressed slowly, alternately pulling on an item of clothing and gazing out of the window. Finally, he seemed to make a decision and turned to Isabelle.

'You must talk to your mother if you want to come to London, and most importantly you must talk to Alain,' he said. 'I don't think that I could persuade him to allow it, and here at least, he is master.'

He rose and rang for Maria.

'The maid will dress you. I leave in six days' time.'

After kissing her lightly on the cheek, Robert walked out into the courtyard. A moment later she heard a splash as he dived into the baths.

'Only six days,' she murmured to herself.

9

The Card Sharp

Early one evening as Charlotte returned from a ride over the hills surrounding Fulstead, she saw that they had another visitor. A black mare, groomed and trimmed in the fashion that the military preferred, stood in the spare stall of the stables. She left her own horse with the groom and went to the house with a measure of apprehension. As soon as she was inside she heard voices and laughter coming from the drawing room and went to investigate. Anne-Marie was sitting at the card table with a man in a cavalry uniform. He rose as soon as he saw Charlotte and bowed.

'This is Captain Weaver,' said Anne-Marie, 'we knew each other in London.'

Charlotte curtseyed.

'Madame, please join us,' said the man indicating the chair opposite his own.

'I am not an accomplished card player,' Charlotte said reluctantly, 'the best that I could hope to do is lose with good grace.'

'If you join us I promise you will not lose a hand.'

Charlotte looked at him in surprise. There was a roguish good humour about the man and his eyes sparkled in the sanguine face.

'I do not quite believe that, sir, but I shall join you for a few hands.'

They played whist. The captain dealt, and each hand that he dealt to Charlotte was unbeatable. She received nothing but aces, kings and queens. After the third hand Charlotte began to watch as the captain shuffled and dealt. His stubby fingers made him an unlikely cheat and, if he was cheating, which he must surely be, Charlotte couldn't see it. Finally, Anne-Marie could suppress her laughter no longer as she watched Charlotte try to work out how it was done.

'Captain Weaver is the most notorious card sharp in the British Army,' she said, 'and it doesn't matter how you watch him, he will fool you every time. I will not play with him unless I deal every hand.'

'My dear!' said the captain as if shocked. 'How can you say such a thing, ruining my reputation before such an attractive and respectable young woman!'

Anne-Marie laughed the more. 'They say that if he was as deft with a sword as he is with his fingers he would have defeated Napoleon single-handedly.'

'I would not have raised a hand against any country man of yours sweet lady,' the captain said gallantly, 'though I would have willingly played your Napoleon for his empire. And won, by Jove!'

The two women looked at each other and Charlotte couldn't help but smile.

'Another hand, madame?' he asked.

'I must go to the kitchens and make the dinner arrangements,' said Charlotte.

'Please stay. Anne-Marie will deal. It will all be strictly above board.'

'Even so . . .'

'Do you ever gamble, madame?'

'Not with the most notorious card sharp in the British Army, sir!'

He smiled and leant forward. 'I have something that you might care to win.'

She looked at the man. His expression was quite changed. Behind the good humour there was something else, something cool and hard. He reached into his pocket and drew out a key, dropping it into the middle of the table.

'Will you play me for that, madame?' He asked in a voice with a touch of ice.

'I imagine that you would persuade the Lord Jesus to play you, sir.'

'I couldn't have staked my soul, madame. I lost that to a lady as fine as yourself many years ago.'

'And now he plays for the souls of others,' Anne-Marie said.

'Play, madame.'

'And what do I have to lose that you don't already have?' asked Charlotte.

'Why money of course! That key must be worth . . . two hundred guineas?'

Charlotte was taken aback.

'I don't have such a sum in the house, sir!'

'Then what do you have?'

'A little over fifty, perhaps.'

The captain looked at the broach that Charlotte wore on her breast.

'That and the broach then. No, that is not enough.'

His eyes swept the room.

'The money, the broach and that silver.'

He pointed to a fine figurine, a woman holding out an apple, Aphrodite perhaps, or Eve.

'You will want my house next!'

'No, those items are sufficient. Though I do need a horse. The one that I have is . . . borrowed'

He smiled.

'Sirrah!' cried Charlotte.

'You are right, we will not think of the horse. It is a disagreeable subject to me as well at present. Let us play for what is already on the table. I suggest three hands of whist. To be assured of fairness, you can deal.'

'Very well,' Charlotte said finally. She found the man likeable, even attractive in a dissolute way, but she did not want to be in his power. Though her chances of winning seemed slender, it seemed worth the gamble.

'Is there a new pack?' she asked, not wholly innocent of the ways of card sharps.

Anne-Marie took one from a drawer in the table and undid the carton. She pushed the fresh cards across the red baize with her fingertips. Charlotte shuffled inexpertly and dealt. She lost the first hand but won the second. In the third she had hopes of winning but he was too clever. He took the final hand with a king of spades laid over her queen and plucked the key from the table. He chuckled as he slipped it into his pocket.

'We must play again, madame.'

Charlotte had gone pale and didn't reply.

The captain rose and went to stand behind the woman. He pushed the sleeves of her dress down and exposed her bosom.

'Such perfect breasts. I would like to see her climax as I slap them,' he said to Anne-Marie, touching the exposed nipples speculatively.

Anne-Marie nodded. 'I would also like to see that.'

'Will Madame Charlotte permit you?' asked the captain.

Anne-Marie leant forward and took Charlotte's chin, raising it so that their eyes met.

'Will you?' she asked. 'Will you let me watch that?'

Charlotte sighed. 'Could I really stop you?'

'No.'

'Then I must permit it.'

The two women smiled at each other, Anne-Marie broadly, Charlotte with a slight quivering of the lips and a plaintive expression as if she wanted something but could not bring herself to ask.

The captain had her stand and allowed her to adjust her dress. 'Perhaps you could show me your house, madame?'

'The dinner . . .' murmured Charlotte.

'Allow me to do that,' said Anne-Marie, rising.

The captain proved to be a jovial companion as Charlotte conducted him around the house. He had good cause to be happy. He had just won two hundred guineas or more and he had the beautiful wife of an old friend entirely within his power. She showed him the music room and he played a quadrille on the piano. She could easily imagine him in the regimental mess, a girl in his lap and a bottle of brandy in his hand. When he asked her to, she performed a few steps of the dance. She missed having a man in the house and when he applauded her at the end she smiled prettily.

Charlotte was nervous though, as she showed him the other rooms. It felt a little like showing a burglar the family silver. If his hands alighted on a timepiece or he picked up a book, she imagined immediately that he would find some way of taking it from her. She was more content to show him the gardens. He could hardly carry off one of the trees.

It was in the gardens that he first kissed her. He was very much the gentleman, first asking her permission, then taking her hands and pressing his lips to her neck before finally reaching for her mouth. It was not one of Robert's kisses but it affected her and she smiled afterwards rather shyly.

'We will have much pleasure tonight,' he told her.

Her heart sank to think of it, even as she believed him.

For dinner they had a dish from Anne-Marie's region of France and it made Charlotte think of Robert. She wondered if he was eating roast pheasant stuffed with rosemary, lemon and olives at that moment. When she voiced this thought, Anne-Marie replied, 'Perhaps, if he is eating with my mother this evening. It is her speciality.' Charlotte couldn't help wondering if Madame Belloque was as attractive as her daughter.

Charlotte led her guests to the drawing room once they had finished eating. The light was fading and the candles had been lit in the large tall-ceilinged room. Charlotte stood by the window for a few moments and watched the sun as it sank over the parkland to the west. It was still warm but she had a footman close the windows, knowing Anne-Marie's dread of even the slightest chill in the evening air. The butler served drinks but withdrew when the captain demanded that they be alone. He had Charlotte rise and, after looking at her for a moment with a disconcerting gleam in his eye, asked her to sit at the card table.

'Now we will devise the evening's entertainment,' he told Charlotte, 'and the cards will help us.'

When Anne-Marie joined them at the table, the captain asked her to keep the score. She took pencil and paper from the card drawer and set them beside her.

'So,' he began, 'what shall we play for first?'

Charlotte looked non-plussed.

'The lady's mouth, I think,' continued the captain, answering his own question. 'Shall I have the pleasure of her mouth?'

Charlotte blushed as he passed the cards to Anne-Marie. She shuffled the pack and dealt two hands, one for Charlotte and one for him. Charlotte's hand was poor and the captain won easily.

'If you would write down the fact that her mouth is mine,' he said to the Frenchwoman, which she duly did.

'Her sex?' Anne-Marie asked.

'Very well,' he replied and she dealt the cards.

This time Charlotte's hand was good and she felt that she would win. She played the cards with assurance but, as fate would have it, his hand was almost perfect and she lost. Anne-Marie duly noted this as well. When it came to playing for her behind they both had poor hands and Charlotte, to her surprise, won. The captain showed no concern at this loss. The game had only just begun.

'I had begun to think that you were losing deliberately, Charlotte,' teased Anne-Marie as she wrote it down.

'Anne-Marie!' said Charlotte, scandalised.

'Will you not give Captain Weaver the opening to your behind, freely? For the sake of your mutual pleasure?'

Charlotte looked at the captain.

'That is not for the good lady to decide,' he ruled, 'it is for the cards alone.'

Rebuked, Anne-Marie shuffled the cards again.

'Your husband told me that the whip excites you, madame?'

Charlotte hesitated before replying. 'Sometimes,' she murmured.

'You have all the usual things?' he continued. 'The straps and canes I assume?'

There was a fierce cast to his eyes as he said this. Charlotte looked down as she told him that they had them all.

'I shall have your breasts regardless,' he told her. 'I have won those already. And I shall use the strap. But we shall play for the number of strokes.'

They played a hand and Charlotte lost again. The margin of the captain's victory, four tricks, was taken as the number of strokes she was to receive. They played in this way for an hour or more.

They played for the number of strokes of the crop that Charlotte was to receive on her behind. The cards decided that she should receive two. They played for the backs of her thighs but she won that hand. Anne-Marie suggested the cat for Charlotte's belly. It was a milder instrument than the one used on His Majesty's ships, but it still had a stinging bite. Charlotte won that hand also. She was not so lucky with the thin strap for her sex. She won only one trick in the entire hand and was thus to receive eleven strokes. As the tally mounted, so Charlotte began to feel dizzy and she played less well. She was to receive three strokes of the dog whip on the inside of each thigh and one from the cat on the areas bordered by her breasts, ribs and shoulders. Her back was to be spared but not her calves. Her stomach was fluttering when they played to see if her nipples should be whipped. She lost badly, each was to receive four strokes. At this, her nerve broke.

'Have some pity, sir,' she pleaded.

'It seems a little harsh,' he agreed, 'perhaps you would care to wager the use of your behind against that rather severe attention to your pretty breasts?'

She agreed and they played another hand but it went badly for Charlotte. Instead of winning a reprieve from the whip, she ceded him the right to plunder her behind. He said that he would wager a doubling of the strokes of the crop on her buttocks against the whipping of her nipples. They played and she lost again. She was now to receive four strokes of the crop, a terrible weapon even when wielded by the slender arm of Anne-Marie. The more that they played, the more strokes Anne-Marie noted down.

When the captain finally closed the game, the Frenchwoman read out the tallies from her notes. She smiled in sympathy at the end, but Charlotte saw a glint in her eye.

'I think the lady has been clothed long enough,' said the captain. 'We deserve to see those charming breasts once more.'

He asked Anne-Marie to strip Charlotte and watched as she stood and drew Charlotte to her feet. The Frenchwoman undid the buttons at the back of Charlotte's dress and pulled it downwards. Beneath this Charlotte wore a narrow corset of yellow satin and nothing else. Her breasts and her belly from the navel downwards were naked. The captain gazed at her with undisguised desire, focusing especially on the pink tips of her breasts, those parts of her that had seemed to fascinate him from the first. Anne-Marie stood beside the naked girl and touched her behind repeatedly, running her fingers across the indented mouth of her anus as if struggling with the desire to penetrate her immediately.

'She has such grace and dignity when she is exposed like this,' Anne-Marie said to the captain. 'It begs to be broken by naked lust but never truly is. Even in the midst of orgasm, even when kneeling to take the strap, her refinement and grace never leave her. She cannot be debauched, only opened by pleasure.'

'We shall see,' said the captain, an edge in his voice as if he took this as a challenge.

Anne-Marie stepped away from her charge as if finally letting go, finally putting her into the man's charge.

'Make your nipples stand for me, madame,' said the captain.

Tentatively, Charlotte reached for her breasts.

'No, not like that. Touch your sex.'

She did so. Her fingers sought out the little bud of pleasure and gently circled. As the arousal spread upwards so her nipples hardened. The captain's hands tightened on the arms of his chair as he watched. Anne-Marie settled into the chaise.

76

'Let me call for the maid, sir,' she said, 'and have her fetch the whips. It softens Charlotte so when she is beaten. Her beauty increases until she breaks the heart with her sweetness.'

It was done. Sara brought the rosewood box from the bedroom and set it on the card table. Anne-Marie had the maid stay, partly for her education, and partly so that Charlotte could be held by the girl when it was necessary. The captain decided to begin with the crop. He pulled a large, comfortable armchair into the middle of the room.

'Madame,' he said, indicating that Charlotte should stand in front of it.

When she did so, the captain took her in his arms and lifted her easily. She gave a little cry as he turned her almost upside down and laid her in the chair. Her shoulders were pressed to the seat while her back lay against the backrest. As her legs opened and her knees bent, so her behind came to be uppermost, presenting a perfect target. Sara pressed down on her mistress's shoulders as the captain took the crop from the box and flexed it. Charlotte's sex jutted from her open thighs in this position and the captain bent over to kiss it. Even though it was only a light brush of the lips, Charlotte responded strongly and groaned.

'Kiss her mouth, Sara,' Anne-Marie said.

The pretty Irish girl smiled her gratitude for this opportunity and pressed her lips to those of her mistress. She used her tongue freely and was exploring Charlotte's mouth when the captain struck the first blow. Charlotte exhaled into Sara's mouth as if she had been winded and gave a deep, shuddering groan as the crop blazed a stripe across her behind. The blow had been low, landing at the top of her thighs rather than her buttocks, missing her sex only by a fraction. The captain aimed the second blow higher and Charlotte cried out, for this time he had put more force into it. She wriggled desperately and Anne-Marie had to rise and put a hand on her thigh to steady her before the third blow could be struck. This intersected the first two, deliberately, and was truly atrocious in its ferocity. Charlotte screamed and struggled furiously. She tried to press her hands to the bruised flesh but they would not let her. It was only when the captain rested a finger on the eye of her behind and pressed in, as was his right, that she became still again. He laid the final stripe across the back of her thighs high up and close to the first, just below her sex.

'I like to hold a woman in these places,' said the captain to Anne-Marie, resting his hand on the scalded flesh at the junction of Charlotte's thighs, 'and I like her to know that she is being held.'

Charlotte was sobbing as he slipped his arm between the seat and her back to lift her up. He turned her over and sat her upright in the chair, telling her to keep her hands on the armrest. The tears ran down her cheeks in streams as he went to the drinks table and poured himself a brandy. Charlotte saw that he was trembling and he would not meet her eyes. She sensed no remorse though, and saw in the set of his jaw that the struggle was a struggle to contain his desire: his desire to beat, his desire to ravish. It was the way of men.

Anne-Marie stood behind Charlotte and rested a hand on her shoulder. Sara pulled a clean handkerchief from her pocket and wiped away the tears as quickly as they formed. Charlotte's thighs clenched and unclenched as she wrestled with the burning pain. As her legs opened and closed convulsively, Anne-Marie pointed out how wet she was, how her excitement was soaking into the fabric of the seat. She told Sara to touch that wetness and taste it.

'Soon I will start whipping you,' Anne-Marie whispered to the maid, leaning forward and brushing the girl's lips with her fingertips, 'and your *cul* will run with pleasure as your mistress's does.'

Sara flushed and gazed at the Frenchwoman with a mixture of fear and love.

The captain took his drink to the card table and sat. He lit a cigar and smoked as the women attended to Charlotte. He seemed to have calmed a little and was able to view Charlotte with more detachment.

'You are right, mademoiselle. The crop makes Madame Charlotte radiant.'

'She is delicious in her simplicity and trust. A fawn, a shy thing you might see for a moment in the woods at dawn,' replied Anne-Marie.

'We will not let this fawn escape, I think,' said the captain.

'Indeed not sir.'

The captain finished his brandy and, taking another draw on his cigar, rested the glass on the table. He gestured to Charlotte.

'Go to the captain,' said Anne-Marie, seeing her charge's reluctance. 'Offer your lips and your breasts, thank him for his efforts. Go on all fours. Show him your behind. He will want to touch it and feel the weals as they rise.'

Charlotte did as she was bid, crawling on all fours like a supplicant to an eastern potentate. When she reached him, she turned around so that he could see the stripes across her buttocks and thighs. He touched her with the cigar still in his hand and she felt its heat against the already burning skin. His fingers found the wetness of her sex and immediately she began to groan. He had her twist around so that he could watch her face as the hand worked and she hurried towards orgasm. He let her climax, but took his hand away as soon as she began so that it was only a taste and she wanted more. When he had her kiss him afterwards, there was arousal and gratitude in the tongue that sought his with such great urgency.

He lifted her into his lap and she rested against his chest while his hand went back to her sex. She closed her eyes as the arousal built again and he told her to open them and look at him. Her behind began to squirm and he took it, squeezing the bruises with his free hand, increasing her arousal. Anne-Marie sat in the chair that the captain had used to beat Charlotte and pulled Sara on to her lap. She and the captain faced each other, each with a girl in their lap. As the captain moved his hands to Charlotte's breasts and touched, Anne-Marie did the same with Sara.

'Lift up your skirt, Sara,' the captain said.

Sara looked at Anne-Marie. Her eyes held a silent plea to be excused from this. Anne-Marie saw the girl's reluctance and frowned.

'I won't let him touch you,' she said, 'but I want him to see how lovely you are.'

Sara looked away.

'There is no evading this,' Anne-Marie continued, firmly.

With a tantalising slowness, Sara raised the dress as far as her knee. Her legs were very fine, the muscles of her calves were full and the skin taut. Their paleness and smoothness made them look as if they were made of marble, as if she were a Greek nymph.

'Lift your bottom,' said Anne-Marie. 'Pull the dress to your waist. The gentleman will want to see more of you.'

Reluctantly, the girl complied. Her thighs were strong and though her hips were narrow they cupped a belly so sweetly curved that to see it was to want to penetrate it. Anne-Marie reached down and applied a pressure to the inside of the girl's thighs until they opened. When they would open no further, Anne-Marie eased the girl around until she was facing the captain and he could see her sex with its delicate moss of fine, auburn hair. As the captain opened Charlotte with his fingers so Anne-Marie opened Sara, parting the lips with the fingers of one hand, touching inside with the fingers of the other. The girls excitement could be seen as a shaking in her legs. Anne-Marie told the captain how she liked the girl's quietness when she was stimulated. She would allow no sound to come from the girl when she climaxed. There was just the shaking and the spasms in her belly and a look in the eye that spoke of desperation and hunger.

As the captain took his charge to pleasure's peak, so Anne-Marie took hers. Charlotte however, was not silent: she could never have been silent when she felt those things. Her mouth was opened wide and she moaned. The captain let her climax begin but took his hand away quickly, as he had done before, so that only the first few waves of pleasure broke and she was hungry again immediately. Sara was also at pleasure's point and Anne-Marie told her to kneel on the floor with her behind in the air. The maid's excitement made her less shy and she complied easily, dipping her back and opening her legs wide. Anne-Marie began the stimulation again, her fingers drawing wetness from Sara's sex and anointing the whole of her behind. The captain slipped his fingers inside Charlotte but did not move them as he watched.

'Uncover her breasts,' he said.

Anne-Marie undid the buttons at the back of the girl's dress and slipped the sleeves from her shoulders. Pale, freckled breasts, small but well shaped, appeared. The girl's nipples were very pale indeed, the coolest pink that could still be called pink, and they were long, arresting in their distension. They looked as if they had been sucked every day of the girl's short life. Anne-Marie's hand was edging the girl to a climax and those long pale nipples shook as the rest of her body shook. Anne-Marie turned the girl's face to the captain and he watched as a dark, hungry shadow crossed her features and then lifted to reveal a look of great release. That is how he knew that she had climaxed, that and an easing of the shaking in her limbs.

The captain rose and carried Charlotte to a chaise longue that stood near the window. He laid her out and went to the rosewood box.

'Three strokes to the inside of each thigh?' he asked.

'Just so,' Anne-Marie confirmed.

The dog whip had a wooden handle and a single short strand of leather, quite thick and heavy. He swung it through the air and it hissed like a snake. He went to the chaise-longue and stood over Charlotte. She was nervous and her tongue licked at the side of her mouth. He bid her open her legs and slowly she complied. The captain pressed the wooden handle to her knee and stretched the leather blade along the inside of her thigh. The tip finished an inch or so from her sex.

'Can you keep your legs wide, madame? Or will you need to be held?'

Charlotte could not reply. He raised the whip above his

head and she looked away, hearing the whistle as it swung through the air. The captain had judged the matter well. By bringing the handle down sharply on to her knee, the whip snaked along the inside of the thigh, lashing her to within a fraction of her vulnerable sex. Charlotte howled and closed her legs tight. He waited for her to open them again. When she did so he struck to the other side and again Charlotte closed her legs as her thigh was burnt by the leather. After this she needed to be held. Her nerve had gone and she was shaking. The captain tied her hands to the armrest of the chaise and Anne-Marie held one leg while Sara held the other. Even then she wriggled so much that the task was not easy. One of his blows fell badly and the tip of the whip cracked into her pubis taking her breath away. Mercifully, it missed her labia. When the final blow had been delivered, the captain and Anne-Marie withdrew, leaving Sara to comfort the weeping woman. The captain drank two more brandies then declared that it was late and time to retire to the bedroom.

There, all of the remaining punishments that he had devised and won from Charlotte were enacted. Sara wept as she watched her mistress tied to one of the bedposts on her knees so that her nipples could be whipped. The captain was severe in the application of this test. When her slight movements caused him to miss his target and the whip found only her breast he struck again to ensure that she escaped nothing.

He took a savage pleasure in slapping her burning breasts later as she masturbated under his direction. His blows were relentless and when she climaxed, they were painfully heavy. Her scream of release could be heard in the distant servants' quarters but afterwards she was oddly grateful that he had not spared her. It had reminded her of Robert and the first weeks after their marriage when she had encouraged him to take everything that he wanted from her, so great was her desire to give.

The captain did not sleep that night and even when Charlotte briefly did, it was with his sex in her behind or his fingers in her sex. As dawn broke he slipped away from the sleeping women, taking his winnings and adding several choice pieces of silver from the house as he went.

10

Crimes of the Flesh

The day after Robert had told her that he was leaving for England in six short days, Isabelle waited impatiently for the carriage to collect her. By the evening, she was frantic. As soon as her mother had retired to her room for the night, Isabelle walked out to the meadow behind the house. She selected a horse and, without saddle or stirrups, mounted it and rode like a peasant girl to the villa. It was dark by the time she arrived. She took her horse directly to the stables and found a groom to attend to the animal.

'Where is Monsieur Robert?' she asked.

The groom, a tall, saturnine man of thirty or so, frowned.

'He is in the library, mademoiselle. But he won't want to be disturbed at this hour, neither will Monsieur Alain.'

There was something disrespectful in the man's tone and demeanour.

'Those are not judgements that you are required to make,' Isabelle said sharply. 'Now find me a lamp, I will escort myself.'

'Mademoiselle! It is for your own good.'

'What is your name?' she said, cutting him short.

'Absolem, mademoiselle.'

'Absolem. Find me a lamp and say not another word.'

The servant shrugged his shoulders and, going into one of the stalls, he took a lamp from the wall, checked that it had sufficient oil and lit it for her.

Isabelle hadn't visited the villa in the evening before and

it seemed larger than ever. The villa of the daytime was crisply defined and open to the senses. At night, shadows filled the long corridors and it seemed unknowably vast and complex. She regretted dismissing the groom after losing her way a number of times. By the time that she had finally located the library, her nerves were on edge and she rapped on the door more sharply than she'd intended to. No reply came and after some long minutes she knocked again. There was a roar from inside demanding to know who was there.

'It is Isabelle, Isabelle Belloque,' she called nervously, unable to recognise the disembodied voice.

There was silence again. Isabelle wondered if, perhaps, she would simply be ignored or sent away without even being admitted to the presence of the two men.

Eventually, however, the door opened and Robert appeared. He pulled the door to behind him so that she couldn't see into the library. He was dressed only in shirt and breeches and his face was flushed.

He regarded her quizzically.

'It is late for you.'

'Why didn't you send for me?' she asked.

'I had things to attend to.'

'You tell me that you are leaving and the next day you will not see me!' she protested.

He took her into his arms.

'I am truly sorry,' he told her. 'But I really did have business that I needed to attend to.'

At that moment there came a sound from the library, muffled and indistinct, but not unlike the sound of a woman groaning.

'It is inconvenient for you to stay,' he said.

The woman's groan was repeated and Isabelle heard it quite clearly this time. She felt the blood rush to her head. It was obvious that Alain and Robert were concerning themselves with someone other than herself at that moment. She pulled away from him angrily.

'This is not the place for you Isabelle. Not yet anyway.'

'I know what is happening in there,' she said.

'Then perhaps you should leave.'

Isabelle remained stubbornly in place.

'Do you think that I would be shocked?' she asked.

Robert smiled. 'Yes. I do.'

'Do you and Alain share girls?'

'Sometimes.'

Against her will, Isabelle had an image of the two men with a girl. It did shock her, as so many things at the villa shocked her, but she would not allow this to deflect her.

'I want to speak to Alain about going to London,' she persisted.

Robert thought about this for a moment. 'And if Alain wanted to share you with me?'

Her face twisted in distress.

'It would be only a part of his price for agreeing,' he warned.

Isabelle felt her shoulders drop. 'Would you allow that?' she asked.

'I would want it,' he told her.

The woman in the library groaned again, although this time the sound was stifled, as if a hand lay across her mouth. Isabelle wondered if she could truly do what she was asking of herself. The mosaic floor seemed to shimmer as she imagined Alain's hands on her and she felt that she might faint.

'He may not want me,' she said finally. 'If you tell him that I am yours.'

'I have enjoyed your sister many times as his guest, I couldn't refuse him the pleasure of you.'

Isabelle digested this information slowly. 'My sister?' she said softly and felt a surge of shame that she should be begging to be admitted to this perverse circle. Equally, she knew that it would be unbearable to be excluded.

'If it is your wish, if Alain wants me,' she stammered.

Robert pursed his lips as he considered her acquiescence. 'You need to know what it is that you agree to,' he said. 'Wait a moment.'

Robert turned and half opened the library door. 'Helene,' he called.

Isabelle heard the soft pad of bare feet on stone and then Helene appeared, dressed in a cream kimono. Her copper coloured hair was free and hung over her shoulders in a shower of gleaming curls. The girl was quite beautiful, transformed somehow from the pale, nondescript maid of daytime. Perhaps it was the colour in her cheeks or sense of satiation in her slow smile that so struck Isabelle. Whatever new quality the night gave her, Isabelle felt suddenly afraid, as if she could not compete with the other girl. Helene's eyes, larger, more luminous than ever, seemed to register this and Isabelle could not meet them.

'Come,' said Robert.

They walked down the long, deeply shadowed corridor together, Isabelle taking Robert's arm and Helene trailing behind them. The procession made Isabelle think of some prince of Araby promenading with two of his wives in the seraglio.

Robert led them to his bedroom and had Helene light the various lamps. Isabelle went over to the open windows and took a succession of deep breaths of the warm evening air to calm herself. The moon was up and cast a blue-white spell across the courtyard. The black bulk of the stone cupola showed starkly against the night sky. Beneath it, the water of the baths caught the moonlight and glistened.

Robert came to stand behind Isabelle and trailed his fingers down the nape of her neck making her shiver.

'What are you going to do?' she asked.

'Nothing to you,' he replied. 'Unless you want it.'

'And Helene?'

'I want you to understand what might be expected of you, if you come to London.'

'I have already said that I am yours,' she said, turning to him.

He smiled. 'Undo the buttons of your blouse.'

Her fingers fumbled in this task but finally her blouse was open to the waist. Robert pulled the fabric aside to reveal her breasts and examined the place where he'd bitten her. The skin had turned blue and when his finger tips explored her there, she quivered.

86

'Is it sensitive?' he asked.

'Yes,' she breathed.

Robert leant forward and kissed her. Her mouth opened immediately and she felt his breath, hot in her throat. He took the whole of her injured breast in his hand and squeezed. An erotic pain shot from there to Isabelle's belly and she moaned. Releasing her, Robert tugged the two sides of the fabric together and turned to Helene.

'The whips and ties, Helene if you please.'

Isabelle saw the girl wince.

'Please, monsieur,' Helene murmured, 'not again. It was only last night . . .' her voice faltered.

'It is important that Mademoiselle Isabelle sees this,' said Robert firmly. 'I can't excuse you this time.'

Helene looked at Isabelle with a silent plea in her eyes. Isabelle looked away for a moment, stricken with guilt, then pressed her hand to Robert's arm.

'I can't allow this,' she said. 'Do not hurt her for my sake.'

Robert turned to her abruptly.

'It is not up to you to allow it or not allow it,' he said sharply. 'If you don't wish to witness what I intend to do, then leave now. But don't imagine that you could ever return.'

Robert said this with such ferocity that Isabelle recoiled. Her mouth opened to make a reply but no words came out.

'Well?' he asked, a little more softly.

'I can't go,' she stammered.

'Then say no more.'

Once again Isabelle tried to speak but Robert pressed his fingers to her lips and sealed them.

'The doors are open. No one is a prisoner here.'

Looking over Robert's shoulder, Isabelle saw Helene cross the room to a tall, thin chest of drawers. The girl opened one of the drawers and pulled out some items that Isabelle couldn't see. Robert glanced at Helene and then back at Isabelle.

'It is settled,' he said.

With those words he took her by the arm and led her to

a chair by the bed. Helene had already laid out the instruments of her torture on the crisply ironed, cotton counterpane. There were a number of canes of various lengths and a collection of leather straps ranging from broad, heavy belts to thin, flexible bands. Returning from the chest for the final time, Helene brought cuffs and ties of thickly woven black silk. Isabelle noticed the dark, bruised circles around her wrists as the girl leant over the bed to add these to the grotesque assemblage.

Robert held out his hand and Helene walked over to him. Without a word she buried her head in his chest.

Isabelle saw that the girl was shaking and this fear communicated itself strongly. Isabelle felt a constriction in her chest as if her ribs had frozen together and would suffocate her.

'Undress now,' Robert said.

Helene stepped back from him and, undoing the tie at her waist, allowed the kimono to slip to the floor. In contrast to her full hips and belly, Helene's breasts were rather small and her arms, though long, were thin and childlike. At that moment, she seemed very vulnerable to Isabelle, young and defenceless, not at all the woman who had stepped from the library. It was all that Isabelle could do to prevent herself from jumping to her feet and throwing her arms around Helene, protectively.

Robert reached out and took hold of Helene's sex. The girl reacted with a sharp intake of breath. Her eyes opened wide and flared with arousal.

'You have found your true home here, Helene,' Robert told her, and she gasped as he thrust his fingers inside.

Robert worked her this way for a time but he wasn't interested in seeing her climax. Pulling his fingers clear he told her to lie on the bed and prepare herself for the strap. Turning to Isabelle, he smiled grimly and stroked her cheek. Where his fingers touched her, a trail of mucous from Helene's sex remained to glisten in the light of the oil lamps. Isabelle raised her hand and touched this, curious, against her will, to feel another woman's excitement.

Helene lay face down on the bed and taking a pillow,

pushed it under her hips. Her legs fell open and she lay still. For the first time, Isabelle saw the dark stripes across Helene's buttocks and thighs and trembled in sympathy.

Robert went over to the girl and taking a number of the silk ties, carefully secured Helene's wrists and ankles to the four corners of the bed.

'Isn't she marvellous?' he said to Isabelle.

Isabelle could not reply but she watched as he caressed the girl.

'She has such fine, smooth skin. So very responsive. It was only after I'd had her half naked at the baths the other day that I really noticed her.'

He smiled at Isabelle. 'She is a natural whore,' he continued.

Isabelle looked away, pained by Robert's affection for the girl and also by his contempt.

'If you don't want to watch then leave,' he told her.

Isabelle turned back to him angrily, biting her tongue.

'There is a deep hollow at the base of her spine. Can you see it?' he asked.

Isabelle shook her head and Robert motioned to her to sit on the bed. There was indeed an unusually deep depression just inside the valley of Helene's behind.

'She is very sensitive there.'

Robert ducked his head and ran his tongue down her spine. The girl groaned when it slipped into that valley and swirled around the hollow.

'Touch her.'

Isabelle shook her head.

'Touch her,' Robert repeated, sharply.

Tentatively, Isabelle reached out. The skin was wet where Robert's tongue had passed over it. Isabelle stroked down the girl's spine following the same path and ending in the same sensitive hollow. Helene groaned again and Isabelle enjoyed that sound, enjoyed extracting it from the girl.

'You see?' asked Robert, smiling at the gleam in Isabelle's eye.

'Yes,' she murmured.

'And further down too. Further down she is even more sensitive.'

Isabelle looked at the cleft in the girls behind. It was easy to understand the pleasure that Robert derived from having this beautiful flesh wide open to him. Being much closer now, Isabelle could see that the marks on Helene's skin were more than simple discolorations. The flesh was swollen and raised. Tiny purplish, pinprick marks framed the stripes which were surprisingly neat and regular. Isabelle couldn't help but touch them, sensing the extra heat in those ridges. Looking at Robert she took the darkest, most sensitive piece of skin between thumb and forefinger and pinched. Helene gave a little cry.

'Is this what you will do to me?' Isabelle asked.

'Perhaps. Will you allow it?'

'It frightens me,' she confessed. 'But you have no need to ask what I will allow.'

Robert pushed his hand between Helene's thighs and worked her sex again. She came back to full arousal quickly.

'Kiss me,' he told Isabelle.

Leaning across the girl, Isabelle kissed him hard, pushing her tongue into his mouth with sudden violence.

'No one is ever truly innocent,' Robert said when they separated. They looked at each other and Isabelle felt that they were two demons in hell, accomplices in these crimes of the flesh.

'If you stay with me, you must allow everything. Do you understand? Everything.'

She nodded.

Helene gave a deep guttural groan at that moment and, looking down, Isabelle saw that Robert had buried his thumb deep in the girl's anus.

'So tight,' he growled. 'But it opens like a flower.'

11

Mother and Daughter

The next day Isabelle rose early when the sun was no more than a promise behind the distant hills. None of the servants were awake and she fetched water from the well herself to wash away the heat of the night.

After a bowl of chocolate and a small piece of bread she wandered the house restlessly, trying to distract herself with minor tasks. She had slept no more than three hours and apart from that brief respite, her mind had been filled with images of Robert and the villa.

She considered herself insane that she could contemplate allowing Robert the kind of liberties that he had taken with Helene. Many times she vowed that she would never see him again. At those times she longed for the security that had existed in her life before his arrival. Since her very first visit to the villa, desire had corroded her peace of mind. Her very body seemed to have changed, centring itself on her breasts and belly and thighs, the very places that Robert had marked as his own. Isabelle's vows evaporated, however, when she remembered how it felt to be held by him and how it felt to have his hands between her legs. Many times she lifted her skirt to examine the blue-green imprints on her thighs and, each time, she experienced a sweet arousal.

When she heard her mother stirring and her voice calling to the maid, Isabelle withdrew to the music room. Seating herself at the piano she idly picked at the keys and gazed through the window at the lightening sky.

She asked herself again if she could allow Alain to touch her as Robert touched her. The knowledge that Robert had enjoyed her sister burnt into her mind, igniting fires of fierce jealousy. She recalled the desperate feeling of exclusion as she stood before the library door. These were the thoughts that flooded through her mind as the house gradually came to life. Listening to her mother as she issued instructions to the maid and the farm boy, Isabelle realised how alien she now felt in her own home. The world that had nourished and protected her hardly seemed of any consequence any more. She would have destroyed it all for one night with Robert. This thought made her feel worthless and she rapped her knuckles hard on the piano as punishment.

To break this introspective spell, Isabelle rifled through the scores in the piano stool and selected a number to play. Stiffly and without enthusiasm she worked through a pretty serenade by Haydn and then a capriccio from Mozart. It was only when she began Beethoven's Appassionata that the music flowed from her. The grand, wild, tragic sonata filled the house as her fingers flew across the keyboard. There was such feeling in her playing that her mother paused in the kitchen to listen. Having finished the piece, Isabelle returned to the beginning and started again immediately, with even greater abandon.

Madame Belloque, perhaps sensing something of her daughter's state of mind, came to the music room and after tapping lightly on the door, let herself in. Isabelle continued playing, oblivious to the interruption, and her mother took a seat by the window.

When Isabelle finished, her mother applauded.

'Bravo,' she said.

Her daughter smiled thinly, a deep tiredness showing around her eyes.

'Is something wrong?' asked Madame Belloque.

Isabelle looked at her mother as if she wasn't there, as if she were the person least likely to help her.

'Tell me.'

'I'm in love,' said Isabelle in a quiet voice, almost to herself.

Her mother smiled. 'It can hardly be love. So soon?'

Isabelle shrugged.

'Don't make fun of me,' she said, closing the lid of the piano and pushing her stool back from its embrace.

Madame Belloque rose and came to stand beside her daughter.

'Is it the Englishman?' she asked.

Isabelle nodded.

'Men of his age and position make a habit of playing with the feelings of young girls,' Madame Belloque said sadly. 'But it will pass.'

'I won't let it pass,' said Isabelle.

Madame Belloque walked around the piano and looked her daughter full in the face.

'What do you mean?' she asked.

'I intend to go to London with Robert.'

Madame Belloque nodded as if this were an everyday announcement but her body stiffened, betraying her true feelings.

'Has he asked you?'

'Not in so many words, but he would let me.'

Madame Belloque's patience broke.

'Will he marry you? No! So what will you be?' she asked angrily.

'A whore, mother,' Isabelle replied derisively.

'Don't speak like that!'

'It is what you thought.'

'The world would think it.'

'And what does the world think of Anne-Marie? Does anyone believe that she is merely a housekeeper?'

Madame Belloque turned away from Isabelle. She had already lost one daughter and now the other was trying to leave.

'If I have to chain you in the cellar, you will not go,' she said with quiet force. 'In November you will marry at Arronville and by next summer you will have a child.'

Isabelle knew how much this meant to her mother and sighed. 'Let me go to London and I will return by November. I swear it.'

'Have you slept with him?' asked Madame Belloque.

Isabelle didn't know how to reply. 'I'm still a virgin,' she said finally. 'And if you let me go, I will remain one until my marriage.'

Madame Belloque turned around. 'Isabelle! What are you saying? I know these kind of men. I know what they want from a woman!'

Isabelle looked at her mother in surprise. Madame Belloque turned her face away to hide the burgeoning tears.

With a shock, Isabelle realised how closely her mother resembled the woman in the painting at the villa. Standing in the pale morning light, her face half-hidden, hair escaping from her ribbon, it was unmistakable.

'There is a portrait of Alain at the villa,' Isabelle began. 'I thought the woman was Anne-Marie ...'

Madame Belloque stiffened as Isabelle thought the unthinkable.

'You and Alain were lovers,' Isabelle finally managed to say.

She recalled Alain's many visits when she was a child and the attentions he showed to the family. She remembered that the visits continued after her father's death and only ended when Anne-Marie went away.

'You gave your daughter to your lover,' she said incredulously.

Madame Belloque sat heavily in the chair by the window. It would have been futile to lie.

'We were lovers a long time ago,' she said softly. 'A very long time ago. As for Anne-Marie, he seduced her and I couldn't prevent her from going.'

'You know what Alain and Robert want from a woman because you have given yourself to such men!' Isabelle continued, following the flood of her thoughts.

Madame Belloque wiped the tears from her cheeks.

'You forbid me what you have enjoyed yourself!'

'I want to protect you!' cried Madame Belloque.

'You betrayed my father!'

It was this last thought that galvanised Isabelle. She rose

and strode from the room. 'I will not stay in this house!' she shouted from the door and, ignoring her mothers pleas, she ran to her room. Methodically, as if she had planned it for many weeks, Isabelle emptied her wardrobes. From the small adjoining boxroom she hauled out a travelling chest and, in a fury, began to fill it with her clothes.

Downstairs, in the music room, Madame Belloque was still seated by the window. A great heaviness lay on her. Memories that she had tried to bury returned, pushing into her mind as a succession of tiny shocks. It seemed that the delirium that had swept through her youth was invincible, returning first for one daughter and then the other. She remembered that delirium and it was sweet, overpowering.

'How could I have thought that Isabelle was pure enough to resist?' she murmured to herself. The sounds from upstairs finally roused her and she rose with an effort.

Isabelle's bedroom was a turmoil of cottons and silks. Discarded clothes and shoes lay cast here and there, as if rifled through by a thief. When her mother appeared in the doorway, Isabelle tried to force the door closed and they struggled. From somewhere, Madame Belloque found the strength to push her way into the room.

'Isabelle, listen to me. You don't know what happened!'

'There is nothing that you can say that will keep me here,' Isabelle replied coldly.

'Well know this at least! I didn't betray your father. He wanted to see me with other men. It excited him. After the first years he never took me, not fully. You must understand. He was your father, always your loving father, but I did not conceive from him.'

Isabelle shook her head and lifted her hands to her ears.

'I won't listen,' she cried.

'Robert will want the same thing from you. He will give you to other men as your father gave me.'

'Did you enjoy it? Did you enjoy being given?' Isabelle asked spitefully.

Madame Belloqe recalled the long nights at the villa, the many beautiful girls, and the men. Yes, she had enjoyed it, enjoyed them, but it was not what Isabelle would want to hear at that moment.

'It is a subject best left alone, Isabelle,' she said.

'Did you climax with them, as my father watched?' the girl persisted with increasing malice.

Madame Belloque slapped her daughter's face for the first time in many years. Isabelle was so surprised that, for a moment, she was absolutely still. Madame Belloque took her in her arms.

'Forgive me,' she begged. 'I'm so afraid of losing you.'

Isabelle began to cry. The tears were long overdue and hotter and wetter because of it. Madame Belloque held Isabelle as her body shook and her chest heaved, then, with an arm around her shoulder, she led Isabelle to the bed and they sat side my side, mother and daughter again.

For a long time they were silent. The sun, finding its way around the house, began to edge through the window and on to the twisted piles of clothes. Finally, Isabelle took her mother's hand and stroked it. Madame Belloque turned to face her.

'If you leave it now and never see him again you will save yourself so much unhappiness.'

Isabelle knew that what her mother said was true, but could only shrug. 'He is all that I think about. He excites me so much.'

Madame Belloque thought of the handsome Englishman and sighed. She understood too well the effect that such a man could have on a young girl. When she asked herself if she envied her daughter, a part of her, at least, could only answer yes.

'Please let me go to London,' Isabelle persisted.

Madame Belloque squeezed her daughter's hands hard. 'Could I stop you?'

Isabelle shook her head. 'But I wouldn't leave you, I will come back in November. And I will still be a virgin. I swear it.'

Madame Belloque smiled. 'What a wife you will make for Monsieur Chabard! He will never have need to visit the whores of Arronville again,' she said ironically.

'You are not bad, Maman. Must I be?'

'You do not see my dreams, Isabelle. They may not be bad but they are not virtuous.'

'Is it my father that you dream of, or the others?'

'All of them,' Madame Belloque sighed. 'But it was your father that I loved.'

12

Readying

Later that day, Isabelle rode over to the villa on her mother's horse. Robert was busy when she arrived and sent a footman with a note asking her to wait in the library. In a postscript, Robert told her that she would be presented to Alain before the day was finished and that the matter of her journeying to London would be settled.

The library was an exceptionally spacious room with tall windows that looked out on to a terraced courtyard with shrubs and fountains. The walls were lined with white lacquered bookshelves crammed to bursting point with volumes ancient and modern, in every civilised tongue. If the walls suggested study and concentration the remainder of the room was established for relaxation. Silk covered ottomans and easy chairs filled the centre of the room. The windows had long, softly padded seats at their base and there was a scattering of cushions with an eastern appearance on the floor.

This restful air did not penetrate Isabelle, however. Robert's note had left her with a sense of foreboding and she spent most of the hour or so that she waited pacing the floor. Images of Alain filled her mind, Alain as seducer and master of her sister, Alain as lover to her mother.

As she thought these things, she glanced through a window and noticed one of the stable boys standing in shadow on the far side of the terrace. He was gazing at her intently. She recognised him; she had seen him in the grounds on the day that Robert had taken her to the lake and had her raise her dress while he sat against a tree. Just as he'd done before, the boy hurriedly retreated when he realised that he'd been noticed. This episode added to Isabelle's uneasiness. It felt as if everyone in the villa were examining her and weighing her in their eyes. It was a relief when Maria appeared and announced that she was to take Isabelle to be dressed.

Robert was already in the bedroom. He was rifling through the wardrobes and all around him were discarded dresses.

'Strip her please, Maria,' he said, as soon as they entered the room, allowing himself barely a glance in Isabelle's direction.

Maria slipped Isabelle's dress off her shoulders and pulled the sleeves down her arms.

'She needs to make an impression,' said Robert pulling out yet another garment. It seemed no more right than any of the others and he discarded it in frustration. Maria pulled the dress off Isabelle's hips and stepped back to examine her critically.

'Alain likes bruises on a woman, perhaps we should leave her top bare,' Robert murmured, glancing at the marks on her breast. 'Or perhaps she should be completely naked.'

Isabelle felt oddly dispossessed as he spoke, as if her body were no longer her own. A rebellious feeling stirred in her heart and she felt an impulse to stamp her foot, like a child and say 'I am here, look at me! Not simply my flesh, but me!' But she did not speak and he did not look at her. He continued to sort through the clothes and his glances in her direction were simple assessments, decisions as to what would display her to best advantage when she was taken before his friend. It seemed that after her visit the previous evening, after she had witnessed him beat Helene and consented to being beaten herself, he no longer felt the need to consult her as to what should or should not be done in her regard.

Maria circled the naked figure. If she was aware of Isabelle's distaste of this examination she showed no interest in it. Her eyes scanned Isabelle's thighs and sex, they wandered across her belly and breasts with the same critical distance she had once shown while dressing Isabelle in the bedroom at Robert's behest. When Robert, standing beside the maid, looked at Isabelle, he showed a similar detachment. Looking at Isabelle's face, he focused only on her lips and something in his expression made Isabelle feel that from now on, her mouth was a sexual organ, a part of her body to be opened and explored for another's pleasure, rather than an organ of speech.

'Mademoiselle Isabelle would attract any man, monsieur,' said the maid, after this full, critical inventory of her body had been taken.

'Yes, but we need something special.'

'Perhaps no dress, monsieur. But underwear. Something that shows off her figure and especially her behind.'

Robert smiled. 'You have noticed Monsieur Alain's preference for women's behinds, Maria?'

'I have experienced it, monsieur.'

For the first time, Isabelle saw Maria smile. It was not a pleasant smile and Isabelle understood why it was usually suppressed. Something in the present situation seemed to excite Maria and for a moment her mask had slipped.

Robert started opening the drawers at the foot of the wardrobe, pulling out bundles of lace and silk. He bade Isabelle stand before him and held up a succession of flimsy garments of all shades and shapes. Isabelle, feeling more and more helpless let her head drop. Robert stroked her hair and kissed her forehead absently, as if he were petting an animal.

'Put this on her, Maria,' Robert said finally, and tossed a bundle of silk to the maid.

Maria knelt at Isabelle's feet and had Isabelle step into the little black slip that Robert had selected. The maid tugged it half way up Isabelle's legs but it jammed against her thighs.

'Excuse me, mademoiselle. It must go on from the top.'

Maria tugged the slip back down and, standing up, slipped it over Isabelle's head.

'It would need some adjustment,' Maria said.

The slip was tight at the waist, loose and open at the bust and very short. At the back there was nothing and Isabelle was naked to the waist. When Robert told her to lean forward, her breasts were completely visible. Bending over fully, the lower parts of her buttocks were exposed, as was the rear view of her sex.

Robert and Maria contemplated Isabelle in these various positions.

'It is very plain,' said Robert, doubtfully.

'It is very exciting, monsieur,' Maria replied.

Robert looked at the maid. 'It excites you, Maria?'

'Yes, monsieur.'

'You desire Mademoiselle Isabelle?'

'It is not my place.'

'If it was your place?'

'Then I would desire her, monsieur.'

Robert smiled. 'One evening I shall watch her with you.'

'Thank you, monsieur.'

Isabelle was standing with her back to them at that moment and breathed in sharply. Robert rested his hand on her neck.

'You must have imagined what it would be like with a girl,' he said.

'Not Maria,' she answered rather coolly. She felt no desire for the maid.

'Then Helene, perhaps?'

Isabelle thought back to the previous evening, recalling Helene's luminous eyes and soft skin. She heard again the howls when the girls buttocks were whipped and the sobs as she lay in Robert's arms afterwards. Most vividly she remembered Helene masturbate to climax as he plied the strap across her breasts.

'I wanted to be a man with Helene,' said Isabelle. 'After you had beaten her, she was so . . . pliant.'

'I think Maria will want to be a man with you, my darling. Perhaps at this very moment.'

Robert rested his hand on the side of Isabelle's head and turned her face to his. He kissed her briefly.

'Maria,' Robert called.

The maid came to stand before them.

'Use your mouth on her sex. There is no need to be gentle.'

'No,' Isabelle groaned.

Robert stifled her protests with his lips and drew her hands behind her back. Maria knelt and pulled the slip up and over Isabelle's belly. The maid took hold of Isabelle's sex with her mouth as a fox might seize a rabbit. Isabelle stiffened for a moment then struggled furiously.

'Must we tie you?' asked Robert, angrily.

He had her wrists so firmly in his grasp that she might as well have been tied.

'Must we?' he asked again.

Isabelle's will to resist drained away and she slumped back into his arms. Between her legs she felt a hard pressure of teeth against her lower lips and a tongue, wet and hungry, at the entrance of her vulva. Robert's erection pushed into the cheeks of her behind like a weapon.

Such were the indignities that had been forced on her, that Isabelle was determined to take no pleasure from these attentions. When Robert took her breast though, and eased it from its silken cage, she gasped. Hearing this, Maria bit hard into the inside of Isabelle's thigh, her teeth marks overlying the fading, but still visible, imprints of Robert's thumb and fingers. When Maria's tongue moved back to her sex Isabelle gave a long deep moan of excitement.

'She is a bitch in heat, Maria,' Robert said. 'One day I will have her lie with the dogs in the stable.'

'She is very wet, monsieur.'

'My sweet bitch,' Robert murmured and stroked Isabelle's hair. 'You should be on all fours in a market square presenting your behind to all the passers-by.'

'I hate you,' moaned Isabelle.

'Make her climax, Maria.'

Maria's tongue moved irresistibly to Isabelle's clitoris and established a steady, knowing rhythm. Isabelle felt her belly inflate and fill with slowly expanding spheres of arousal. She moaned repeatedly.

'Wait,' said Robert suddenly.

He took Isabelle by the arm and led her to the bed. Shakily, she climbed on to it and knelt as he directed her to. Feeling the pressure of his hand in the small of her back she bent forward so that her bottom was high in the air and her breasts were crushed against the counterpane.

'Spread your legs,' he told her.

'Now I am your bitch,' she said thickly and edged her knees apart.

'You want it?' he asked.

'Yes,' she said.

Her eyes were hooded and her face had dissolved. She felt as if she had crossed into another country, a country whose landscape was flesh. In this land, it seemed, there were no constraints on what could be done to her or on what she would consent to.

'Finish it now, Maria,' Robert said.

The maid climbed on to the bed and, taking Isabelle's buttocks in her hands, she opened them. Maria plunged her tongue into the girls sex and began again the alternate soft and harsh, teasing and probing arousal.

Robert went over to the open door and looked out into the courtyard. A peacock had found its way in from the gardens and was drinking from the baths. He watched as it drank then strutted a few paces and drank again. Before the bird had finished, Robert heard Isabelle climax in a series of high, tiny cries.

'Wash her, Maria,' he called over his shoulder. 'And attend to that slip. It will have to do.'

After Isabelle had been washed and her clothes had been taken away, Robert sat on the bed and asked her to stand before him. He examined her still wet thighs, remarking on the red marks left by Maria's teeth and the gross inflammation of her sex.

'There are some gags in the chest and some cuffs,' he said. 'Would you bring a selection?'

She looked at him quizzically.

'I think you should be blindfolded, gagged and cuffed when I present you to Alain. The more desirable that he

103

finds you the more likely he is to agree to you coming to London.'

Isabelle went over to the tall, thin chest that Helene had opened the night before. Each drawer was lined with red velvet and there was a strong smell of leather. The first drawer contained a bewildering variety of brass and steel instruments whose function she couldn't begin to guess at. One in particular, a large forceps like device with rows of sharp teeth on the closing surfaces, caught her eye and made her shudder.

In the second drawer there was a collection of smooth black rods, some as thick as her wrist, others thinner than her little finger. She guessed that these were designed to go inside a girl. They had an ancient appearance and she noticed that carved on each was an Egyptian hieroglyph. Somehow, they made her think of necromancers and alchemists, of men in black cloaks surrounded by fire and molten metals. It was only when she opened the third drawer that she found anything resembling a gag.

'Is this what you want?' she asked, holding up a satin band with a ball of tightly folded fabric sewn into its centre.

Robert nodded.

There were a number of different colours and she picked one of each. The cuffs were easy to identify when she came across them. She had already seen Robert use them on Helene.

'Am I not to be allowed to speak for myself?' she asked, as she presented these things to Robert.

'Perhaps not,' he replied, holding up the satin gags to her face to see which most complemented her hair and skin colour.

'Do you prefer the gold or the red?' he asked.

Isabelle looked at the innocent seeming strips of satin. 'Neither,' she said.

Robert discarded the red. 'Silence is golden.'

He had her turn around and folded her wrists together behind her back. She felt the broad silk cuffs tightening and Robert pulling at them to make sure they were secure.

Excitement began to smoulder in her belly again. When Robert was satisfied with the knots, he had her turn around a number of times and she saw in his eyes that he too was aroused. For Isabelle, the cuffs made external what she already felt, a prisoner in a cell of desire. But if she was constrained on one level she was also opened and liberated on another. Since she was now unable to cover herself with her hands she was doubly aware of the passages that led into her belly. She thought of twin rivers open to the sea, down which any ship might choose to pass, peaceful merchant man or rapacious corsair. This very openness made her wet.

Robert reached out and wrapped a length of her pubic hair around his fingers. Using this as a lead, he drew her to the bed.

'Lie on your belly,' he told her.

Without the use of her hands, this was impossible to achieve gracefully and she ended by tumbling on to the counterpane. Robert pushed a pillow under her hips so that she was in the position that Helene had adopted the previous evening. His hands dragged her legs apart with savage force, stretching the tendons at her groin. She knew from this violence how much he wanted her. When his fingers dug into her buttocks and opened wide the area around her anus, her heart began to race.

'I want you to be the first,' she said.

Robert used his tongue in that sensitive, subtly shaded well until it opened.

'Keep it open,' he told her.

She turned her head and looked over her shoulder.

'It is for you, not Alain,' she told him.

Robert said nothing. Instead he took her hands and placed them on her behind. Even with her wrists tied she was able to hold apart the two cheeks. He pressed her head to the pillow and pulled her hair across her face so that she could see nothing.

From the small movements of the bed and the faint sounds of fabric and buttons grating, she realised that he was undoing his breeches. After a few moments she felt his fingers at her sex. He dipped them inside her several times, gathering the moisture. She realised that he must be lubricating his sex and her anus fell wide open to receive him.

Robert must have seen that sudden dilation but made no attempt to penetrate her. Instead, he masturbated over Isabelle's prostrate body as if seeking a simple release. Finally understanding his intention, Isabelle raised her behind from the pillow, presenting it more fully and opened her buttocks still wider.

'Let me see you,' she said urgently.

Robert continued masturbating steadily.

'Please.'

Hearing neither assent nor reproof, Isabelle raised her head tentatively. Through the partial veil of her hair, she saw his face, nakedly savage. At that moment he climaxed and she felt his seed spattering on to her behind. A rivulet of the lukewarm, viscous fluid ran slowly down the widely spread cleft. Slipping into the well of her open anus, it ran inside her. In a reflex reaction to the tiny irritation, the ring contracted and then expanded again as if to gulp down more.

Afterwards, Robert was very gentle with her. He bathed her behind like a loving father would bathe a young child and released her hands. They lay together on the bed in the afternoon heat and Isabelle held him while he dozed. There was such an innocence in this, that it was hard to remember what he had done to Helene and what he had had Maria do to her.

As the time drew near for Isabelle's appointment with Alain, Robert roused himself. They walked together in the courtyard for a while. Dipping his hand into the baths, Robert gathered a handful of water and splashed her with it. She ran laughing into the shadows of the colonnade disturbing the peacock that was sheltering from the fierce sun. It flapped its huge wings and flew up on to one of the terra-cotta rooves, noisily. Isabelle had become so accustomed to nakedness that she felt no self-consciousness when a boy, a stable boy it seemed by his dress, looked out of one of the windows to see what was causing the disturbance. Catching her eye, the boy flushed scarlet and withdrew hastily.

Before long, Maria returned with the black slip and a variety of cosmetics which she lay out on one of the dressing tables. It was decided that Isabelle should be blindfolded and cuffed but not gagged. Robert judged her lips too tempting to be hidden. They tried a variety of make ups but her natural skin colouring was so good that eventually they discarded them all. To display her hair to best advantage it was simply left untied to fall across her shoulders.

Maria had adjusted the slip so that it moulded itself to her belly and hips like a second skin. She had also shortened it, so that unless Isabelle stood absolutely still and absolutely upright, her sex could be seen.

When she was ready, Robert had her walk ahead of him down the long corridors to the library. Against the white of the marble walls she looked astonishing. The short black slip accentuated the length of her slender, well shaped legs and the narrowness of her waist. With her wrists tied, her shoulders were pulled back, fully displaying the rich fruit of her breasts.

At each corner, Robert gave instructions on which way she was to turn, as the blindfold cut out all clues to her whereabouts. Since he insisted that they hurry, Isabelle was terrified that she would bump into one of the many pillars that she knew lined the corridors. Without the use of her hands, she felt that she would crash heavily to the mosaic floor at any moment.

After some minutes of proceeding like this, Robert stopped her and pushed her against the wall. She was grateful to be stationary, with a firm surface behind her.

'You are a whore,' he said in an even voice, as if teaching her some simple fact.

She felt his hand ease one of her breasts from the slip.

'Tell me what you are.'

'A whore.'

'Anything that Alain asks of you, you will comply with immediately.'

'Yes,' she said.

'Open your legs.'

She splayed out her thighs.

'Wider. And lift your pelvis as if your cunt is hungry and searching for the fingers that will open it.'

Isabelle's bare feet edged apart still further and she tipped her pelvis upwards.

'Rock it up and down, slowly. Make me want you.'

As she performed these obscene movements, there was a tingling in her labia and soon, she knew, her moisture would be running.

'Slut,' he said.

'Your slut,' she breathed.

'And Alain's.'

Although all of this seemed no more than a lesson in an unusual form of etiquette, Isabelle's heart missed a beat as she thought of Alain watching her do these things.

'And Alain's,' she agreed eventually.

Robert pushed his fingers against her sex and held them still.

'Excite yourself against my hand,' he told her.

She did so, rocking her pelvis slowly at first, but then with increasing speed. When she was panting with arousal he lowered his hand gradually so that she was forced to bow out her legs to keep in contact. With the fingernails of his free hand, he flicked her exposed nipple hard several times. It stung and made her gasp but when he stopped, she wanted more. Isabelle's head was twisting from side to side in the extremity of her desire.

'I don't want you to climax yet,' he told her and abruptly he removed his hand.

She lay against the wall breathing heavily. Her belly was full and swelled out and over her sex.

'Turn around. I'm going to beat you,' he said evenly.

Isabelle shuffled around to face the wall. He had never beaten her before and though she had always known that he would it was a surprise, especially so at that time and in that place. She pressed herself against the cool, smooth surface and waited for him to begin.

'Bare your behind,' he told her.

This was difficult with her wrists tied, but by scrabbling at the material with her fingers she was able to raise it into a bunch at her waist. He started to slap her steadily. At first, the blows only stung, but as the slapping proceeded, first to one side of her behind and then to the other, the pain became unbearable and she started to struggle. Robert pressed his hand into the small of her back and pinned her to the wall. He increased the force of his blows and she began to howl. By the time he had finished, she was hardly able to breathe and tears flowed from her eyes in hot, salty rivers.

Robert allowed her to rest for a few minutes. She must have seemed especially pitiful in her distress for he could not help but kiss her cheek and murmur soft words of affection. When she had quieted, he told her to push out her behind and open her legs. Isabelle did this slowly, as if she were in a dream. Her torso slid down the wall and her freed breast, crushed against the marble, spread outwards so that the nipple peeped to the side.

He placed his hand against her sex again, this time from behind, and told her to continue with her masturbation. As soon as she moved, the feelings were deep and strong. She groaned and her lips curled back over her teeth. There was an unselfconsciousness in her movements as if she had lost all track of where she was and what she was doing. She ground her pelvis into his hand in the way a man might grind his sex into a girl.

As soon as Isabelle began to climax, Robert took hold of her arm and pulled her along the corridor. The orgasms continued as she half stumbled, half walked beside him.

13

The Library

Reaching the library door, Robert pulled Isabelle into an upright position and knocked. Almost immediately, the door was opened and Isabelle heard Helene murmur 'Monsieur', by way of greeting.

Isabelle took a deep breath and struggled to gain control of her body, wracked as it still was by the aftershocks of orgasm and by the numb pain of her beating.

'Straight ahead,' Robert said, giving her a gentle push. 'I will tell you when to stop.'

With her heart racing, Isabelle walked slowly forward.

'That will do,' said Robert, when she'd reached the centre of the library floor, 'turn around if you please.'

She turned until he told her to stop. Given the many small sounds in the library, Isabelle guessed that it was more than just Alain and Robert who were present. From one corner came the rustle of a dress, from another the clink of glass and the creak of a chair.

She imagined the picture she must present in that elegant and civilised room. One of her breasts was bared, her thighs were damp with excitement, and her cheeks damp with tears. She would look as Robert intended her to look, like a woman pulled from the midst of orgasm.

As she thought these things she heard the library door being closed and footsteps approaching her. She stiffened, sensing that a man was circling her, a man who was large and powerful. His heat and bulk seemed to impress itself on to her skin and made her tingle from head to toe.

'So,' the man said abruptly, and from his deep, heavy voice, Isabelle knew that it was Alain. 'This is the virgin, Isabelle.'

Fingers trailed down the length of her naked spine and she shivered.

'How is the beautiful daughter of my old friend Madame Belloque?'

'Well, monsieur.'

Isabelle felt the back of her slip being raised.

'And your behind.'

'A little sore.'

Alain made a small, amused, snorting sound.

'Indeed.'

The fingers trailed around the hem of her slip so that the front portion was lifted to her navel. After a moment's examination the fabric was released and the footsteps receded. Isabelle felt herself colouring as she realised that all who were present in the library had seen her reddened behind and inflamed sex.

'So you want to come to London?' asked Alain.

'Yes.'

'As Robert's courtesan?' His voice was weighted with irony as he said this.

Isabelle started, realising that what she had said in confidence to Robert, intimate things that related to Alain and her sister, had been passed on.

'Well?' Alain persisted.

'As his lover.'

'You love him?'

'Yes.'

There was a silence. Almost a silence. From directly in front of her came a sharp intake of breath and then a sigh. Isabelle felt sure that it was Helene and that either Alain or Robert was playing with her.

'Does he love you?' Alain asked.

'I don't know,' she stammered, taken aback by this question. 'It doesn't matter. I love him.'

Without realising it Isabelle was struggling against the cuffs. It took a great effort of the will to calm herself and still her hands.

111

'Do you love her?' Alain asked Robert.

There was a long silence, during which Isabelle suffered agonies of hope.

'I'm fond of her,' Robert said finally.

'Fond?' There was a cruel mockery in Alain's voice as he said this. 'And you want her in London?'

'Yes.'

'And what are you offering me, Isabelle?'

Isabelle knew that this question would come and she had rehearsed her answer many times.

'Everything but my virginity,' she said firmly.

'Everything but your cunt?'

'Yes,' she replied.

'Be specific if you will, I want to know exactly what our bargain will entail.'

Isabelle knew quite well from his teasing tone that this was part of a game. Alain was seeking to embarrass her with these questions in exactly the way that Robert's presentation of her sought to embarrass and discompose. It was the cruelty of small boys who have caught a mouse and torment it with fire. Such understanding did not help though and she blushed freely.

'I offer my mouth,' she murmured.

'Speak up.'

'My mouth,' she repeated in a louder but still shaky voice.

'And what might I want your sweet mouth for?'

'You are making fun of me, monsieur!'

'You offer it as substitute for your cunt?'

'If that is what you want.'

'I have three fingers inside Helene at this very moment. Could your mouth offer more than this hot, wet tube?'

'No,' she replied, stung. 'But what I offer is as good.'

'Perhaps,' murmured Alain, 'but I shall want more. What else can you offer me?'

'My behind,' she said coolly.

Alain laughed. 'I will accept that graceful invitation one day, perhaps.'

At that moment a woman, almost certainly Helene, gave

a series of little cries. There was a slapping sound, a sound of hand against thigh or breast. This was followed by a half-stifled groan whose soft, unreserved sweetness sat oddly against the sharpness of the inquisition that Isabelle endured. She longed to exchange places with the girl who could give herself so easily before others and who had already conceded such liberties. It was the conceding that was hard. If Robert had simply pushed her over a chair and pulled open her behind for his friend she would have struggled perhaps but not as fiercely as she struggled now to speak, to assent to what she both feared and desired. Isabelle steeled herself once more and waited as patiently as she could for the game to unfold. Alain, who seemed to make all the rules and who was still deciding Isabelle's fate also seemed to decide that the girl must wait. Helene's moans subsided and in a small voice, but one imbued with a hardly resistible sensual longing she whispered, 'please'. She repeated this word three times in succession, each time with more desire and more desperation as the certainty of refusal increased. The word seemed to cast a spell over the room. All the sounds that Isabelle had heard, the faint rustlings, the sighs of pages turning and glasses being filled or emptied ceased and there was absolute silence as if this small word had the power of kings. Isabelle knew then the power of desire and the power that she herself possessed when everything seemed to be surrendered.

'And if I want to have you whipped?' Alain asked abruptly, breaking the silence and directing his attention to Isabelle again.

A chill passed through her. 'I give you that right.'

'Bravely spoken now, ahead of the event.'

'If my sister can bear it, I shall.'

Something about this reply, perhaps the tone with its youthful pride or perhaps the reference to Anne-Marie seemed to infuriate Alain.

'What I shall expect of you, in place of your virginity, is your honesty,' he said angrily. 'You will never lie to me or evade telling me the truth. Do you understand? If I suspect that you are withholding anything at all from me, you will be beaten past any point that your sister has ever experienced. Make sure that you understand what I'm asking for before you reply.'

Isabelle did understand. If he couldn't rape her sex he was intent on raping her mind. She hesitated.

'Isabelle, answer.'

This was Robert's voice and it gave her the strength to reply.

'I will never hide anything from you, monsieur.'

There was silence for a moment as both parties digested the meaning of this agreement. When Alain spoke again he had regained his usual, heavy calm.

'There is one other obstacle. Your mother's agreement in full to all that has been talked of here.'

'She has agreed, monsieur.'

'Understand that I shall speak to her in person.'

'I have told her that I shall travel to London if you permit it. She has ceased trying to dissuade me.'

'Good. Then let us hope that the matter is settled.'

There was another silence.

'Maria,' Alain called after a time. 'Fetch a chair for Mademoiselle Isabelle and remove her blindfold.'

Isabelle heard Maria's quick footsteps and the sound of a chair grating on the mosaic floor.

'Place it further to the left.'

When the chair was placed as Alain wanted it, Maria approached Isabelle. Fingers tugged at the knot of the blindfold and after a few moments it was removed. The sudden light made Isabelle wince and it was a while before she could see clearly.

The first figure that she became aware of was Robert, standing to her left and leaning against a bookshelf. Beside him was Anna, slight, pretty Anna, the wanton Anna with the smile that teased and beckoned. She pressed herself against Robert's side as Isabelle watched and he looped an arm around her waist bringing his hand to rest on her breast. Her erect nipples were clearly visible through the thin fabric of her dress and his fingers played across them lightly. She kissed his cheek and whispered something that

114

Isabelle couldn't hear. Robert smiled, first at Anna and then at Isabelle who looked away feeling betrayed. Her eyes scanned the rest of the room.

Directly in front of her was Alain, seated on one of the ottomans. By his side was Helene, naked, her knees tucked up to her chest and her widely spread feet gripping the silk covered seat. Alain was working his hands between her legs and her head rolled slowly from side to side. As Isabelle looked at the girl, she saw a bead of sweat run from her forehead, down between her glazed eyes and to the corner of her trembling mouth.

It was the realisation that another man was present in the room that shocked Isabelle. This man was young and well dressed, clearly a gentleman and a complete stranger. He was turned away from her at the moment that she saw him, pouring a glass of brandy from a crystal decanter. His hands, she noticed, were unusually long and the fingers were thin, almost feminine.

Before Isabelle could study the man further, she felt Maria's hand on her waist. The maid gently guided her to the high backed wooden chair set out in the middle of the room. Alain had deliberately had the chair placed so that the afternoon sun, falling through the library window, lit it like a stage set. Stepping into the burning square of sunlight, Isabelle realised that the glare made it difficult for her to see the others in the room. At the same time she realised that nothing of herself could be hidden. When she was seated she was directly facing Alain, who regarded her unemotionally as another might regard a familiar painting.

'Put your feet on the crosspieces at the sides of the chair,' Robert told her.

This required that she open her legs wide and raise them so her heels could gain a purchase on the smooth wooden bars. Inevitably, the slip rode up on to her belly exposing the space between her legs.

'Play with her breasts, Maria,' Robert said when he was satisfied with Isabelle's position.

Maria reached over Isabelle's shoulder and ran her hand inside the slip. It felt to Isabelle that Robert was keen to

115

display her to full advantage as he might show a racehorse to a friend in its finest livery. She glanced at the young stranger to see if she was having the desired affect. The stranger's blue eyes slipped away from her, almost shyly, but Isabelle knew in that brief glimpse, that he too desired her. There was some pride in that realisation and a satisfaction that Robert would not be disappointed. Maria's fingers worked on her nipples gently at first but from time to time she would give a sudden sharp twist that made Isabelle gasp. As Maria leant over her, Isabelle felt the warmth of the other woman's body and this intimacy softened her. She gave up her struggle for self-control and began to breathe heavily. Her eyes opened wide then half closed as the feelings deepened. She was aware of Robert's close attention and she turned to him, offering him this growing excitement, an excitement that he sanctioned, almost commanded, not for his own sake, but for his friend Alain and for the stranger. Maria pulled the slip completely clear of Isabelle's breasts so that she could reach underneath and lift them for the men to see, and so that she could separate them and squeeze until the nipples stood proudly. They blushed a milder pink than the lips of her sex, lips which gleamed now with the juice of fresh arousal. When Robert told Maria to stop, she left Isabelle's breasts uncovered so that only her waist had the protection of clothing.

Alain's eyes probed between her open thighs. Her sex, starkly illuminated by the strong sunlight, clearly fascinated him.

'Your sister's sex is entirely bare,' he told her. 'I like to see her lips become engorged with blood when she is excited.'

He looked Isabelle full in the face to see how she would react to this information. Isabelle could hold his gaze for only a moment before looking away.

'She is made quite differently from you,' Alain continued. 'Her sex is so full, so visible, so external.' Alain turned to Robert. 'Is that not so, my friend?'

Robert nodded.

'Isabelle's sex is more discrete,' he agreed, 'but charming. Would you like her to be depilated?'

'I like to see a woman completely,' Alain replied.

'It will be done,' promised Robert.

Alain's fingers seemed to find a particularly responsive area at that moment and Helene uttered a long guttural groan, arresting in its intensity. All present turned to look at her. She was oblivious to this attention, her eyes were closed and focused inwards. Her breasts, no larger than Isabelle's when Isabelle was twelve years old, rose and fell on her broad ribcage with a deep tidal rhythm. She might have been taken for a woman dreaming some powerful dream whose spell held her from consciousness but gave her no true repose. The world for her was the hand that invaded her and kept her poised in this purgatory of ever escalating arousal.

Robert walked over to the girl, casually, and tipped her head back so that it rested on the top of the ottoman. He leant forward and whispered something to her. Her eyes opened reluctantly and she reached out her hands to him. Taking them, Robert pulled her long arms into the air and then back so that her body arched and her pelvis lifted clear of the seat. Alain's fingers still did their work but Helene, too, worked now, raising and lowering her sex to meet his thrusts. Seeing that she was close, Robert told her to look at Isabelle and Helene's drowning eyes turned to the other woman. Isabelle was held by them, by their neediness and by the sense that she was looking deep into another's desire. She so much wanted to give the girl her release but was powerless. The two men who played with her exchanged little glances, nods, hardly detectable signals as they acted together to slow her as they felt necessary or to add new sources of pleasure, a finger tip at her behind, a series of kisses on her neck, the tantalising brush of a palm across her nipples. Isabelle watched them with the growing realisation that they had done this a thousand times before and that their judgement and control was as fine as any virtuoso musician's might be with a favourite instrument. It was clear that they could keep Helene in this

117

state of arousal for hours if they wished or could tip her into orgasm with the merest graze of a finger across her sex. She both envied the other girl this attention and dreaded that one day she too would become just a plaything, addicted to arousal as Helene so clearly was.

Robert let go of Helene's arms with the instruction that she should continue to keep them raised and walked over to Isabelle. He crouched beside her and by no more than resting his hand on her belly pulled feelings to the surface that were the invariable prelude to climax. It was as if she had already been caressed in some subtle way as Helene had been caressed, as if the fingers at Helene's sex had had ghostly companions at her own, preparing her for Robert's hand, a hand that did not move but simply warmed and drew longing from its bottomless reservoir. She groaned as he slid that hand to her sex and allowed it to rest there.

'You are so sensitive my darling,' he told her, 'you cannot watch another girl being given pleasure without feeling it too. I knew it when you watched me beat Helene. You felt every blow of the belt and afterwards every kiss and every thrust as I took her.'

He seemed to track Isabelle's thoughts and feelings with the ease of a bloodhound, scenting each shy desire or flickering anxiety unerringly. And he had the power to give or to take away as he now demonstrated, removing the hand that she craved and returning to Helene. The girl was still crouched, legs wide, back arched against the ottoman, arms high above her head like some captured soldier. Alain had abandoned her to watch Robert with Isabelle and she waited with a patience that Isabelle would have found impossible. Positioned as she was, all of her weight pressed down into her sex pushing it out into a ball of flesh, a ball that had burst to reveal its vulnerable, tempting interior. Reaching her, Robert immediately thrust his fingers into this ball and she cried out. His other hand took her neck and forced it back so that her face was open to his. His hand fucked her very slowly but it reached deep. When he gave his permission, she climaxed with a pumping of her hips and a shuddering from head to toe. Robert was right,

Isabelle felt that climax, felt it deep inside and had to fight a burning desire to touch herself.

Robert pulled his hand clear and Helene slid down the ottoman close to a faint, her arms falling to her sides and her head lolling on the pale flesh of her shoulders. Glancing at Isabelle, Robert ran his fingers through the girl's hair. His face shone triumphantly and Isabelle wanted him back at her side doing those things to her.

There was a relaxation in the room after this, as if everyone had somehow participated in the release. Alain called for a scotch and Maria fetched it on a silver tray. Robert sat at one of the desks turning the chair outwards so that he faced Isabelle. He motioned for Anna. She sat at his feet, as he told her to, and leant her back against his legs. Her dress fell open to reveal the nakedness of her legs and behind but she made no effort to cover herself. Isabelle was reminded of a well trained dog, a dog that wished only to please.

'How did she respond when you beat her?' Alain asked, directing his attention to Isabelle once more.

'She was aroused.'

'Is that true, Isabelle?'

Isabelle shifted uncomfortably in her seat. When Robert had slapped her in the hall, there had only been pain and a feeling of humiliation, but afterwards when he touched her, it had been electrifying. The experience had confused her. Haltingly, she tried to explain this.

'If Robert asked you to bend over that desk and receive the same again would you comply?' Alain asked.

'Of course.'

'Imagine it now. You bend over the desk. Your slip is lifted. Helene holds open the cheeks of your behind so that Robert can spank inside, so that he can reach the most sensitive parts, imagine that and tell me how you would feel.'

Isabelle thought how it would be. 'I would be ashamed to be seen in that position. It would hurt me.'

'But still you would consent?'

'If Robert wanted it.'

'And you? Do you want it?'

She blushed. Part of her did want it but she could not say.

'In your belly now,' Alain asked more insistently, 'how do you feel?'

She regarded each of the men in turn, lost. 'Aroused, frightened . . .'

They looked back at her silently, digesting the meaning of these contradictions, participating in her dilemma, as an audience participates in a theatre. This feeling of being studied unnerved her and she looked at Robert with a silent plea in her eyes. She wanted to consent, wanted to allow everything as he had said that she must but it was so very difficult. Robert's face had a serious cast and she knew that he understood. It was also clear that he could do no more for her than smile encouragingly.

'And if Robert or Helene or Maria were to run their tongue inside your sex at this moment what would you feel?' asked Alain.

'I think that I would climax,' she said softly, looking down, away from the probing eyes. 'I wouldn't be able to help myself.'

'Shall I ask Helene to do that for you?'

She shook her head.

'Perhaps you should show us how you would do it for yourself.'

Isabelle's mind shook at the thought and she could not reply.

'You have done it for Robert?'

'Yes,' she groaned.

'But then you love him?'

'Yes.'

'Wouldn't it be even more exciting to do it here, before all of us?'

These words had a strange effect on her and for a moment she felt dizzy, as if something were stirring deep in her mind. She took a deep breath and looked at Robert, still vainly hoping that he might rescue her.

'I couldn't,' she began.

'Do it,' he told her.

It was the arousal in Robert's eyes that allowed her to move her hand to her groin. Keeping her eyes on his she dipped her fingers into her sex and moistened the apex of her labia, labia that were as fully engorged with blood as her sister's ever were. The excitement that Robert had stirred in the hall had never truly faded, and every moment in the library had increased her sexual tension so that Isabelle's first touch sent a shiver through her belly, a shiver of pure wanting. As she continued to caress herself, tiny spasms seized her legs and she felt an urge to be seen, somehow to be seen inside. The image of herself bent over the desk with Helene's hands holding her wide came into her mind and she groaned. She turned to look at Alain, wanting him to see her, to see the power of her arousal. She remembered what he'd said about Anne-Marie's sex being so external and wished that she could turn her own inside out. Most of all she wished to be penetrated by a man, any man, by Alain or the handsome stranger whose eyes she felt burning her, as much as by Robert whom she loved.

'That is enough,' said Alain, suddenly.

Isabelle was in such a trance that she did not respond.

'Maria, her hand.'

Maria seized Isabelle's hand and dragged it from her sex. Isabelle howled her disappointment and struggled to return it.

'Enough!' said Alain loudly and Isabelle, stunned, looked at him in disbelief and confusion.

'Ask,' he told her.

At first she didn't understand. When she realised what he meant, that she should ask his permission to climax her mind rebelled. Sensing this stubbornness Robert intervened.

'I want you to watch something,' he told her.

Robert pushed Anna to her feet and had her stand with her legs wide. He pulled the girl's dress to her waist and pushed her forward so that she bent from the waist and her elbows came to rest on the surface of the desk. Isabelle looked at the slender hips and boyish behind that presented themselves so gloriously. She could not prevent her mind kissing that dun coloured skin with desire, desire that turned to envy as Robert unbuttoned his breeches and drew forth his erect member. Anna looked over her shoulder and smiled, then arched her back lazily, catlike. Her behind swayed and Isabelle saw the girls slit pouting between the slim thighs and above it the eye of her behind already opening, blinking its invitation.

Robert presented his sex to the open flesh and rubbed the tip up and down, nudging aside the sexlips one moment and pushing fractionally into the other opening the next. Anna rotated her hips, following him, pushing back when his sex pressed at one of her openings as if to catch him and suck him in.

'Where do you want it?' Robert asked.

'My cunt,' she said, in her rich low voice.

Robert pushed into Anna slowly, savouring the first moment in that soft sleeve. His arousal was as quick and sharp as her yielding. Her mouth opened to show its teeth, small and white like a terrier's.

'I've taken this girl many times,' he told Isabelle. 'And I've learnt that we share many things,' he took Anna's breast and squeezed hard. Isabelle saw his finger nails sinking into the girls flesh and saw her face twist into a snarling knot. 'We share desire to tear, for instance,' Robert pulled harder at the already distorted breast until Anna growled and reached for the hand that tortured her with her teeth; Robert pushed her head away with his free hand, 'a desire to tear and be torn by extremes. As soon as a hand rests itself on her breast like this or pushes itself into one of her openings, a chasm opens in her soul and she falls deep into places a young girl shouldn't know of. I have read desires in Anna's eyes that would frighten the most depraved of libertines . . .' He grunted as he forced himself into her with exceptional violence. 'I have been goaded to acts that no sane man would own in daylight. There is no love, only the chasm and a sharp ruthless hunger.'

Isabelle trembled as she listened to him and as she watched him thrust into the girl as if he wanted to kill her. Anna had lifted herself on to tiptoe and pushed back, bracing herself with her hands on the desk against the steadily increasing violence of his thrusts.

When he wanted the girl naked, Robert reached for the neck of her dress and split it asunder with his hands so that her sinuous body, increasingly obscene in its movements, lay among rags.

'One day I will take her to England,' Robert continued, 'I will have her in the woods and fields of my estate. I will watch her writhe beneath me in the autumn mud, her body covered in leaves. I will have her over the fallen trunk of a tree, her behind spread by a broken branch while I fuck the life from her cunt –'

He seized her arm and bit into the flesh below the elbow. She groaned loudly and struggled furiously until he opened his jaws. When he did, Isabelle saw a trickle of blood and gasped.

'Like this,' he said and gave Anna her arm to lick before taking it to his own mouth and sucking hard.

'She tastes of iron,' he told Isabelle, his eyes narrow and hardly recognisable.

Isabelle looked at the girl again as her groans became a howl. Robert began to slap her, hitting sharply at her behind and the breasts already reddened from mauling. The girls hands were fists. Her back was alternately a man's, with every muscle contracted, defined, hard, and a woman's, softly suffused with the flush of surrender.

When she was at the point of pleasure, when it was a sword that seemed to impale her from sex to throat Anna turned to him. Her eyes were black with desire, mutely pleading, threatening, beseeching. Robert said nothing, only speeding his movements and driving to his own pleasure. He climaxed as she watched him, and they visibly burned together in that climax, he with release, she, with frustration.

Finished, he ripped himself clear of her flesh and sat down, drained. Anna remained open legged, presenting herself as if he were still inside her, quivering. Her sex, expanded and grown hot, seemed to taunt Isabelle, who watched from her chair like a beggar girl at a feast. She wriggled as if imagining the pleasure of having a man inside her and that imagining did nothing to ease the heat between her thighs.

'Stand up,' Robert told Anna.

The rags fell from her as she raised herself from the desk so that she was quite nude. Her breasts, large for such a narrow frame swayed as she waited before him. He touched her rounded nipples as they shone in their distension like grapes, tempting the teeth to crush out the wine.

Robert pushed forth his leather-clad foot.

'Squat,' he said.

Anna frowned, as if uncertain of what he wanted.

'Use it,' he told her, looking first at her sex and then at his boot.

Finally she understood. Lifting one leg she placed her feet widely either side of his. She lowered her body slowly and reached between her legs to open her sex. As her flesh kissed his foot her eyes narrowed. At first when she moved, the friction seemed uncomfortable for her. As her secretions soaked the leather and it became slick she moved into a steady rhythm swinging her pelvis from her waist, using the whole length of his boot. She rested her head on his knee and he gave his fingers to be sucked, even allowing her to bite. Occasionally he stroked her hair and whispered encouraging words, driving her to even greater lewdness. She slipped a finger into her behind at his behest, turning it this way and that, stoking pleasure into her bowels. She began to move in a staccato way thumping her sex hard into his foot and grunting.

'Now?' she asked but Robert shook his head. This denial did not slow her, the cruelty of waiting seemed only to excite her more.

Robert pulled his foot back after a while, as if he doubted she could contain herself any longer and lifted it to her face. She sniffed the leather that was now wet from

124

heel to toe and licked it. The taste seemed good to her and she smiled at him taking his foot in both hands and sucking the toe lasciviously.

When he replaced the boot for her to use, she asked again for her pleasure and, taking his hand, she kissed it in the way that a supplicant will kiss the hand of a priest. The way that she moved so urgently and the way that she kissed his hand was so affecting that finally he gave her his permission. She smiled, thanking him, running her hands across his legs excitedly. Her legs opened wider and she squatted lower, sawing back and forth with great speed, greedy or perhaps fearful that he might change his mind. As the arousal became extreme her teeth sank into the fabric of his breeches and pulled at it. She began to grunt again and finally, as she lost control, she threw back her head and screamed full-bloodedly. The orgasms continued for a long time and towards the end she clasped her arms around his leg holding on tightly as if she might be swept away.

Robert looked at Isabelle, a look which asked her if she finally understood.

Isabelle did understand. It seemed that Robert had showed her this to demonstrate many things. Partly, it was to demonstrate his power, as it had been with Helene. Partly, it was to show that he could find his satisfaction in many places other than her arms. Mostly, it was to make clear that her compliance was expected in all things, including the taking and giving of pleasure. If Anna with her extremes of arousal could defer her climax or abstain completely, so could she.

'Ask,' Alain said to her again.

She understood that she must do this for Robert's sake, if not her own, but her head shook its refusal.

Alain snorted, amused rather than angry.

'You are cruel to yourself, *ma chère*.'

When she turned to Robert she saw that Anna had crawled between his legs and rested with her head in his lap. Her lips were clamped about his sex and he was hard again. Isabelle looked away as she saw the girl push the tip of her tongue into the moist opening of that member.

125

'She has much to learn, but take her to London if you wish.' Alain said to Robert.

In her disappointment, this hardly registered with Isabelle.

Robert thanked him.

'I would advise you to teach her some control though. Arouse her as you wish but limit her releases. She is to learn that she is no longer mistress of her desires.'

'That might be the best course,' Robert agreed.

'I would like her to be brought here tomorrow, at the same time. I intend that she shall be beaten on each of her remaining days at Severcy.'

With these words Alain turned and left. To her surprise Isabelle felt a tear squeeze itself from the corner of her eye. As Alain quit the room it was as if a great weight passed from her. But the result of this was her tears, tears of relief, tears of frustration, tears of gratitude that she should be travelling to London with Robert. She felt foolish as they overwhelmed her, running down her cheeks in a bewildering downpour.

Robert stood and detached himself from a clinging Anna. Rearranging his clothing, he walked over to Isabelle and rested his hand on her head.

'You must excuse us, Ferrier,' he said to the stranger.

'Of course, monsieur.'

Reaching his hand under Isabelle, Robert lifted her and cradled her in his arms. Safely enfolded in this way her tears flowed even more freely.

'The mademoiselle is tired and over-strained.'

The stranger bowed and Robert carried his slender charge from the room and down the marble corridors. They encountered no one on their journey and, reaching the privacy of his bedroom, Robert laid the girl down on the bed, allowing her to curl into a ball. He sat with her as the sobs continued to shake her body, stroking her hair or back from time to time.

It was a while before Isabelle calmed enough to sleep.

14

The Edge

When her eyes opened, Isabelle found Robert sitting in a chair by the bed watching her. The simple joy that she felt on seeing him made her smile of welcome brilliant and he rose and kissed her deeply, sucking the air from her lungs.

'I love you,' she said when he released her mouth.

It was such a relief to say these words that the tears returned to her eyes. She wiped them away quickly and looked up at him.

'I'm so foolish,' she said softly, 'these tears . . .' she shook her head.

Robert smiled and sat beside her. She laid her head in his lap with a sigh and they remained quiet as she slowly came to full wakefulness. Then, feeling a stirring at his groin, where her cheek rested against his sex, she put her lips to the very tip of the lengthening organ and bestowed a long sucking kiss through the thin fabric.

He marvelled at how different she was, how unreserved, when no one but himself was present. While he valued this lack of reservation he knew that Alain was right when it came to the issue of self-control. When he broached the subject she stiffened.

'Alain hates me.'

'He desires you too much to hate you, but there is something, something that I don't understand.'

Isabelle looked at him carefully, wondering if what he said was true, if Alain did, in fact, desire her. She had never felt that in him, not for a moment.

'Has he ever touched you, I mean touched you sexually?'

'No,' she answered.

Robert dismissed the matter from his mind temporarily and returned to the main issue.

'We must agree that from now on you will not climax without permission.'

Isabelle rolled on to her back. Her head still rested on his lap as she looked up at him.

'Am I so greedy?'

'Do you agree?' he persisted.

'I agree,' she sighed.

Robert slipped his hands between her knees, knees that were raised and pressed together but which opened at his touch. Sleep had softened her and she seemed as innocent and fresh as a newborn infant. She responded to his caresses without any inhibition. One thumb he slipped into the entrance of her sex, the other into her mouth. She suckled at each gratefully.

'You make me greedy,' she said, when the thumb in her mouth withdrew. 'And then you deny me. It is cruel and contradictory. It isn't surprising that I cry.'

'And is it also why you are so excited now?'

Isabelle thought about this question, but before long Robert's hand between her legs had begun to move, pushing her beyond the point of reasoned thought.

'Lie quite still,' he told her. 'Enjoy the feelings, give yourself to them, but do not allow yourself to climax.'

Isabelle tried to do as he asked. She could prevent herself from clutching at him as she wished to, she could quiet the legs that needed to coil and uncoil, and the neck that wanted to arch; she could control all of the larger movements. What she could not prevent was the trembling in her shoulders, or the sudden spasms that rocked her pelvis. Finally a shaking began in her calves that spread inexorably throughout her whole frame.

'It is too much,' she gasped.

Robert withdrew the finger that was playing across her clitoris. He rested the hand that was already damp with moisture from her sex on her sweat drenched brow.

'When we begin again, I want you to keep yourself on the very edge and if it becomes impossible to control the feelings I want you to move my hand away. Do you understand?'

She nodded her assent.

'We will do this often and in future should you climax without permission you will be whipped severely and each time that you move my hand away I shall slap the insides of your thighs until you weep.'

Isabelle took a deep breath. 'You will make me mad.'

'Then I shall visit you in the asylum and we will continue this pleasure.'

Robert began again but, almost immediately, the arousal, after what he had just said, was overwhelming.

'Please!' she groaned. 'I cannot stop myself.'

She seized his hand and pushed it aside.

'Am I demanding too much?' he asked.

'No!' she said. 'I couldn't bear the thought that there was anything that I couldn't give you. But please, a moment or I really shall go mad and end my days chained in a padded cell.'

Robert laughed. 'In future when we do this you will be gagged.'

'Yes,' she agreed, knowing that this was the only way that it could be done.

'For the time being, rest.'

Half relieved that it was over, half desiring that the attentions should continue, Isabelle rolled on to her side once more and curled her body around his where he sat. His erection was full and taut against her face now and she could feel it's heat burning through the breeches.

'I want to stay like this,' she said. 'I want nothing else. I shall give myself to you so completely that you will always want me and will always be hard. And if you take other women I shall enjoy that for your sake. And if you beat me I won't complain because you will be no more than a whip's length away.'

She was silent for a moment.

'Are all women like this when they are in love?' she asked.

129

'Almost none,' he replied.

'So I am already mad?'

'Yes.'

'Then you must protect me. You are my illness. You must be my physician.'

'But if I nursed you back to health, you would no longer want me.'

'I shall be a terrible patient. I shall prefer the sickness to the cure. I shall keep you as the fever that is inside me and as the nurse that comforts me through its agonies.'

'Your greed will devour me.'

'Never. No more than I could drink a whole ocean.'

'Then I shall devour you.'

'Yes. And I shall curl up inside you, like this, content.'

They were silent for a while, then Robert, resting his hand on her hip, gently pushed Isabelle on to her back.

'You must wash now,' he told her.

'No,' she groaned and rolled back into a ball.

'You must be dressed and ready for dinner soon.'

'And this?' she asked, kissing his sex once more. 'Will you let me?'

'Not yet.'

'Then let me ring for Helene. I worry for you, it is so hard.'

Robert laughed. 'It will not burst.'

'Was it hard all the time in the library?'

'Yes.'

'I'm glad.'

'And before that too. In the corridor.'

'Then let me call for Helene.'

Robert thought for a moment.

'Very well.'

Isabelle rose unsteadily and walked first to the bell pull and then to the adjoining wash room. Reaching the doorway, she turned around.

'Can I watch you with her?' she asked.

'When you have washed.'

She smiled. 'You make me feel like a little girl.'

'Little girls don't ask for what you ask.'

130

'Will you beat her?' she asked with a sudden seriousness.

He thought for a moment. 'Do you want me to?'

'No, I would feel responsible.'

'Should I beat you instead?'

She smiled again. 'Isn't tomorrow soon enough? Is my bottom so tempting?'

'Show it to me,' he said, returning her smile.

'You might not be able to resist.'

'Show it or wash it.'

'I'll wash it,' she said, and laughing, skipped into the bathroom.

Weary suddenly, for all the events of the afternoon had drained her, Isabelle pulled the slip over her head and turning to the mirror she examined herself. To her surprise, her face shone with health. She had half expected to find herself aged or marked by overindulgence. Instead she appeared younger rather than older and her skin was as smooth and clear as the child Robert sometimes took her for.

Taking the sponge, she soaked it in the cool fresh water from the ewer and ran it across her breasts for the pure pleasure of the surprise. Her breath caught and she watched the skin around her nipples contract. It was only since so many others had taken such an interest in her body that she had been able to attend to it herself without either anxiety or shame. To be seen by so many, naked and aroused and to feel no fear was not something that she could have imagined unless Robert had imagined it for her first. The many compliments she had received before meeting him had never made her feel desired, neither had they made desire seem good. The compliments had seemed mere courtesies, the smiles deceptive, self-serving. The look in the stranger's eyes in the library was beyond such niceties, as was the constant evidence of desire that Robert displayed. Even Alain, as cruel and as indifferent as he appeared, had surveyed her breasts and her sex as if they were precious items, coveted and rare.

The sound of the bedroom door opening broke into these thoughts and Isabelle, hearing Helene's voice, washed more vigorously, scrubbing her legs and feet mercilessly. When she was finished, she took the towel and stepped into the doorway, drying herself as she watched Helene undress. There was a pleasure in this and a pleasure in watching Robert reach for the girl's sex. It was not the pleasure of the pimp who profits by supplying a girl, perhaps his own girl, to a stranger. It was the selfless pleasure of giving something to her lover.

Robert lifted the girl on to the bed with the hand between her legs and she stood precariously on the yielding surface as he turned to look at Isabelle. He smiled, then guiding Helene further into the centre of the bed he knelt between her thighs and applied his mouth to her already wet lips and to the opening that Alain had so recently explored with three fingers. It was not long before Helene was gasping and Robert, sucking at her without pause, took her swiftly to a series of climaxes, steadying her with a hand on her behind as she cried out.

Isabelle remained rooted to the spot as she watched all of this, as involved as she always was when she saw Robert with another woman. She heard Helene thank her lover and watched as the exhausted girl sank to the middle of the bed, her tall, slender frame collapsing into an untidy, almost boneless tangle.

'Poor Helene,' Robert said softly. 'The favourite whore. The more she is taken, the more she responds and the more she responds, the more she is drained and the more she is drained, the more her pale, fragile beauty increases, until none can resist her.'

Isabelle looked at the girl's face. Framed by the brilliant, copper coloured hair, her skin seemed almost transparent and her features as fluid as water. The slightest feeling, as it moved through her body, registered in those features and was as clearly visible as the whip marks that covered her behind, for there were fresh marks on that tender flesh as there always were, one set overlying the next like a series of fading echoes. Helene's smile was so sweet in response to this attention that Isabelle felt her heart contract, pained that such goodness should ever meet such cruel treatment.

Robert bent and kissed the girl gently then turned once more to Isabelle.

'Fetch some ties,' he told her. Quite suddenly his tone had that irresistible authority which indicated she was not allowed the luxury of dissent. When his voice had that edge he was most surely her master and if she wanted her lover she could only wait until the other Robert returned, the Robert whose voice was soft and whose eyes were warm.

Isabelle walked slowly to the chest that held such things and opening the correct drawer she pulled out a handful of black silk.

'And something else,' Robert said, considering for a moment what would be most suitable. 'One of the gags, perhaps two. Yes, two.'

Isabelle found these as well then took them to the bed.

'Sit,' he told her, indicating the nearby chair.

She sat as she thought he would want her, her legs wide, her behind on the edge of the seat.

'You learn the little tricks of the coquette quickly,' he told her.

'I want to please you,' she said, hurt by this implied criticism.

Taking the ties, Robert secured her wrists to the arm rests. Then, taking her knees, he lifted them so that they overlay her hands. Tied and exposed she felt the excitement in her belly renew itself. Harsh or gentle, he could stir her so easily. She felt like a scrap of paper that the wind could lift or let fall as the caprice took it.

Leaning over, Robert took a few strands of her pubic hair in his hand and pulled. She started as they were torn from her flesh.

'Afterwards, Helene will pluck your cunt bare,' he said, resting his hand on the stinging skin. His eyes, finding hers, held her quite still as his fingers opened the moist lips.

'I have just washed,' she said foolishly, as if this was of any consequence.

It didn't stop his fingers working, neither did it stop her arousal.

'Do you want to climax?' he asked.

She nodded and his fingers squeezed the whole of her overheated sex sharply.

'Remember that this climax will be for my pleasure. It is not yours to take but mine to give. If I decide to withhold it you will not protest. If I permit it you will not hold back.'

His eyes left no doubt that she must obey.

'As you wish,' she murmured.

He took the gags that she still held and tied one of them tightly around the inside of her left thigh. The balled fabric in the middle of the satin strip, the part that would normally go in the mouth, he allowed to rest against the crossroads of her thighs. When he lifted her legs down and pressed them together, the fabric crushed itself into her sex.

'Do it by squeezing and relaxing,' he told her.

She did as he asked, tensing and untensing her thighs. The pleasure was slight, tantalisingly so. As he watched her arouse herself in this way he undressed. She had never seen him completely naked before and she was surprised by how deeply she reacted. His arms and shoulders were strong and she longed for them to surround her. She desired his broad chest as a pillow for her head. His erect penis she longed to suck. Yet he did not intend to offer her such comforts and sat instead on the bed, his back against the headboard.

'Climax for me,' he said.

It took a long while, the pleasure building only slowly. When she became too excited the desire would be to open her legs wide and then she would lose the stimulation and the pleasure would fade. It required discipline to reach a plateau and to stay there long enough to climax. Robert watched her all of this time and Helene lay beside him, sometimes with her mouth around his penis, sometimes rubbing her sex against his leg and groaning as Isabelle groaned, half in pleasure, half in frustration.

When the climax came for Isabelle it hurt her with its strength. She had waited for so long, had been denied so many times that when it came it felt as if her belly had burst open and her mind had torn. She screamed with such

134

an intensity, with as much pain as pleasure, that Helene sat up, suddenly afraid for her.

Robert placed his hand on Helene's shoulder and pressed her back to the bed. Rising, he went to the bathroom and took the sponge from the bowl where Isabelle had left it. With this he washed her between the legs.

'Now you are clean again,' he said.

She looked at him through exhausted eyes.

'Did it please you?' she asked.

'Very much.'

He smiled and kissed her. His voice was soft again; she had her lover back.

Leaving her tied to the chair, Robert returned to the bed and there he made gentle love to Helene. Isabelle watched without envy, delighting at the end as he cast his semen on to Helene's breasts.

That evening at dinner, Isabelle was introduced formally to the stranger in the library. His name was Ferrier and he was the new steward. Sitting beside him throughout the evening was his wife, a pretty, vivacious but very respectable woman not much older than Isabelle. Alain was charming throughout but towards the end of the evening when no one else could hear he reminded Isabelle that tomorrow she would be whipped. Even before he had spoken, this knowledge had begun to prey on her mind and an uncharacteristic tension had rendered her almost silent as the others ate and talked.

'Let me give you one last chance,' Alain said, almost kindly. 'Take the carriage tomorrow morning and return to your mother. If you stay here I shall take it as a sign that whipping is agreeable to you, and you will suffer greatly.'

'I understand that you dislike me, monsieur. But I cannot leave.'

'I don't dislike you Isabelle, quite the reverse,' he told her, surprised that she should think so. 'Besides, I would not let my likes or dislikes influence me in these matters. It

135

is entirely a matter of what you need, what Robert needs and what I need. It is a question of what will provide all of us with the greatest pleasure.'

She turned away from him sharply, ignoring these words. To her they had the ring of hypocrisy. Robert had given her to suffer the humiliation of being beaten before others, this she accepted, but there could be no pleasure in it for her, beyond the satisfaction of demonstrating her devotion. Alain had no place in that devotion.

15

The Ball

A month or so after Robert had left for France, Charlotte received an invitation to a ball in Richmond at the home of Lady Olivia Mayerland. Charlotte would have preferred to avoid the dirt and clamour of the city but Anne-Marie was too excited by the prospect of seeing old acquaintances to allow her objections.

They travelled down a few days early so that Charlotte could be fitted for a new dress and stayed in the home of one of her uncles near Hyde Park. Charlotte's two young cousins, sweet girls of fifteen and sixteen, were beside themselves with the excitement of the ball and soon Charlotte herself was caught up in the flurry of preparations.

It seemed that the whole city was similarly affected. When Charlotte and Anne-Marie visited the dressmakers, the fitting rooms were crowded with ladies having final adjustments to their gowns and discussing who was invited and who was not.

Anne-Marie had a dress of the purest, lightest cream silk made for Charlotte. The seamstresses had to work long through the night to finish it, but on the day of the ball it was ready and it was perfect. The high waist and deeply cut bodice clasped her breasts in a delicate embrace, the light fabric clung to her body like a lover as she walked. When her cousins first saw it they gasped. Her uncle frowned, then looked at Charlotte in the way an uncle should not look. It was not the dress of a married woman and though it was entirely decent and very fashionable, it had the scent of the courtesan, the woman who exists for men. Charlotte begged to be allowed a silk shawl to cover the great expanse of naked skin but Anne-Marie allowed her nothing but the dress, and pumps of pink satin for her feet.

It was a long journey to Richmond, and when they arrived there was a queue of carriages that stretched back a full mile from the entrance steps of the great house. Despite their father's reproaches, Charlotte's young cousins hung out of the open windows as they edged forward, chattering without pause. When the party finally disembarked, evening had begun to fall and great torches were being lit on the verandas around the first floor of the house, casting a shifting orange glow across the whole scene.

Inside, the great entrance hall was full of people in high spirits calling out to friends, embracing, and exchanging the most graceful of curtsies and bows. Anne-Marie quickly detached Charlotte from her uncle and led her into the first of the large drawing rooms. As they made their way through the crowd, Charlotte was surprised at the number of gentlemen who greeted Anne-Marie as if she were an old friend.

In the centre of the room stood a group of two men and two women. It was this party that Anne-Marie had been seeking and she made straight for them, pulling Charlotte along with her. The older of the two men took Anne-Marie's hand and kissed it.

'James, I believe that your lips are warmer and more amorous than ever,' Anne-Marie said, as the man held her hand for a moment longer than was customary.

'He is drunk with his new conquest,' said the older woman.

'Marietta, you will make the child blush,' chided James, releasing Anne-Marie at last.

The 'child' – the young woman he was referring to – did blush, but then her fine, pale skin seemed fashioned for it and she made the prettiest, most innocent of pictures.

'This is Coutts,' Anne-Marie told Charlotte, indicating

the young man who had been staring at her with the sharpness of a hawk. 'Robert might have mentioned him.'

Robert had indeed talked of him and Charlotte stiffened as she remembered her husband's descriptions of the man and his preferences with women. There was a cruel gleam in his eye as he took Charlotte's hand and brushed it with his lips. Then, instead of releasing her, he pressed a cool metal object into her palm. When she turned her hand over and opened it, she saw a key and the colour drained from her face.

'James and Marietta also possess keys,' Anne-Marie told the suddenly frightened woman. 'I will leave you to their pleasures.'

With that she kissed Charlotte and took her leave.

Charlotte had a feeling that she had been abandoned in a forest with wolves. The colour and noise of the ball receded and all that was left was the close predatory circle.

'Your card, madam,' demanded Coutts.

Charlotte fumbled in her bag for the dance card. Coutts took it and scribbled his name across three dances in the middle of the evening. He passed it to James who took several towards the end. Marietta said that she would have Charlotte much later, when the dancing had finished.

After these arrangements had been made, James suggested that Charlotte rejoin her party. As she was turning to leave, Coutts took her arm and whispered fiercely in her ear.

'Do not let your nervousness dry your mouth. Tonight it is mine.'

Then he released her and, numbly, she went in search of her uncle. Before she had even found her party, Charlotte's card had been filled by young men anxious to make the acquaintance of so beautiful a woman and she had only had a moment with her cousins before she was swept on to the dance floor.

At first, the music and the sight of so many fine men and women dancing drove the keys from her mind, and she was able to dance with the lightness and elegance that she remembered from the time before her marriage. Yet, as the moment for Coutts to take her approached, the spring in her legs deserted her. When she saw him approaching her legs almost buckled.

He took her arm without a word, and not caring who saw them, led her through the hall and upstairs to a bedroom on the second floor. There was already a collection of whips on the bed. He didn't ask her to strip, instead he had her raise her dress to her neck and told her to hold it there, no matter what he might do to her. So, with her hands imprisoned by this simple instruction, he bade her kneel on the bed facing the open window.

He began with the cane on her behind. On the third blow she cried out loudly and he paused to push a piece of cloth into her mouth. This stifled the sounds that proceeded from cries to screams and finally to howls.

When he was finished with the cane, when she was already quaking uncontrollably and tears already covered her cheeks, he took up a thin strap with a triangular, weighted tip and asked her to turn around. Miserably, she shuffled around on her knees. Her hand had slipped so that the dress covered her breasts. He made her raise it fully again, then began on her breasts and belly. The black tip left deep triangular marks wherever it landed and soon the front of her body was covered completely by its cruel bites. The sweat poured from his brow as he worked. Finally, he dropped the instrument and undid his breeches. He was as hard as iron as he stood on the bed and went into her mouth. As he fucked her there, he described the times that he and Robert had treated other women like this. Most especially, he gave details of Robert's seduction of a young girl in Hertfordshire, the daughter of a lawyer. With a sinking feeling, Charlotte recognised Coutts' descriptions of the girl and the village. She realised that she had met the girl and that the seduction must have occurred when she and Robert were newly married and staying nearby with his family. As Coutts pushed for the back of her throat and she gagged on his thickness, she remembered a number of times that Robert had ridden to the village to meet his friend, a man unwelcome in the family home because of his

140

notoriety. Then, holding on to the back of her head tightly and pushing hard, Coutts climaxed and, after a final thrust that bruised the back of her throat, he sank to his knees in front of her. He glared at her for a moment, as if he might take up the whip again, and Charlotte's hands shook as she held her dress at her neck.

'I would have paid for that, madam,' he told her with evident satisfaction and worked his hand into her sex.

She was wet and he smiled.

'And I'm glad that it gave you pleasure too.'

The tears that had ceased flowing from Charlottes eyes began again. Coutts admired her for a moment, then rose and left the room without another word.

Charlotte composed herself and returned to the dance floor. She was acutely aware of the reddening of her breasts where they showed above the line of the dress and equally aware that her dancing partners must be seeing her stiffness and her instant, pained, reaction to the slightest touch. Even so, she made a brave show of it until her appointed time with James and the young girl. James took her to the same bedroom and had her strip completely. He was not interested in her for himself, he simply wanted to show her to the girl.

The girl looked on in shock as Charlotte removed her dress and revealed the souvenirs of her beating. James had the girl touch Charlotte all over, especially between the legs. Charlotte was obliged to pull her opened legs to her chest so that the girl could do this. It was obvious that the girl had never touched a woman in this way before and at first she was tentative. James had to encourage her with constant soft reassurances, especially when he told the girl to penetrate Charlottes sex and behind. When the girl saw that Charlotte was aroused by this treatment she gained confidence and even kissed her full on the lips without being instructed to. Finally, James had the girl suck Charlotte until she climaxed. Then he began to undress and dismissed Charlotte abruptly. As Charlotte saw the excitement in the girl's eyes as the man approached her, it made her think of Robert and she felt a sudden wave of longing for him.

Marietta came for Charlotte only after the dancing had finished. She was a guest at the great house and stripped and spanked Charlotte in her own bedroom, then made love to her in the manner of a man, except that, instead of penetrating her, she ground her sex into Charlotte's mound until both had climaxed. Afterwards, she asked Charlotte to call her 'aunt', which seemed to have a special significance for her. As soon as Charlotte used the word, the older woman became very tender and offered her breasts. It was a great luxury after all the ordeals of the evening and Charlotte took suck like a starving lamb.

16

The Whip

The next day, in the middle of a sultry afternoon, Isabelle presented herself in the library. Alain and Ferrier were working through some papers at one of the desks and Isabelle waited silently for them to reach a conclusion. She was grateful to have been allowed to enter the library without the terrible attentions of the previous day, and grateful to be allowed to remain unremarked and in silence as the enormity of what was to happen seeped into her consciousness. Since that morning she had felt drugged, stripped of all volition. Her dreamy passivity had excited Robert enormously. He had washed her lovingly, fed her and dressed her, kissing her constantly on her mouth and breasts as if he could not believe that she could have come to be so completely his. After watching her swim naked in the baths, he had taken her in his lap and held her gently, murmuring all of his desires, describing all that he wished to do to her. She had stroked his hair and kissed his forehead, endlessly grateful that fate had allowed them to meet.

Isabelle stood then in the library awaiting the whip or cane, wrapped in the soft protection of her love, her simple gown of blue muslin swaying slightly in the faint breeze from the open windows. From time to time Ferrier would look at her, his desire making him nervous, his awe at her tranquility giving him the appearance of a boy stealing furtive glances at a grown woman.

After some minutes, Robert entered the library with

143

Helene. He smiled at Isabelle and, in passing, squeezed her arm affectionately. Helene was exceptionally pale and drawn. She walked stiffly over to one of the window seats where she sat with great care. Isabelle wondered if the girl had been beaten that morning, and if so, whether it had been Robert or one of the others. She wanted to ask but it would have been impossible for her to initiate a conversation in that room which was so thoroughly the domain of Alain.

Robert browsed through the library shelves taking out a succession of books and thumbing through them before settling on a collection of the writings of Tacitus. This he took to one of the ottomans and opening it at random, he began to read.

Left alone with her thoughts, Isabelle found herself wondering if she would be tied, perhaps to one of the bookshelves, or whether she would be laid across a chair or desk. She wondered if it would be the whip or cane and whether it would be Alain or Robert who used it. These images of herself being constrained and of her body being stung and cut while she was powerless finally broke the protective barriers that she had erected against the reality of her fate. She felt her stomach somersault. Glancing at Robert, engrossed in his book, she saw a man thoroughly at home in his world while her own shook. Yet it was knowing that he was present now and would be present after her ordeal that strengthened her, and she steadied herself, breathing deeply and evenly.

Alain and Ferrier still showed no signs of finishing their work and continued to pore over the ledgers and bills of sale that crowded the desk top. Isabelle half-listened as they discussed plans for a new vineyard and the problems of supplying water to the various proposed sites.

These murmured exchanges were finally interrupted by the opening of the library door and the entrance of Madame Ferrier. All eyes turned to her smiling face. Her husband seemed the most surprised by this sudden intrusion and seemed on the verge of anger. He checked himself, however, and acknowledged his wife civilly.

'You must excuse us while we continue with our work, my darling,' he said after the various greetings had been concluded.

'Of course,' replied his wife brightly. She went immediately to Isabelle whose heart had risen to her mouth at the moment Madame Ferrier had entered the library. For reasons that Isabelle did not fully understand it would be absolutely intolerable for her if this woman were to know of her situation.

'Mademoiselle Belloque, perhaps you can help me. I want to embroider a shawl and I need a pattern. Do you think that there is such a thing in the library? If not, would there be some illustrations of birds or plants that I could use in my own design?'

Isabelle found it almost impossible to respond to this question. The bright innocence of the woman, and her commonplace concern with embroidery, a subject that Isabelle might have relished a few weeks ago, were now so alien to her thoughts that no words would form in her throat.

'Are you well, mademoiselle?' asked Madame Ferrier, seeing Isabelle's distress. The two women had barely spoken the previous evening, but Madame Ferrier had thought of Isabelle as sensible and intelligent. The half paralysed creature before her now, whose eyes she noticed were ringed with the dark evidence of sleeplessness, surprised and concerned her.

Isabelle looked to Alain in her confusion.

'Madame Ferrier, allow me to help you. Isabelle is not familiar with the library,' Alain said with great courtesy, rising to his feet. 'We have many illustrated volumes, perhaps one of those would be useful.'

Madame Ferrier, pleased by this attention, took Alain's arm and allowed him to guide her along the bookshelves.

Monsieur Ferrier, temporarily relieved of the burden of work, leant back in his chair and looked at Isabelle. The uncertainty that Isabelle normally found in his eyes had been replaced by insolence.

'I am looking forward to watching you being whipped,

145

mademoiselle,' he said in a low, intense voice. 'I didn't understand until yesterday how exciting a woman's tears can be.'

Isabelle looked away from him. She had known from his first glance that he would seek possession of her before she left Severcy. At the other end of the library, Madame Ferrier was studying a large volume that Alain had found for her. The animated responses and expressive gestures of the other woman reminded Isabelle of what it was to be free. Her own limbs were heavy with waiting and her belly too, she realised, was weighted with the same pregnant desire that she always felt in the presence of the men in the villa.

Isabelle's eyes returned to Ferrier. She noticed that his hands were shaking.

'You want me,' he said.

Isabelle shook her head unconvincingly and glanced at Madame Ferrier, concerned that they may be overheard.

'Your wife is so charming, monsieur. Surely she is enough?'

'I love my wife, mademoiselle. When I have you in my bed it will not be for love.'

Madame Ferrier brought the manuscript that she had been studying over to her husband.

'Look,' she exclaimed. 'Aren't these birds marvellous?'

She laid the book on the table before Ferrier. He glanced at the handsome, vividly coloured illustrations of ibis and flamingo and at his wife's excited face.

'No more so than you, my darling.'

Ferrier took his wife's hand and raised it to his lips. She flushed with pleasure and embarrassment and in that instant Isabelle had an image of their lovemaking. A blush came to her own face and an envy stirred for what she imagined were such simple, natural pleasures.

'Which would you like to see on a shawl?' Madame Ferrier managed to ask, tracing the outline of the flamingo with her recently kissed hand.

'You must choose, and you must excuse us, my dear, Monsieur Alain has already been most gracious with his time,' Ferrier replied.

146

Madame Ferrier smiled at Alain.

'My husband is right,' she said. 'You have been most kind, monsieur, and I must leave you to your work. Can I take the book for a little while?'

'It would be my pleasure.'

Alain bowed and, bestowing the same bright smiles that she had bestowed on entering the library, Madame Ferrier left, book in hand. As the door closed behind her, Alain turned to Ferrier.

'You have not told your wife of our practices here, I assume?'

'I have not. She knows and accepts that I was once in the habit of visiting whores, but she has never before seen one in the flesh.'

Isabelle stiffened at the implications of this remark.

'Perhaps we should deal with Isabelle before we resume our work,' suggested Alain.

Ferrier nodded and Alain resumed his seat.

'So Isabelle,' he began. 'You are here to be beaten?'

Isabelle shivered. 'If that is your wish.'

'Robert has left the matter to me, the instruments to be used and so on. You do not object, I hope?'

Isabelle glanced at Robert who was still engrossed in his book.

'He has chosen this for me, I cannot object.'

'I understand that your sex has been depilated?'

'Yes, monsieur.'

'Kindly show us.'

Isabelle raised her dress to her waist. Her belly fluttered as the two men looked at the smooth mound and at the lips that protruded, pink and fresh, from the deep rift of her sex.

'How does it feel to be bare?' Alain asked her.

'I have so little protection here, and now I have less.'

They spent a number of minutes simply looking at her, having her turn first to the left and then to the right. Isabelle was aware of the intense desire that Ferrier felt for her. It charged the air around them. Alain too must have noticed it for he turned to the other man and studied him.

147

'I have a strap that is ideal for beating the sex of a woman. Have you ever watched a woman beaten in that way, Ferrier?' he asked.

The blood rushed to Ferrier's face. After a moment he shook his head.

'It is a great pleasure,' Alain assured him. 'You will allow us that pleasure I hope, Isabelle?'

Isabelle could not imagine such a thing.

'I don't . . . If Robert wants it,' she stammered.

'Robert has already used such a strap on your sister. I wouldn't imagine that he would want to spare you. Besides, when the time comes you will desire it.'

Isabelle knew that she would never want such cruel treatment and would never descend to such a level of debasement. She glanced at Robert again, wondering if he would require this of her. Seen in profile, his eyes gleaming with a steady pleasure as he read one of his favourite writers, it seemed impossible that such a man could follow so cruel a practice.

'This time, however, I intend that you shall be whipped only on your behind.' Alain continued, when her eyes returned to him.

These words of Alain finally caught Robert's attention and he laid his book on the silk surface of the ottoman.

'You will be beaten by Absolem, who is master of the stables. I believe that you have already met him?' Alain told her.

Isabelle was so surprised that it would not be one of the men already present, that she could not place the name for a moment. Finally, she remembered. On the night that she had ridden to the villa bare-back, she had left her mother's horse with a tall, saturnine servant. She had been forced to reprimand him for his presumption in attempting to block her wish to see Robert. In her mind's eye Isabelle could already see the satisfaction that he would gain from beating her.

Alain produced a leather whip from one of the drawers of the desk.

'Take this to him,' he said.

Isabelle stepped forward and keeping her dress raised with one hand she took the whip in the other. The smooth black handle rested heavily in her moist palm. The cutting part of the instrument was short and thick, cruelly square in section, and, hanging downwards, it tapered to a point like a rapier. Nothing could have seemed more alien or more horrifying to her. She could not have brought herself to use such a vicious weapon on a rabid dog.

'Tell him that it must only be your behind and that there is to be no blood.'

The three men watched the colour drain from Isabelle's face until she appeared no more substantial than a ghost.

'He may keep you for as long as he wishes, employ whatever restraints he deems fit and afterwards, or indeed before, he can ask you to reward him with your mouth. Do you understand me?'

Alain's eyes showed a peculiar, grey satisfaction as he spoke.

Isabelle dropped the whip as if it had burnt her. Her other hand released the fabric of her dress and she stepped back. Close to panic, her eyes roamed the room as if searching for an avenue of escape.

Robert rose to his feet quickly and, coming to stand behind her, he slipped his arm around her waist. His free hand came to cover her wildly beating heart.

'I can't do it,' she moaned. 'Don't ask me.'

'It has been decided,' Robert told her firmly.

'No.'

'You have already agreed.'

'Not Absolem. If it has to be done, let it be you.'

Robert slipped his hand down between her legs and cupped her sex. The desire that had smouldered there for so long, ignited immediately.

'Absolem won't miss his mark,' he told her. 'I might.'

'Then take me first. Don't send me to him a virgin.'

She twisted her head and buried it in his chest. She sensed that Robert was looking at the two other men, engaged in a silent debate. At the same time her hips began to move involuntarily, rubbing her behind into his groin.

His penis stiffened and she rubbed herself against him harder, deliberately, almost desperate to arouse him.

'Take my mouth, at least,' she whispered, kissing his ear.

Robert stepped back quite suddenly and Isabelle almost fell.

'Helene,' Robert called. 'Remove the mademoiselle's dress, please.'

Helene hurried over to Isabelle and began to undo the buttons at the front of her dress. The girl's smile was so tender that Isabelle wanted to kiss her in gratitude. When the dress was open to the waist, Isabelle pulled the sleeves down by herself and Helene, kneeling, slipped it down her legs. Gathering the light muslin in her hands the maid carried it over to one of the ottomans where she laid it out carefully.

Robert ran his hand down Isabelle's naked back.

'Are you asking Robert to sodomise you?'

Isabelle had almost forgotten that the other men were present and Alain's voice jolted her. It was not a question that she could answer.

'Is that what you want?' asked Robert.

Isabelle looked at him shyly and after giving the smallest of nods, her eyes fell to the floor.

'Wet her with your tongue, Helene,' he said, and stepped aside so that Helene could reach her from behind.

Isabelle, still with her eyes downcast, felt Helene's gentle hands parting the cheeks of her behind and her tongue, soft and wet, running down the sensitive cleft. Helene suckled first at Isabelle's sex, softening her, making Isabelle want that tongue when it moved to the tighter opening. Isabelle closed her eyes and her hips began a steady circling as if she were rotating upon the pointed tongue of the other woman. The men watched in silence, listened to the little gasps and sighs, followed the spectacle as if mesmerised by Isabelle's slow dance of desire, the sudden fearful retractions, the renewed surrender and excitement.

Robert rested his hand on Helene's shoulder and guided her to a kneeling position in front of Isabelle. Here, she concentrated on Isabelle's naked sex and, as if becoming hungry herself, Helene sucked hard, drawing all of the opened flesh into her mouth and nipping with her teeth. Robert, standing behind Isabelle, freed his sex from the constraint of his breeches and taking her waist in his hands immediately pushed at the opening to her behind. Isabelle, momentarily losing her courage, twisted away from him.

'It's gone too far this time,' Robert told her hoarsely, and seized her hair, pulling downwards so that she was forced to bow her knees and arch her back.

Robert found his mark again at that virgin ring of muscle and pushed hard. Isabelle gave such a cry that he almost withdrew. Finally, it was Isabelle, pressing her pelvis back with a grimace of pain, that united them. Her eyes opened into wide circles of surprise as Robert slid deep into her bowels. Her breath came in quick short, gasps as she tried to master the discomfort.

Helene, still squatting between Isabelle's widely spaced knees looked up into her tortured face with pity. Ferrier, at the desk, betrayed his feelings with a sudden uncontrollable spasm that ran through his body like a thunderbolt. His hand, jerking suddenly, upset the ink pot that he had been using, and it fell to the floor with a clatter, casting its black liquid contents across the marble. Attracted by the sound, Isabelle turned to him but her eyes had no focus. All of her awareness had coalesced around the burning sword of flesh that had invaded her and that inverted all of her senses.

Robert had to work hard against her tightly contracted behind but, with his steady plying back and forth, the passage eased and quite suddenly, as if some crisis were passed, she opened to him.

The two men would have seen that opening, each would have known well the moment that a woman surrenders to the man who uses her behind. They would have seen the softening of the features and deepening of the breathing that signals the onset of that deep, dark pleasure a woman can take from such treatment. A pink flush spread from Isabelle's neck to her breasts. From deep in her belly came a sound that rose unhindered through her opened throat and spilt into the room as an animal chant, rhythmic and hypnotic. For a long while the couple moved together, until finally Isabelle tensed.

'I am close,' she groaned. 'Finish with me now or I shall climax.'

Robert had no intention of finishing with her but he did withdraw and, for a moment, left her teetering on the very edge.

'The desk,' said Robert hoarsely, looking at Alain.

Alain nodded.

Robert took Isabelle's arm and guided her to the desk. Alain swept it clear with a single motion of his arm. The neat piles of paper scattered across the floor in a brief snow storm.

Robert turned Isabelle to face him and after kissing her, lifted her buttocks on to the polished surface. He looked at the sweat running down her breasts and the moisture that oozed from her neglected sex. She sensed the growing cruelty in his desire and it excited her.

'Do you want more?' he asked.

'Yes,' she breathed.

Robert placed his hands under her knees and lifted them so that her pelvis rotated, presenting the two gaping portals.

'Then put it in,' he told her.

She grasped his sex and guided it to her behind. Even though he held her legs high and forced them back against her breasts she had to edge forward on the desk to give him easy access. Once she had him in place he pushed into her hard with a single deep thrust. She had contracted and the first few strokes made her cry out with pain.

'Kiss me,' he told her.

She slipped her tongue into his mouth, grunting at each of his thrusts. Soon the pleasure came again and she began to buck, so much so that he came out of her more than once. Clearly losing his patience, he pushed her down on to the desk top and pinned her hips with his hands. Lying now within easy reach, Ferrier could not resist the temptation to touch her, tentatively at first, but soon without reserve. His fingers stroked, then dug into the soft flesh of her breasts and he looked into her eyes until the pain that he inflicted finally drew a pleading glance in response. Since she did not try to push away his hand, even when it went to the smooth, prominent mound of her sex and pursued its callous work there, she knew that he would take this as an acknowledgement of his right to use her as he chose.

Robert began pounding into her hard, and inexorably the pleasure mounted until once more Isabelle felt herself on the edge of dissolution. Alain watched this; he watched her lungs filling to capacity, watched her hands desperately clutching the sides of the desk, and as if he had been waiting for this moment, he took her head in his huge hands. She struggled as he turned her to face him fearing that he would somehow poison the joy of receiving her lover for the first time.

'Do you agree to take the whip to Absolem?' he asked, his eyes piercing her own like hot steel. 'And to offer him your mouth?'

She tried to shake her head free but his grip was unyielding.

'Let him whip me,' she moaned. 'But not my mouth.'

'It is already promised to him, so agree,' he said. 'And then take all the pleasure that you desire.'

Isabelle felt Ferrier parting the lips of her sex, pulling at their very apex until the clitoris was free and exposed. He blew a stream of air across that most sensitive of places and a great shiver ran through Isabelle's body. It would have been be so easy for her to let go, to slide into the dissolution of orgasm.

'No man has taken me there,' she managed to say. 'I can't.'

Quite abruptly, Robert withdrew from her and there was a terrible sense of deflation. Where she had been full, suddenly she was empty.

'No!' she cried.

Alain released her head and she turned sharply, looking for Robert. He stood above her, his eyes fierce and his penis taut. She knew immediately that he was going to use her mouth. Smiling shyly, she reached out to him. Taking his penis in her hand she drew him forward, wondering at her own courage with such an audience. Looking into his eyes, she tried to divine if this was right, if this was what he wanted from her. When his hand cupped the back of her head she knew and her lips kissed the very tip of his sex. The smell of her bowels was sharp and she licked him clean, as a cat might clean a kitten.

Between her legs, Isabelle felt Ferrier's hand renew its labours, but this time he sought to arouse not hurt. This pleasure was a distraction when she wished to concentrate only on Robert and she closed her legs against the other man. Robert, however, pulled back from her mouth and Isabelle knew that she had displeased him. Immediately she opened her legs wide and lifted her feet from the surface of the desk so that nothing would be hidden. Robert rested the crown of his penis against her lips once more and she swallowed him deep into her throat.

'Helene,' Robert groaned. 'Use your fingers in her behind.'

Isabelle sucked at him and he allowed her to spend a long time doing this. Occasionally he would withdraw to trail his straining penis across her cheeks or forehead, sometimes he would push her head underneath so that she could lick his sac and the root that led down to his own narrow opening. All the time that Isabelle did these things, Helene was stretching her behind with two, sometimes three fingers. These writhed inside Isabelle like snakes, opening and closing, pushing and pulling until she was so stretched there that the girl's whole hand might have slipped in.

When Robert eventually tired of being sucked he pushed Isabelle's shoulders to the desk.

'Now will you agree to Alain's demands?' he asked.

'You haven't climaxed in me yet,' she said. 'Am I so undesirable?'

Robert looked at her carefully, as if unsure whether he should be angry or not. He must have seen how excited she was and he must have noticed that from moment to moment her expression changed as the fingers between her legs stirred and probed. Her hair was drenched with sweat and her mouth gulped air as if she were drowning.

'She reminds me of women that I've seen with a high fever,' he said to Alain, 'those who cry out in their delirium and reach for figures that no one else can see.'

'Her arousal is extreme, even for a Belloque,' agreed Alain.

'If I climax in your mouth will you then offer it to Absolem?' he asked Isabelle.

'If you command it,' she said.

'And will you offer your behind freely as well?'

She knew well that her acquiescence to such a demand would excite him but it was still difficult to agree.

'If it pleases you,' she said finally.

Robert took hold of her shoulders and pulled her down the desk until her head hung over the edge. In this position he could work himself into her mouth easily, and she, with her neck bent tightly back, was entirely helpless.

'Lay your hands, palm up, by your sides and don't move them until I'm finished,' he told her. 'Climax if you wish but keep still and keep your lips soft and open.'

With these words he pushed into her throat deeply, so deeply that at the bottom of each stroke she was prevented from breathing. At first he moved slowly, expecting her to gag, but when this didn't happen, when he realised that her throat was as open to him as every other part of her, he abandoned all inhibition. Once Isabelle began to climax, and that was soon, very soon after he gave his permission, a strange shuddering took her body and she gave a long wail of release. His own climax was so copious that she thought he had lost control of his bladder in the frenzy that seized him at the end.

As soon as Robert was finished, Helene hurried to fetch a cloth and kneeling, she washed his sex. When she moved to clean Isabelle, however, Alain raised his hand and waved the maid away.

'On your feet, Isabelle,' Alain said.

155

Isabelle struggled first into a sitting position and then, easing herself from the desk, she managed to stand.

'Give her the whip, Helene.'

Helene picked the whip from the floor and offered it.

'Mademoiselle,' said the maid and curtseyed.

Isabelle opened her hand and took the whip, all resistance gone.

'Absolem is waiting for you,' Robert told her. 'And remember, allow everything.'

Isabelle didn't even ask if she was to be allowed the dignity of clothing for her long walk to the stables, and turning, made for the door without a glance at anyone.

17

Father and Son

The stables lay on the north side of the villa and were most
easily reached by walking through a long series of gardens
enclosed by the building. There was a great temptation to
stop at one of the fountains to wash, especially to wash the
stickiness from between her thighs, but Isabelle resisted
this. She was aware that Alain had deliberately wanted her
to present herself to Absolem in this soiled condition.
Somehow it seemed right that she should do so.

It was impossible for her to know how many people saw
her as she walked whip in hand through those sunlit
spaces, overlooked as they were by window after window.
Certainly she herself saw no one until she reached the
stables.

At the sight of the long, low building she paused. She
could smell the rich mixture of hay and manure and could
hear the sounds of horses hooves as they shuffled in their
stalls. At the far end of the building a boy was sweeping
the cobblestone driveway. Inside, she knew that there
would be more of these stable boys and somewhere among
them would be their master, Absolem. For the first time
since her climax in the library she felt the protective shield
of self-abasement crumbling. Her pride, reasserting itself,
froze her legs and she remained fixed where she had halted,
in the lee of the villa. By sending her alone and by asking
her to carry the whip that she was to be beaten with, Alain
had given her both reason and opportunity to run away.
At that moment she almost turned.

She imagined with a terrible clarity the trial that lay ahead. She saw the faces of the stable boys, she imagined the derision and the desire, she saw herself being beaten, and afterwards submitting to whatever demands Absolem might make of her. Yet as her heart pounded she felt a curious security, as if nothing that might happen could touch what mattered to her. When it was over she would be returned to Robert, and she would be more desirable in his eyes than ever. She remembered how the marks on Helene's behind constantly fascinated and excited him and how jealous that made her feel.

Isabelle's feet burned as she crossed the strip of sun heated cobbles which separated the villa and stables. Inside, the smell of horse and leather was almost overpowering, and the gloom was impenetrable after the brightness of the sunlight. She halted on the threshold while her senses adjusted.

When her eyes were able to function she saw the startled figure of a young man, the same young man she had seen once from the library and who had been familiar to her then. He was rooted to the spot, staring at her like a startled fox. She looked at him calmly and after a moment he spoke haltingly.

'Can I be of assistance, mademoiselle?'

At the sound of his gentle voice, Isabelle blushed deeply. He looked at her with a mixture of concern and astonishment, his sensitive eyes avoiding her naked body in a vain effort to preserve her dignity. Such respectful awareness of her situation was the thing that she could least bear at that moment. She had steeled her mind and body for this ordeal but not her heart. Isabelle took a step backward and might have fled if it were not for the sound of another voice, one sterner and stronger than the boy's.

'Mademoiselle Belloque. Come forward.'

Isabelle looked in the direction that the voice had come from. At the far end of the building she could just make out a figure.

'You don't have to,' said the boy quietly, glancing at the whip.

Isabelle frowned and looked at him in surprise. 'A child cannot save me,' she said with deliberate cruelty, hardening herself.

The boy winced.

'Come,' said the voice again.

Isabelle walked forward across the prickly straw. She was aware of faces turning towards her, of scuffling, of boyish sniggers, of sudden intakes of breath as she passed along the long line of stalls. The heat and the smell intensified as she penetrated further into the gloom. To be naked in such a place, such an intensely male place, stirred her. The air was thick with the boys' desire. Her skin registered the passage of their eyes like so many small hands. Her breasts tingled as imaginary mouths, hopelessly young, clamped on to the hardening tips. Gradually the figure who had spoken became clearer. Absolem, dressed as darkly as he had been on their first meeting, stood waiting for her with his legs apart and his arms folded.

'Monsieur,' Isabelle said simply, when she finally reached him. She handed him the whip. There was a silence and Isabelle realised that she was expected to speak again. 'Monsieur Alain says that you are to use it only on my behind and that there is to be no blood.'

Absolem nodded and examined her naked body carefully. He couldn't have failed to see the erection of her nipples or the looseness of her thighs.

'The stables always have a strong effect on young women,' he told her and brushed the back of his hands across her belly. 'Is it the horses with their outsized organs, I wonder, or the boys with their many, much smaller hardnesses?'

Isabelle ignored this coarseness and returned his gaze with a steady mildness. She realised that he might have been a handsome man if it were not for the expression of weary contempt that soured his features. His eyes were the deepest black and shone with an unhealthy energy as if something demonic was only just suppressed.

'And what am I to receive in return for my labours?' he asked after a moment.

159

'My mouth and my behind,' she intoned as if repeating a familiar litany.

He laughed. 'Such an obedient whore!'

'I do this for the man that I love,' Isabelle replied, stung by his laughter.

'I want nothing to do with love,' he said. 'Or your foolishness. You will not speak again until I tell you to.'

Isabelle lowered her eyes.

Absolem reached out and took first one breast and then the other in his hand. Looking over her shoulder, he called out.

'Benjamin!'

There was the sound of hurrying feet behind her. Absolem had clamped his fingers on to one of her nipples teasing it out, pulling at it in a testing way, as if to see how easily she was stirred.

'Yes, Father.'

'Take the mademoiselle to the harness room.'

'Yes, Father.'

It was the boy that Isabelle had first seen on entering the stables, the boy whose concern had caused her to hesitate and almost to flee from the threshold. And this was Absolem's son! Isabelle looked at him as he stood next to his father. The boy was almost as tall as the man and they shared the same strong, regular features but there all similarities ended. Where the father was hard the boy was soft, where the father was sour the boy was sweet. Absolem released her breast after giving her a final fierce pinch that made her gasp.

'Play with her until she climaxes. Then tie her to the beam.'

Benjamin shot a quick, questioning glance at his father.

'You have your instructions,' Absolem rasped.

'Yes, monsieur.'

Isabelle saw that Benjamin was more afraid of his father than she was.

'Mademoiselle, please,' Benjamin said nervously. 'This way.'

'She is yours to command in all things. Remember that,' were Absolem's final words.

Isabelle followed Benjamin as he led her to the end of the stables and through an arched door. The harness room was large and square with a paved floor and stone pillars supporting the roof. Unlike the area with the horses' stalls there was no wooden ceiling and the terracotta pan tiles were visible. This lack of insulation made the room oppressively hot, despite the windows that were open to the gardens at the back and the double doors open to the courtyard at the front. Benjamin closed the door to the stalls behind Isabelle as she walked into the centre of the room. She looked around at the towering racks of oiled and polished leather of every kind. It was not difficult to imagine the long hours that the stable boys spent maintaining this collection so that the house parties Alain hosted from time to time could ride in pursuit of boar and deer.

Isabelle turned as she heard Benjamin approach her. She felt no apprehension with this boy. She felt rather, on seeing his flushed face and uncertain expression, a tenderness that was almost maternal and might have been entirely so if his eyes were less warm and his lips less full.

Isabelle, lowered her gaze for his sake, but only after smiling at him encouragingly.

'I have never been commanded to do this before,' he said. 'I have heard my father whip girls, girls sent from the villa. I have seen them tied and waiting for him. But . . .' his voice trailed away and for a moment he seemed quite paralysed.

'How can you allow it?' he asked after a moment. This must have been the question he had wanted to ask her from the first, from the moment he had seen her half-naked with Robert in the grounds by the lake.

Isabelle remained silent. She was thinking of Robert's final words in the library. He had told her to allow everything and he had told her to take pleasure in it. Could she explain either the excitement or the deep satisfaction of allowing everything to her lover? Isabelle looked at the boy, seeing his concern and realising that he felt shame on her behalf. She wondered if it was his own desires that caused him such mortification.

'Speak,' he said after a moment.

'I am yours to command,' she said, 'but if you try to make me explain why I allow these things, I don't think that I fully could. But I am not forced, I give freely what is asked.'

'I had dreams of rescuing you,' he told her.

She sighed. 'There is nothing to rescue me from.'

'I understood that as you walked through the stables.' He gave her a weary, resigned smile, the smile of someone who belatedly realises his foolishness.

'I have my duty to perform,' he told her, 'but I may not be very expert.'

She lowered her eyes once more. 'I won't make it difficult for you.'

Benjamin approached her then halted. Glancing up, Isabelle sensed his confusion.

'How should I do it?' he asked.

Isabelle suddenly felt embarrassed. It was as if he expected her to take the lead. She shrugged and they stood in silence for a few moments.

'How would Monsieur Robert do it?' he asked.

Isabelle had to force herself to be calm as she thought of the many ways that Robert might choose to give her pleasure.

'He might have me standing or lying down. Sometimes I will be kneeling.'

'You make me feel dizzy when you say these things.'

'What things?' she asked in surprise.

'Kneeling. The thought of you kneeling makes my head spin.'

'Is that exciting for you?' she asked.

He turned away from her. 'It makes me feel cruel. I don't want to be like my father.'

There was a sudden commotion in the courtyard and Benjamin walked to the doors to see what was happening. A groom was struggling with a black Arab mare that was kicking wildly. Benjamin called to the boy and then went to his assistance. Isabelle waited and listened as the two boys struggled with the animal.

* * *

When Benjamin returned he found Isabelle standing exactly as he had left her. As he watched, she slowly sank to her knees on the paved floor. Her legs parted and she lowered her eyes simultaneously. He gasped. Slowly, as if approaching something inexplicably dangerous, Benjamin walked around her. Isabelle was trembling. He saw that in the soft flesh of her breasts and behind. The realisation that she too was excited made him even dizzier. For the first time he allowed himself to examine her body thoroughly. The narrowness of her waist, the slender curves of her opened thighs, the nakedness of her sex, all of these things seemed perfect, as if sculpted by his own desire.

'You are the loveliest woman I have ever seen,' he told her. 'Perfect.'

Isabelle smiled, her silence allowing this illusion.

Walking around her again, he had a powerful urge to seize her and to sink himself into her flesh. Checking this impulse made him angry both with her and himself. Suddenly her posture and demeanour, the way that she offered herself, made him want to hurt her.

'Do you know why men beat you?' he asked.

She seemed taken aback by this question, and by the anger in his voice that must have appeared to come from nowhere. She shook her head.

'I could beat you, if I chose to.'

She said nothing but he saw her body stiffen in response to that threat.

'Do you want to?'

'Yes. I hate you for making me feel that.'

She looked at him with soft, apologetic eyes that prompted further cruel impulses.

'My father calls you a whore, and what other kind of woman would kneel before a man like this?'

Isabelle raised her shoulders slowly, smiling as she shrugged. The word didn't seem to offend her. 'I know that to the world I am Robert's whore. But if I am, I am paid only in pleasure. To myself, I am something quite different, something that would sound foolish if spoken aloud.' She

163

looked at him with a sudden shyness, a shyness that made him want to press her.

'Tell me.'

'You will laugh.'

'I promise you that I will not.'

She lowered her eyes for a moment as if gathering her courage then looked him full in the face.

'I am his ocean and my lover can swim in me or drown as he chooses, and I will make it safe for him. If he invites others into the water, I cannot complain.'

'He exploits you and you do not even know it!' Benjamin cried out in exasperation.

'I exploit him,' she replied.

Benjamin shook his head wearily. 'When my father has whipped you I will ask the same questions again,' he told her. 'Perhaps you will give me other answers.'

'Will you watch me being whipped?' she asked, raising her eyes to his.

Benjamin felt a nakedly savage desire burn through his body at these words. As they regarded each other, a drop of moisture fell from between her legs and stained the grey stone floor black.

'You are half witch,' he told her.

'Then I should be burnt.'

Benjamin felt a surge of rage, stronger and hotter than he thought himself capable of. 'Lean back,' he told her, 'support yourself on your hands.'

Isabelle complied, arching her back, and raising her belly as she did so.

'Open your legs further.'

She strained every muscle to open herself, as if revelling in this, revelling in the freedom of her whoredom. Her sex split open, as an overripe pear bursts beneath a man's thumbs. There was an aroma of sweat and mucous, but clean and good as only a young girl's cunt could be.

'I will whip you myself.'

She looked up at him as he stood between her legs with flaming eyes and set jaw.

Earlier, he had compared her to an angel, but now it was

164

he who shone bright. The power of his undiluted desire made him something more than a mere human boy. But she smiled at him as if he was still sweet, sweet and glowing.

'I wouldn't refuse you, even if it was in my power to do so,' she murmured.

'Then I shall, and after I have done it, my father may choose to whip you again.' With these words he crouched down and began to caress her thighs. Reaching between and under her legs he invaded the valley of her behind, seizing the flesh of her separated cheeks and squeezing hard. He used the heel of his other hand on her sex, crudely massaging the whole area. Her head fell back so that her hair trailed on the stone floor. He watched her belly tauten into a perfect arch, her navel stretching to a slit that mimicked her sex. Sweat ran from her breasts into the hollows beneath her arms. He wanted to drink from her, to taste all of her hot, salty places. When he could resist her open mouth no longer he abandoned her sex and leant over her. His shirt stuck to her breasts as he kissed her lips and neck and ears.

'You want this,' he hissed, 'you want me.'

'Yes,' she moaned into his mouth.

'Say it.'

'I want you.'

'You want the whip.'

'Yes.'

His hand went back to her sex and found her bud.

'Give me your permission,' she implored.

He nodded and she climaxed. Her body stretched higher so that her sex was uppermost, the pinnacle of an arc of flesh that vibrated with desire. He allowed her to go on for as long as she wanted to, but as soon as her cries subsided he pulled her to her feet and led her to the whipping beam. She stood meekly as he looped the leather ties around her wrists and raised her bound hands to the hook above her head. He took the dog whip and used it with the fury of a convert. Her pleas for mercy only whetted his appetite for more. Finally he dropped the whip and clasped her

165

twisting body from behind. He ran his hands across her breasts and belly in a fury, his pelvis bucking into her behind until he climaxed without even penetrating her. It was a long time before his breathing returned to normal.

Afterwards, Benjamin cut her down and she collapsed across one of the saddles that was laid out on the floor. He watched as she shuddered and writhed, pressing her hands to her behind in a way that made him feel both guilt and a desire to whip her again. It was only when she had calmed a little that she looked up, showing in her reddened, swollen face something close to exultation as if some great test were over. His own eyes, already moist, suddenly flooded over.

He groaned with such heartfelt remorse that she reached for him and he fell to his knees burying his head in her breasts.

'There is nothing to regret,' she told him. 'You performed a service for me.'

Still he cried like the boy that he was.

'When you have your own girl you will understand,' Isabelle said kindly. 'She will want to give a boy like you everything.'

'But I want you,' he groaned.

The hopeless tone of longing in his voice seemed to move her and her own tears came. They wept together, wrapped in each others arms until Absolem appeared at the courtyard door. He smiled thinly as he saw the two figures and the livid marks on Isabelle's behind. The moment that Benjamin heard his father's familiar tread he rose abruptly and left without a word.

'You have seduced my son,' Absolem remarked as he looked down at Isabelle's prostrate body. 'For that at least I should thank you.'

At the sound of Absolem's rasping voice Isabelle curled into a ball burying her head in her breasts.

'I will come back for you in an hour,' he told her. 'At that time you won't be allowed to hide from me.'

Absolem did indeed choose to tie and whip Isabelle, though not as cruelly as his son. For Absolem, this second

166

beating was a matter of duty to his masters. His disinterest did nothing, however, to soften the scalding blows that bit into the already scorched flesh.

Isabelle was allowed a brief respite before she was released and instructed to take his sex into her mouth. As she sucked, Absolem's eyes were closed and as he sodomised her, he hardly glanced at her heaving body. It was an image of his wife, Benjamin's mother, when she was newly his bride, an image of her tenderness as she opened the cheeks of her own behind that occupied his thoughts and drew his desire to its climax. Isabelle received Absolem's sperm in her entrails as a proxy to this distant, long-dead figure.

18

Don Luis

A stable boy was sent to fetch Maria when Absolem was finished. The maid took the exhausted Isabelle to the bedroom by the baths and said she was to rest. It was a disappointment that Robert wasn't waiting for her and, once the heat in her behind had subsided and she had dozed fitfully in the sultry afternoon air, Isabelle became restless. She took a towel and went out to the baths. The afternoon sun was hot on her breasts as she stripped and she was frightened of being burnt. She was especially conscious of her sex, newly bare and not exposed to such fierce rays since she was a child. She hurried to the water's edge. Her nude behind displayed the whip's livid designs as she stepped in.

The baths cooled and relaxed her and she lay on her back, drifting beneath the flawless blue of the sky until afternoon became evening. Still Robert hadn't come for her. Ringing for Maria she asked where Robert was, only to be told that no one knew. She sent the girl to the library with a list of books for her to find. It was pleasant to command Maria, she who had lifted Isabelle's breasts for the men to see. It was Anna though, not Maria, who returned half an hour later, her arms loaded with leather-bound volumes and carrying a small leather case.

'I am to attend to your hair, mademoiselle,' the girl said when she saw Isabelle's surprise.

'My hair?' asked Isabelle.

'Monsieur Alain says that it is too long. He doesn't want it to cover your breasts when you are standing.'

Isabelle was even more surprised by this but said nothing before the serving girl.

'I also have wax for between your legs,' Anna reported.

She said this with a little, apologetic smile as she lay the books on a secretaire near the windows. The case she carried into the courtyard, placing it beside a chair that Isabelle had taken out earlier when she had swum.

'Please, mademoiselle,' Anna called.

For a moment, Isabelle thought of protesting. In the courtyard she would be exposed to the eyes of any who might be using the corridors or surrounding rooms as she suffered the indignity of being plucked and waxed. But then, she thought, what could they see that hadn't already been seen?

As Isabelle walked over to Anna, the girl was setting up a little copper bowl on a stand. She lit the alcohol burner beneath it and broke up some aromatic beeswax, dropping the pieces into the bowl where it slowly melted.

'Your dress, mademoiselle,' Anna said, the pitch of her voice rising, surprised that Isabelle hadn't already removed it.

'Can you not simply raise it when you need to?' asked Isabelle.

'The wax! Even a drop and it will be ruined.'

Anna came to stand before Isabelle and undid the tie below her breasts. The serving girl's fingers were small and quick, the movements neat, like those of a seamstress. Her breath smelt of cloves as if she had recently drunk absinthe. Looking down on her, for she was three or four inches taller than the other girl, Isabelle took in the fineness of her skin and softness of her lips. She remembered the library and how those lips had closed over the head of Robert's sex. It stirred her to think of those things with the beautiful girl so close, the girl who was soon to perform the most intimate of services.

When at length Isabelle was naked she seated herself on the chair. The sun had lost much of its strength and was reddening as it sank to the horizon. There was a magic to the light at that hour and it touched the two women, gilding and softening features and forms already lovely. Anna took a brush from her case and ran it through the length of Isabelle's chestnut hair. The strands shone with a vibrant health, gleaming red as they were lifted and combed. Isabelle remembered the times that her sister had done this in her bedroom at home, sometimes pulling too hard, deliberately cruel as sisters can be, at other times with a care amounting to love and a delicate, half-hidden sensuality. She gave herself to the pleasure of being groomed, prepared for whatever Alain might have devised for her. She watched the shadows of the building creeping towards her and listened to the squabble of peacocks in the distant grounds. A stray hair fell on to the smooth swell of her stomach and she brushed it aside, watching as it tumbled and glistened in the slanting light.

When Isabelle's hair was free of even the smallest tangle, Anna took up the scissors and began to cut. It was a slow process. The girl was anxious to achieve just the right length and to leave it even and appealing. Her evident concentration and dedication to this task touched Isabelle in its simplicity. It was too easy for her to see Anna as a rival as much as she disavowed such childish feelings, and this could sour her view of the girl.

From time to time Anna would stand directly in front of her mistress to check that the two sides matched. Outlined against the sun, the thin fabric of her dress became translucent. Her slender legs and the rounded space between them, the space at the very top of her thighs, could be seen clearly. Isabelle found herself wanting to see more. In the library the girl's sex had appeared between her legs as a smile of invitation, demure when cool, full and pouting when heated. Isabelle made no effort to hide this examination or to shield her interest. Anna, sensitive to such things, smiled.

'Do you have sisters?' Isabelle asked.

'One, but she is far away,' the girl replied a little sadly.

'So is mine.' Isabelle reached out her hand.

'Could we be sisters?' she asked.

Anna took the hand and squeezed it lightly. 'I would like that.'

They smiled at each other for a moment before Anna resumed her task.

If the odd hair had settled on Isabelle while it was combed, she now found herself covered in a glistening dust of fine trimmings. They began to irritate her and Anna took a dusting brush from her case. It had an ornately carved ivory handle and long, fine bristles, white for most of the length but tipped with brown. When Anna tried to dust Isabelle's skin she wriggled as if ants were crawling all over her.

'Keep still, mademoiselle,' Anna told her. 'It will only be for a moment.'

Isabelle tried to ignore the brush but the more carefully and the more lightly that Anna used it, the more it tickled. Her breasts were the most sensitive and it was impossible for her to remain seated when the brush swept across these. She jumped to her feet with a cry, clasping her breasts as if they had been stung. Both girls began to giggle as Anna continued trying to use the brush and Isabelle retreated across the courtyard.

'I will run,' threatened Isabelle.

'I will run faster,' replied Anna.

Finally, Isabelle was backed against the boundary of the baths and, as if she was being pursued by a man with a rapier, she edged sideways, still trying to dodge the thrusts of the brush. Reaching the stonework of the cupola Isabelle found that she had nowhere left to go. She was hemmed into a corner.

'No more,' she pleaded.

'Stand still,' Anna told her, her eyes gleaming with the pleasure of the chase.

'Anne-Marie used to tickle me when I was little, she'd make me shriek until I was hysterical and then tickle me again.'

Anna reached out and rested her hand on Isabelle's hip. Her expression, intent suddenly, compelled Isabelle to silence. 'Turn around.'

Isabelle complied. The girls hand stroked gently across the raised welts on Isabelle's behind as if this simple

171

attention could heal them. Isabelle felt a small kiss on her shoulder, a kiss of something shared and understood without words. Because of that kiss she allowed herself to be pushed forward against the carved stone work when Anna's hand settled in the small of her back. The surface was rough against her belly like a pumice stone and where she rested her cheek there was a damp stone scent like the caves at Marabar. Anna drew the brush slowly down Isabelle's spine. It was as delicious as it was tormenting. As the brush passed over the outswell of her behind she squirmed, and as the bristles reached into the divide she gave a little gasp. Anna took the brush all the way to Isabelle's feet before returning to her neck and beginning again. When it reached her behind this time it curved under her buttocks quite deliberately, the bristles opening her cheeks and tickling across the well of her anus. Unconsciously, Isabelle pushed her pelvis back and the brush caught the sensitive skin that led to her sex before passing on and down the inside of her thighs. She shivered as it made its maddening way over the backs of her knees and across her calves to the soles of her feet, exposed because she had raised her self on tiptoe. She gave many small cries before Anna had finished with her back and asked her to turn around in a voice that was low and charged with feeling.

'Put your hands above your head,' she said.

Isabelle felt as if she were being dared, as if this were one of the games she used to play with the farm boys, games that had her climbing trees that were too high or kissing lips that were too wet.

She raised her arms slowly, leaning back against the stonework. Her hands sought out projections, a cupid's foot on one side, a carved pomegranate on the other, and clasped them tightly.

'Close your eyes,' Anna told her.

The girl made Isabelle wait, made her wonder where and how she would be touched so that her skin tingled without even being touched. Isabelle remembered how she had felt the first time that Robert had tied her, how it had excited her to feel so offered. It was an excitement that never

172

faded, a riskiness that made her heart race even now when she was not tied but only offered, and this by her own will.

Anna began on the inside of her left elbow, slowly working across the slight swell of her arm muscles and down to her shoulder, rounded above but open underneath and squeamish to the touch of the brush. Isabelle's breasts, drawn high in that pose, quivered on her lean, indented ribcage as the brush approached them. Anna did not spare her. The bristles explored all of that taut flesh lingering on the nipples which pushed out like spring buds, smooth and shining in the last of the sun's light.

'If I was a man and you were mine this is how I would have you,' murmured Anna. 'I would have you painted like this, I would show you to my friends like this.'

The brush kissed its way to her belly, drawing large slow circles around the epicentre of her navel. Her sex was wet and the bristles caught some of the moisture there drawing it out into fine glistening threads. Anna turned the brush around and pressed the smooth ivory handle against the opening of Isabelle's sex. Isabelle groaned and her belly rippled.

'If I go any further we will be punished,' Anna told her, but the brush did not stop its insistent probing. 'If you climax without the permission of one of the men we will be whipped.'

Isabelle opened her eyes. She knew that what Anna said was true but she wanted it.

'If I tied you perhaps they would only whip me,' the girl murmured. 'I could say that I forced you to pleasure.'

Isabelle smiled. 'If I used my hand they would whip me instead.'

'They might whip us side by side.'

'Sisters.'

'I could lick the tears from your eyes afterwards. They would let us comfort each other, I'm sure.'

Isabelle groaned again. The brush was at the entrance of her behind, teasing, opening. She was close, too close to continue this game and her arms came down to rest on Anna's shoulders.

'I can't betray Robert,' she said, and watched the disappointment form in Anna's eyes.

'He takes other women. Perhaps at this very moment,' Anna murmured.

'I want him to.'

'And you? Don't you want me?'

Isabelle did want her. She wanted the girl's trembling lips and she kissed them lightly. She wanted the firm breasts and she reached for them stroking, squeezing.

'Let me see you,' Isabelle whispered, 'all of you.'

Anna stepped back and taking the hem of her dress in both hands she raised it to her neck. Isabelle ran her hands across the girl's belly, savouring its smoothness. There was a swelling beneath her navel, a fullness that was so sexual. Isabelle cupped it in her hand, weighing the desire that bred there. The girl's sex was hidden in deep shadow and dropping to her knees, Isabelle pressed at the inside of Anna's thighs until they opened. She turned the girl so that the sun fell directly on to her front.

'So beautiful,' she murmured, her eyes expanding with pleasure as the mound was revealed. She kissed the neatness of Anna's sex but it was only one kiss, a gesture of affection, a reassurance that the girl was wanted in the most intimate ways.

'I will ask Robert to give you to me,' Isabelle whispered.

Anna quivered at these words.

Isabelle ran her fingers along the crease where Anna's thigh met her belly. The bluish mark that nestled there, close to the sex, the mark that Isabelle had seen in the library, was indeed a tattoo, a miniature emblem surrounded by a spiral of Latin text in tiny letters. Isabelle peered more closely, deciphering the words with difficulty.

'Don Luis of Estragon,' Isabelle read aloud, 'has enjoyed every pleasure with this girl. Take her with my blessing, she will refuse you nothing.'

The emblem was a rearing bull that clasped a naked woman with its front legs.

When Isabelle stood and looked into Anna's face, the girl blushed.

174

'He was my lover.'

'In Spain?'

'Mexico.'

'And you refused him nothing?' asked Isabelle with a smile.

'He would court me very properly during the day, coming to my father's house in his fine clothes, talking to me romantically, talking very softly so that my chaperones wouldn't hear; but at night I would walk out into the darkness of the desert and wait for him, naked. There in the desert I refused him nothing.'

The image of the girl waiting for her lover, naked beneath the stars sent a thrill through Isabelle.

'After nearly two years of this courtship I was caught. Two of my brothers followed me and found us in the desert. They watched and listened as Don Luis took me, then as soon as he left they fell on me and dragged me home naked.'

Isabelle inhaled sharply.

'When I was presented to my father I thought that he would kill me.'

Isabelle took the girl's hand.

'I don't know if it was my father's love that saved me or his fear of Don Luis. Don Luis was a great and powerful gentleman and he had many men. In the end, my brothers took me to the coast to wait for a ship to Spain. I was to be put in the charge of an aunt in the mountains of Andalusia. Her house would have been my prison. I would have been allowed to see no one. But as I waited for the ship Don Luis's men found me and stole me from under my brothers' noses. They took me into the desert and left me there naked. When darkness fell and the moon rose, Don Luis came for me with another man. The stranger watched as Don Luis took me, as we played all the special games that my lover liked. I began to climax almost as soon as he touched me that evening and it seemed that I didn't stop until morning. Then as soon as the sun rose, Don Luis bade me farewell and gave me to the stranger, who was Monsieur Alain. My lover's last act was to draw the design for the tattoo so that I would bear some constant testimony of our passion. Monsieur Alain allowed me to have the mark made even though I had come to be his.'

'Have you been happy with Monsieur Alain?' asked Isabelle, touched by the story.

'He is not Don Luis but he has ways with a woman, ways that are even more refined perhaps. He excites me with a glance, because I know all that he can do.'

Isabelle was tempted to ask what these ways were but checked herself.

It had grown so dark that when Anna came to her final task, the depilation of Isabelle's sex, she was forced to fetch an oil lamp from the bedroom. She laid out a towel so that Isabelle could lie on her back on the paved ground and set the oil lamp between her legs. The alcohol burner had gone out and Anna refilled it from a small bottle in her case. As they waited for the wax to melt once more in its copper bowl, Anna used tweezers to pluck the tiny hairs that would be difficult to reach. These were mainly in the creases of skin where her thighs met her behind and the indented area around her anus. Each time that Anna plucked, Isabelle would quiver and Anna would bend to bestow a healing kiss on the afflicted skin. Anyone looking into the courtyard that evening would have seen the two women, would have seen Isabelle holding her thighs to her chest so that her sexual parts were stretched tight and were exposed to the tweezers; they would have seen Anna's great tenderness and regret at each tiny injury and would have thought that the two were lovers, such was their absolute engagement with each other and their oblivious disregard for all else.

When the wax was melted, Anna poured it over Isabelle's sex causing the girl to buck with the shock. Anna quickly laid strips of coarse woven muslin into the molten wax so that when it set, she could strip it clear, bringing all of the tiny hairs with it. This was far more painful than the tweezers and Anna had to spend far more time making amends with her healing lips. It required all of the girls' discipline to keep themselves in check, to hold back their shared desire and not to take it to completion.

19

Giving

Anna had long completed her task, and it was late in the
evening, when Robert finally came to see Isabelle. She was
lying belly down on the bed clad in a chemise of soft, white
silk. In front of her was a favourite book, *Mort D'Arthur*.
She allowed Robert to sit on the bed and rest his hand on
her shoulder before she raised herself on her elbows and
turned to him. He searched her face for signs of welcome,
but her eyes slid away.

'Are you angry with me?' he asked.

'I wanted you earlier,' she said simply.

'But now you don't?'

'No.'

Isabelle turned back to her book. Visions of Gawain and
the monstrous Green Knight filled her mind.

'Shall I leave?' he asked,

'You understand nothing,' she told him coldly.

'Then I won't leave until I do understand, or until you
tell me to.'

His hand stroked across her back and down the side of
her body. When it strayed across her behind she stiffened.

'Is it tender?' he asked.

She didn't reply.

'Lift your nightdress,' he said softly.

Isabelle continued to read, ignoring this command.

'Lift your nightdress,' he told her, more firmly.

When she turned to him there was an interest, even a flicker
of arousal in her eyes but she made no move to comply.

'Should I spank you?' he asked.

'You will have to tie me first.'

'No. If I tie you it will be for the pleasure of tying you. If I beat you I will expect you to offer yourself freely.'

'Why didn't you come for me, after the stables, after Absolem?' she burst out suddenly. 'I've waited for you all evening.'

He looked steadily into her accusing gaze.

'You exhausted me, the library – sometimes I need to rest from you.'

'I went to Absolem for your sake.'

'I know, and it pleased me very much.'

'And then I waited for you.'

'Forgive me.'

She turned away from him, burying her head in the pillow so that he wouldn't see her tears. Taking her hand he slipped his fingers into her's and squeezed. Her fingers were limp, unresponsive even when he carried them to his mouth and kissed each in turn.

'When I asked where you were no one could tell me.'

'I walked to the lake. I tried not to think of you because I would have wanted you again immediately.'

'You once promised to keep me near you always,' she said reproachfully.

'For as long as you want me, I shall,' he promised.

These words finally satisfied her and she reached down with her free hand, pulling the chemise to her waist. The perfect twin rounds of her behind were covered by an ornate pattern of dark marks. When she turned to look at them they reminded her of the medieval embellishments that ornamented her book. Robert's eyes gleamed as he ran his finger over the bruised flesh and seeing his pleasure, she was content. Impulsively, he leant forward and kissed each taut mound in turn, then, sucking in some of the flesh, he bit. It was only a teasing bite but it made her start.

'No,' she said, giggling, 'no more.'

He growled with mock fierceness and nipped her several times, following the dark welts with his teeth. She struggled for the pleasure of struggling but when his tongue swept down the valley to her narrow opening she became very still.

'Lift up,' he told her.

She pushed her behind into the air. In this position, Robert could reach her sex and his tongue split the lips apart in a single motion. She was wet, as she'd been wet all day. His tongue became an eel, slipping into the saturated opening, undulating, seeking out those places that made her groan. As soon as she began to move strongly, his mouth clamped on to to her behind again and he bit, harder than before, enough to send a shock deep into her belly. When his tongue returned to her sex, her movements became even less restrained. He used this way of exciting her; biting or spanking her bruised behind and then sucking at her sex until she begged to be allowed to climax. Giving his permission, he had her hold open her sex and used his tongue on the fresh, pink bud until the pleasure broke.

She lay sated and still afterwards. One hand clasped his thigh, the other cupped her sex, as if it, and all the feelings that it contained, were too precious to leave unguarded. When he tried to pull away from her, she held him tightly. When he pulled harder, laughingly saying that he had no more to give, she rolled on to her side and with the smile of an angel told him that it was her turn to give. The seraphic quality in her expression transfixed him as she rose to kiss his cheeks and neck.

'Let me give you pleasure,' she whispered, 'let me do it all, I won't tire you. If I drain you it will only be your seed.'

'I must go to my bed,' he told her.

She looked at him and saw the sleep already creeping into his face, saw the yawn that softened his features and made him almost boyish.

'Please,' she murmured, 'I want to do this.'

With these words she took his sex, half erect inside his breeches and began to squeeze. Seeing that she was determined, he lay back on the bed.

'Tell no one that I allowed a woman to rape me,' he said with a smile.

Isabelle felt such a feverish desire to possess him that it was only with a great effort that she slowed herself, undressing him, rather than tearing the clothes from his body. Immediately that his sex was free, though, she seized it with her mouth and took it deep into her throat sucking hard.

'Steadily, my darling,' he told her, 'let me still be a man when you have finished.'

This cut her to the quick and she softened her mouth. As gently as she might, she eased back the mantle of skin that protected his crown and rained tiny, tiny kisses on that most sensitive skin. When he was fully taut, when the head of his sex glowed in its distension, she swallowed him deep and used her tongue at his root, tasting the silk of his hair. Her hands gathered up his heavy sac and she pressed it to her lips wishing that she could take all of him into her mouth. She alternated between these two extremes, at one moment lightly sucking at his exposed crown and the next taking him deep, offering the soft velvet of her throat. Her sex she rubbed against his shins so that he could feel her wetness and know that she was excited. Her breasts she pressed into his thighs. All the time that she had him in her mouth she murmured soft, half-stifled endearments, the gentle phrases that lovers use. When he climaxed she gave him the depths of her unguarded throat to anoint and kept him inside until he was small again and sleeping.

20

Alain

Isabelle had dreaded her meeting with Alain from the moment that Robert had told her of it. She knocked at the door of his study with the resignation of a schoolboy summoned by a headmaster. When the door opened, Alain seemed to fill the entire frame. His stony, pock marked face, as broad as a mountainside, showed no smile as he acknowledged her.

'Thank you for being so prompt, mademoiselle.'

Isabelle curtseyed and he stepped aside so that she could enter. The room was small and the few items of furniture were strictly functional. A large desk occupied one wall. Two armchairs stood facing each other by glazed doors that were open and led into a tiny courtyard. The courtyard itself was paved, but a single tree, a cedar, stood in its centre. The branches cast a deep shadow so that even at noon, the room was gloomy. Isabelle had a sense of something subterranean, like the caves at Marabar. Her eyes scanned the room rapidly. In the semi-darkness she saw no whips or machines of torture, not even a bed or couch where he might take her if that was his desire. Her heart still raced and she realised that it was her inability to read his feelings that caused such apprehension, rather than a fear of what he might do to her. That, and the sense that she could never move him to anything other than anger or disapproval. As the door closed, it felt as if she were being sealed into the lair of an implacable giant.

'Please sit.' Alain indicated one of the two black leather

armchairs close to the window. He remained standing while Isabelle made herself comfortable and arranged her skirt so that it wouldn't crease. He could never be faulted for his patience in these small matters. When she was quite settled he sat in the remaining chair and gazed at her with the thinnest of smiles. Isabelle tried to return this gaze with a forced equanimity but, inevitably, her eyes fell to her lap.

'You grow lovelier every day. Life at the villa seems to agree with you,' he said finally.

Isabelle looked at him sharply but saw no irony in his eyes.

'Have we ever been alone like this before?' he asked.

'No, monsieur.'

'I know that you wouldn't voluntarily seek my company.' There was regret in his expression, but also a sense that this was inevitable and ultimately immaterial.

'I've never felt that I know you, monsieur. I feel awkward.'

He smiled. 'That is strange, because I feel that I know you very well. Far better than you could imagine. Did you know that I was present at your birth?'

Taken aback, Isabelle shook her head.

'Your father held one of your mother's hands and I held the other. I was granted the privilege of choosing your second name, Elizabette.'

His smile broadened and, for a moment he seemed quite human.

'And now Isabelle, you are my oldest friend's . . .' he searched for the correct phrase, 'sexual companion. I am curious to know how that came to be.'

She looked at him quizzically, feeling that there was no mystery. It was clear that he wished to hear something from her but she didn't know what that was. 'I liked him from the first,' she said, 'I found him attractive . . .' Her voice trailed away. Who could say what forged such bonds or stirred such desires?

'But I want to know everything. I want you to tell me about every kiss, every caress, every impulse, every doubt, disappointment, pleasure. No detail is too trivial.' He said this with such an unusual intensity that Isabelle drew back into her seat.

'Remember your promise in the library, and mine too,' he continued, sensing her reticence.

Isabelle's promise was that she would withhold nothing from him. His promise, she recalled, was that he would beat her as her sister had never been beaten if she failed to keep her word.

'Where shall I begin?' she asked.

'From the moment that Robert and I visited your mother's house.' Alain glanced at the clock on the wall opposite his desk. A moment before Isabelle had arrived it had struck noon.

'There is no hurry,' he told her. 'Absolem isn't expecting you until four o'clock.'

It was a difficult task and unnerving. It was difficult to remember every detail as Alain required. It was unnerving to be so open and to hide nothing. She could not hide her childish desire to compete with her sister or her duplicity in pretending to her mother that her innocence was being safely guarded during her visits to the villa. Her sexual feelings, the great pleasure she took in being overwhelmed by Robert and the excitement of seeing his power over Helene and Maria, these things she was forced to describe as well. And Alain wanted the details of their sex acts, compelling her to describe how Robert had touched her or had her touch herself. If she said that Robert had climaxed over her breasts or face he would want to know if she had been kneeling or lying, if anyone else was present and how it felt to clean him afterwards with her tongue, as Robert often required. All these acts and all of the very private feelings that they stirred, were the subject of his endless questions and clarifications. He wanted to know if she was aroused as she described these things to him and in truth she was. But it was an ordeal, as much of an ordeal as the whip. It frightened her that he should know so much and it frightened her that her sex grew wetter and wetter as she talked. There was a giddying sense that somehow he was touching her from inside. Even as she thought these things

184

more questions demanded answers. Alain wanted to know about the other men in the villa. He was fascinated by her perceptions of the Ferriers and her sense of the purity of their marital relationship, hardly being able to suppress a smile as she described her envy of them. When Isabelle talked of Benjamin he grew thoughtful and asked if she found him attractive. She replied, 'Yes, but he is only a boy,' and he nodded, murmuring that perhaps she would help Benjamin to become a man.

Once she had finished speaking, once everything had been told that she could think of telling, Isabelle glanced at the clock. She realised that she had been talking for over two hours and that she was shaking. Every sentence that she uttered had made her feel more vulnerable. It felt as if she had been stripped naked in some very public place and that every part of her body had been opened to the eyes of strangers. She recalled that Robert had once said that she should be presented on all fours in a market square for the pleasure of passers-by. The image had stayed with her and now she knew how it would feel: arousing and shocking, shocking that she should be so aroused.

'You are tired, mademoiselle.'

'Yes, monsieur,' she admitted.

Alain rose and opened a cabinet behind Isabelle's chair. She immediately began to think of whips and ties. A moment later though, there was the sound of a bottle being opened.

'Will you take some wine?' he asked.

She nodded, grateful for his consideration, and took the proffered glass.

'Rest for a moment,' he told her. Alain took his own glass out into the courtyard and sat down on a stone bench beneath the cedar.

Left alone, Isabelle drank deeply and asked herself why it was so difficult to describe the facts of her experience at the villa. Alain had certainly not condemned her for anything that she had done or allowed to be done. On the contrary he had murmured encouragement when she said how this act had excited her or that act made her want more. Perhaps, she thought, it was the way that he made clear truths about herself that she didn't care to acknowledge. He would never let her escape responsibility for her desires or allow her to pretend that somehow she was forced to this act or compelled to that pleasure. He rendered her carnality plain and her desire for self-abasement obvious. Where Robert took pleasure in opening her body, Alain took pleasure in opening her mind. As she was thinking these things, Alain called through the open door.

'Remove your clothes, mademoiselle. I will have you naked for the rest of your visit.'

Alain too, it seemed, would have her body opened and a bolt of nervous excitement passed through her. She forced herself to be calm and undressed without haste, folding her clothes carefully and arranging them neatly on the desk. She could see Alain in the courtyard as she did these things. He drank his wine slowly and at one point, yawned. It stung her that he could be so apparently indifferent to the woman who prepared herself for him, the woman who waited to do as he wished. There was a small mirror on one wall and Isabelle stood before it examining herself. She tucked a few stray strands of hair behind her ears and, wetting the tips of her fingers, smoothed the line of her eyebrows. There was a small sound from the courtyard at that moment and she turned quickly, thinking that Alain might be watching her. He had not moved but still she blushed, the colour rising to her cheeks as she accused herself of inviting caresses from a man that she did not desire.

'Light the candles if you please,' Alain called, still not troubling to turn around. If he had, he would have seen Isabelle standing quite naked, gazing at him as a child gazes at a stranger, apprehensive and curious, wishing to run and to approach, both at the same time. She brushed her fingers across her nipples so that they stood erect. At the very least she wanted him to desire her. She wanted some small measure of power.

When his glass was empty Alain returned to the small

room. The light from the candles was weak in the partial daylight but it still gave a soft warmth to Isabelle's flawless skin. She blushed as he stood over her and stared first at her breasts and then at the hairless space between her legs. No one else's mere presence could make her so self-conscious and she felt panicky as if there were no air in the room. All ideas that she might have some power over him evaporated immediately.

He placed his glass beside her clothes and sat. 'Some women think that I am a monster,' he said with a smile. 'I am not good looking, I have terrible scars from smallpox, I am . . . oversized. In the drawing rooms of Paris and London I have seen young ladies wince as I am introduced, the very young ladies whose sisters I have already had perform acts that would make a soldier blush to ask for.'

He laughed to think of it, a heavy rolling laugh like a wave breaking in a deep cave. Isabelle had not heard him laugh before and looked at him in surprise.

'Monsieur! Please don't think that I see you as a monster.' Isabelle sat forward in her chair as she said this and her hand faltered as if on the point of reaching to him.

'Those women, seeing us in this room would think of beauty and the beast,' he said softly, with the gentlest of smiles.

Isabelle lowered her head with a sigh. 'I don't see you as a monster, monsieur,' she assured him once again, 'but I've always been frightened of you. I don't know why.'

'A little fear is no bad thing, mademoiselle. It excites. Is that not so?'

She looked at him but could not reply.

'Open your legs. Touch yourself.'

Beneath the coolness of his scrutiny this was not easy, but she did it. He watched as her fingers moved and as her eyes liquefied.

'That is enough,' he told her after a few minutes.

She took her hand away as soon as he spoke but the excitement stayed in her belly.

'Yes, I can see it in you. The fear and the uncertainty adds something to the pleasure,' he paused for a moment

187

before continuing in an almost dismissive tone. 'Touch yourself as you wish. I shall not ask it of you again but I will not stop you.'

Isabelle wanted to immediately. It was the same feeling that she had in the library, but here there was no Robert. She wanted to take herself to a climax and she wanted a man who she did not love, a man who frightened her, to watch. Yet as much as she wanted it, she could not move her hand, not entirely of her own volition. She wanted him to order it.

'I need you to make the rules,' she said.

This was not something that she could ever have imagined saying. The words seemed to come from nowhere. He nodded, understanding the import of those words, savouring them.

'Then let us say, when you desire to touch yourself, I shall expect you to do it. But it will not interfere with anything else that I ask of you. Is that clear?'

'I understand, monsieur.'

Alain rose from his chair and held out his hands. 'Your feet, mademoiselle.'

She raised her legs and he took hold of her ankles, pulling her forward until her behind rested on the edge of the seat. He opened her legs wide and lay them one on each of the arm rests. He held one of her feet for a moment longer than he needed to and stroked her instep with his thumb making her shiver. Her sex opened as he watched, as Isabelle herself watched. Again she wanted to touch herself and he seemed to know this and waited for her. When she froze he fetched a cushion from his own chair and placed it behind her so that she was comfortable. As he leant over to do this she thought that he would kiss her. For a moment at least, she had wanted him to, but that was not his intention and he sat again, looking at her coolly.

'You lost your courage, mademoiselle.'

'Yes.'

'Next time you will be punished.'

She nodded. If she asked him to make the rules and then

188

failed to follow them, punishment was to be expected. They were silent for a few minutes. Isabelle was overly aware of the clock ticking. There was a desire to touch herself again, a sort of nervous reaction to the tension in the room. The thought that, at some point she would do this, was strangling her.

'There are some details,' he began again, 'omissions, errors, lies perhaps in what you said earlier.'

She made to protest but he raised his hand.

'When Robert asked if you'd ever been with a woman, had sex with a woman that is, you said that you hadn't. You also told him that you had never shown yourself naked to a man, and that no one had ever touched you between the legs to give you pleasure.'

She looked at him oddly but held her silence.

'What of Anne-Marie?' he asked.

'What did she tell you?' Isabelle asked quietly, a sinking feeling in her stomach.

'What Anne-Marie said is not important. I want to hear what happened from you.'

'That is my family. I will tell you anything that has happened at the villa, but I beg you not to ask for more than that.'

'You promised complete openness. There were no time limits, no areas that were out of bounds.'

Isabelle knew that this was true but couldn't bring herself to speak of the summer that her own sister had seduced her and made her behave as one day Robert would make her behave.

'I could have you beaten until your skin hangs in tatters,' he told her, 'or I could banish you from the estate.'

She looked at him helplessly. Banishment would mean never seeing Robert again. Alain knew the power that he wielded and she realised that he never doubted that he would make her speak. Just as it seemed that it was possible for her to cede everything that he wanted, he made demands that were impossible to meet. The room swam before her eyes.

'You know it all,' she said, 'this is simply to humiliate me.'

He frowned. 'I have no need to tolerate any dissent,' he reminded her.

Even knowing that it would be so much simpler to speak, she shook her head. 'I was so young.'

'Tell me.'

'I cannot.'

'I understand your reticence, Isabelle. You want to protect that younger self, but speak now and there will be no more secrets, no more burdens for you to carry. You will be known, seen completely, and you will realise that in your nakedness is freedom. Your shame is sweet, child, but sweeter will be the freedom of revealing all.'

His words sank into her slowly, dissolving and moving through her thoughts like a drug. She barely understood what he meant but from somewhere had come an excitement; a renewal of the desire to expose herself to his gaze and something else, a wish to stir him with what she had done with Anne-Marie.

He watched as she wrestled with her anxieties and with this new temptation. He must have known that she could not consent easily to describe the events that interested him and offered her a beginning.

'Close your eyes, Isabelle. Don't speak, simply think back to what happened. Think and remember while I'm with you.'

She closed her eyes, grateful to escape his scrutiny for a while. Within that security she could have chosen to think of anything, but it was Anne-Marie who came into focus, Anne-Marie and the summer three years ago.

21

The Sisters of Severcy

Isabelle remembered the year that Anne-Marie had changed, the year that they had stopped bickering as sisters do and Isabelle had fallen in love. The family had gone to Paris in March as they always did. There were the usual diversions; walking or sometimes riding in the parks, the dances and river outings. That summer though, the family attracted young men as it had never done before. Anne-Marie had suddenly blossomed into a young woman, and a women of such charm and poise and such sexual élan that any man who saw her was immediately drawn. In the hope that Anne-Marie would make a good match, their mother had invested in new dresses for the entire family and employed all of her charm on the more eligible suitors. For three months there was an excitement as everyone, Isabelle's cousins and aunts included, were swept into a vortex of courtship and adolescent desire. Her uncle's small house on the Boulevard St Etienne was full of intrigue, speculation, raised expectations and dashed hopes as suitors vied and occasionally fought for the hand of Anne-Marie. Yet, while she encouraged the attentions of many men it was clear by the end that she wouldn't settle for any as a husband.

It was with some disappointment that their mother took them back to Severcy in July. The only person not sad to return was Anne-Marie herself. On her seventeenth birthday, two days after the long journey from Paris, she received a gift from the villa, a pure white gelding, and no one could have been prouder. She rode it almost every day, neglecting her household duties and putting aside her studies.

If Anne-Marie had changed in Paris it was nothing to the change that came over her at that time. It was impossible for the young Isabelle to understand. Her sister seemed to radiate a heat and light and wasn't quite earthly. The transformation was in no way religious though. Anne-Marie seemed to have slowed to a state of absolute tranquility, and was enveloped in a haze of rapture so that every small pleasure, every smile from another, every touch was taken in, magnified, enhanced and reflected back. It could be taken for love but there was a physical quality to all of this; she seemed to take sensual pleasure in every movement, every impression of the world on her senses. Looking back, Isabelle knew that it was at this time that Anne-Marie had first fallen into the hands of Alain. Perhaps he had done to Anne-Marie what Robert was doing to her, slowly peeling back layer after layer of desire to reach its electric centre. Perhaps, after all, Anne-Marie was in love and if not, Isabelle certainly was, or at least in a kind of love. She had fallen under the spell of the woman who could drown a man with a smile and it should have surprised no one who knew the quiet, impressionable, younger sister.

Isabelle recalled the first time that Anne-Marie had kissed her. They were walking together among the fig trees that surrounded their home. It was early August and they were talking about things that had happened in Paris a few weeks before. Isabelle was teasing away at Anne-Marie, trying to draw out the secrets of her affairs. She especially wanted to know about an exceptionally handsome boy, Lucien, who had fallen hard for Anne-Marie and who had a rather melancholy air that appealed to Isabelle. A few weeks before they had left Paris he had taken Anne-Marie to the Avenue Foche, and Isabelle had followed them guiltily as they turned into a side street and entered a small restaurant. There was a sign beside the door saying that private rooms were available and Isabelle had known that the couple had taken one when she glimpsed them climbing the stairs to the first floor through the street window.

'Do you really want to know what we did?' Anne-Marie asked.

'Of course.'

'Do you think that you're old enough?'

'I'm sixteen!' Isabelle replied in exasperation.

Anne-Marie looked at her and Isabelle knew what she was thinking. She was thinking that her sixteen was a very young sixteen, a sixteen that hardly counted when it was burdened with such innocence.

'What do you think that men and women do when they're alone?'

All of this was a tease designed to send Isabelle mad.

'All sorts of things.'

'Tell me.'

'No.'

'Tell me. Or I won't say another word about Lucien, ever.'

'They kiss.'

'And?'

'Touch.'

Anne-Marie nodded and pulled Isabelle to face her. 'How do they kiss?'

'With their lips of course.'

'Show me.'

Isabelle had leant forward and brushed Anne-Marie's cheek with her pursed lips. They both laughed.

'How do they touch?'

Isabelle reached out her hand and laid it on Anne-Marie's hip. It made Isabelle giggle uncontrollably when the older girl did the same to her.

'It tickles,' said Isabelle.

Anne-Marie had shaken her head as if Isabelle was a hopeless case. She took the hand that still rested on her hip and led her deeper into the woods.

The figs were ripening, turning from green to brown and emitting that characteristic scent, sweet and thick. They went to the seat by the old stables. When Isabelle had seated herself, Anne-Marie looked at her with a peculiar expression. It was intent, questioning, as if Anne-Marie were assessing something, judging if it was right or perhaps if it was the right time. Whatever occupied her mind it was something complex, something that might go awry. Quite abruptly, she sat, and taking Isabelle's chin she kissed her sister. It was a light, sucking kiss, applied deftly to Isabelle's lower lip drawing it out, enveloping it in moist warmth, electrifying the young girl.

'That is one of the ways that men and women kiss,' Anne-Marie said, her expression serious yet tender. Then she released Isabelle's chin with a sigh.

'What are the other ways?' Isabelle asked after a moment, her voice low and tense.

'There are so many.'

They had looked at each other as if trying to read each other's thoughts.

'I will come to your room tonight,' murmured Anne-Marie. 'It will be very late so don't try to stay awake. I will show you something and I will tell you about that boy, the one that you liked.'

Isabelle considered this. She knew that what Anne-Marie proposed was a prelude to something that should not be done, should not even be thought of, but she wanted to know about the boy and nodded. They were silent for a while, then Anne-Marie jumped up and said she would race her to the house and that the last there would make lemonade. They ran off screaming through the woods. Nothing more was said of the nocturnal visit for the rest of the afternoon. After the evening meal Anne-Marie had ridden off on her horse and hadn't returned by the time that Isabelle had gone to bed.

The house was absolutely quiet when Isabelle was awoken by a hand on her shoulder. Anne-Marie was sitting on the side of the bed, her face flushed, as she looked down at the drowsy girl. Their was a candle burning on the chest of drawers and Isabelle's eyes flinched away from it.

'I'm sorry, my angel,' Anne-Marie murmured. She

shielded her sister's eyes from the unwelcome light with a warm hand.

'I can smell horse,' Isabelle murmured.

'Don't you like it?'

Isabelle kissed Anne-Marie's hand by way of an answer and Anne-Marie slipped into the bed, holding the younger girl from behind.

'Your heart is racing,' Anne-Marie murmured.

'I'm frightened.'

'Shall I go?'

Isabelle didn't want that. It was so good to be held, so good to feel the softness and heat of her sister's body. But it was wrong to feel another warmth, the warmth that stole into her loins unbidden. She remembered seeing Anne-Marie with a man in Paris, an older man who had once pressed his hands to Anne-Marie's breasts in the garden at the Boulevard St Etienne. Isabelle had felt a similar warmth then but she hadn't desired the man, it was the look on her sister's face that had stirred her; a look of giving into something, a low pleasure, seductive and wordless. It was the beauty of Anne-Marie that had made the warmth funnel up Isabelle's young thighs and had made her heart somersault. And now that beauty enfolded her.

'Take this off,' Anne-Marie whispered, tugging at Isabelle's nightshirt.

Isabelle wriggled her way free of the silken encumbrance and Anne-Marie sat up to look at her.

'Turn around, let me see you.'

Reluctantly, half expecting to be teased, Isabelle turned on to her back and with her eyes still closed, allowed the bedclothes to be pulled down to her waist.

'Your bosom is very fine,' said Anne-Marie, with little real surprise. 'My sister is a swan after all.'

Isabelle opened her eyes and smiled. 'Let me see yours.'

Anne-Marie was wearing a white muslin dress with a high waist and delicate print of pastel flowers. The neckline was low and by slipping off a shoulder she was able to free one of her breasts. It was as sumptuous as Isabelle had imagined, large and firm, the skin flushed with health and

195

the nipple full. Isabelle thought of a painting of Artemis that she had seen in the Gallerie D'Or.

'We are being very bad,' Anne-Marie said softly.

'I know,' Isabelle replied.

'Do you want to be bad with me?'

Isabelle nodded.

'Very bad?'

They looked at each other intently and Isabelle nodded again.

Anne-Marie lifted her exposed breast and brushed her thumb across the nipple until it became erect.

'Suck on it,' she said.

Isabelle propped herself up on her elbows and reached with her lips. There was a slight salt taste. As she sucked it made her dizzy, as if the skin were soaked in some narcotic. Anne-Marie stroked the side of Isabelle's head murmuring soft endearments, telling her to suck harder, to use her tongue, to eat as if she were starved. Even when Isabelle forgot herself and bit, Anne-Marie kept on whispering encouragements. She pulled the other breast free and offered this one too. The young girl moved from one to the other quickly, as if she might miss something. Isabelle was breathing heavily when Anne-Marie finally eased her mouth away.

'You can have them any time,' she said as Isabelle lay back on the bed. 'You have only to ask.'

Isabelle reached out her hand and grasped the breast that was nearest to her.

'Did the boy suck it?' she asked. 'The sad one, Lucien?'

Anne-Marie nodded.

'Did you both take your clothes off?'

'Yes.'

'Did you touch him all over?'

'Every part.'

Isabelle nodded and looked away.

'Are you jealous?' Anne-Marie asked gently.

'Yes.'

'I will tell you everything, if you want to know. If it will excite you.'

Isabelle looked at her. 'He knew that I liked him but he didn't even look at me because of you.'

'I'm sorry.'

'Are you?'

'Next year they will all want you.'

Isabelle shrugged. 'Tell me about him.'

Anne-Marie smiled. 'First, let me see all of you.'

Isabelle hesitated for a moment and then pulled the sheet down past her knees.

'He was a very silly boy not to look at you,' Anne-Marie sighed, as Isabelle's slender thighs emerged into the candle light.

Anne-Marie rested her hand on the slight swell of the girl's belly, just above the place where the sparse hair began. The warm flesh moved as Isabelle breathed.

'Open your legs, let me look.'

Isabelle parted her thighs and Anne-Marie moved her hand downwards making her sister gasp as it passed over her virgin sex. The fingers trailed all the way to the inside of Isabelle's knee and back again to rest over her mound. They looked at each other, reading the shared desire until Anne-Marie asked if Isabelle still wanted to hear about the boy. Isabelle nodded and Anne-Marie felt a heat grow beneath her hand as she told her story. She described the evening of their first kiss in the Luxembourg Gardens, how she had lost her hat as Lucien bent her back against a tree, how he'd been embarrassed that a woman he knew had seen them in the twilight. She described the first time he had touched her behind and the first time he had unbuttoned her blouse to touch her breasts – this in Isabelle's bedroom while she was visiting a market with her aunt. They had lain on the bed and he had said that he loved her, and that she was his only happiness.

Isabelle listened with a mixture of jealousy and desire, asking for details, asking if he touched her gently or hungrily, wanting to know how Anne-Marie had touched him and what they had said. When Anne-Marie described the little room they had gone to, the room off the Avenue Foche, Isabelle began to get very excited. From

Anne-Marie's description she could visualise so clearly how the boy looked as he undressed and how he had lifted Anne-Marie on to the bed once she too was naked. She could imagine his sex hard against her sister's stomach and the way he had held her hands above her head so that she felt vulnerable and exposed. She could imagine how Anne-Marie had liked that feeling and had left her hands there as his fingers took her sex and squeezed. She imagined it all, the kissing and the sucking, the penetration, the sweet relaxation afterwards.

'Was he the only one?' Isabelle asked, when Anne-Marie finished telling the story.

The older sister shook her head with a smile.

'Who were the others?'

'I will tell you another night. I'll tell you it all. That boy was a lamb. Not all boys are like that. Some of them know quite different ways to excite a girl.'

Isabelle's curiosity was so strongly stirred she could not leave it at that. 'Tell me now.'

'Shhh!' Anne-Marie pressed her fingers to her sister's lips and turned to the door. In her eagerness, Isabelle's voice had echoed through the house. They remained absolutely still until they were sure that no one had heard. When Anne-Marie spoke again it was in a whisper. 'Do you touch yourself here?' she said, pressing lightly on Isabelle's sex.

'Yes.'

'Show me.'

Isabelle was embarrassed and had to be encouraged with little kisses, with teasing, with soft promises not to make fun of her. Finally she lay her hand over her sex and began to squeeze the whole area. She became excited quickly, thinking of what Anne-Marie had told her of the boy, but no matter how she squeezed there was nothing more than the steady excitement. Eventually she stopped because she was tired.

'Don't you take it to completion?' asked Anne-Marie.

Isabelle didn't understand.

'Do you ever feel more? Do you climax?'

Isabelle remembered what Anne-Marie had said about

the boy in Paris, how at the end he had groaned and his back had arched as he stabbed into her sister and how she had felt his sperm, warm and wet in her sex.

'Like a boy's?' she asked.

'Yes, like that but better. The pleasure can go on for as long as you want it to.'

Isabelle felt foolish that she didn't know this and looked away.

'Let me show you,' said her sister.

While Isabelle knelt at the foot of the bed, Anne-Marie slipped off her dress and sat up against the head board. She opened her legs wide and showed Isabelle her sex.

'It is almost bald,' said Isabelle in surprise.

'I pluck it,' said Isabelle, 'men like that, it makes us more naked.'

Isabelle had too recently acquired her sexual hair to think of losing it again, but she could not deny how beautiful her sister's mound looked with the lower part bare and just a carefully trimmed triangle below her navel.

Anne-Marie pulled the lips open so that Isabelle could see inside. She showed her the opening to her belly and she showed her, most especially, the little bud that nestled at the apex of her lips.

'Is this part of you sensitive?'

Isabelle nodded.

'Do you touch it?'

'When I'm excited it is so – it makes me feel dizzy.'

Anne-Marie smiled. 'That is good, but you need to go further. Let me show you.'

Sitting quite upright, astonishing in the soft light of the candle with her flat broad belly and full, high breasts, Anne-Marie caressed herself while her young sister watched. She did not hurry. She let the pleasure take her slowly as she ran her finger in the groove beside her little bud. When she climaxed it was with soft groans and a shaking of her head from side to side. She exercised control so that the pleasure went on and on, so that climax after climax took her. Isabelle knew by watching her that this was something she had never felt herself; she wanted to.

When Anne-Marie finally finished, she smiled the most marvellous smile that Isabelle had ever seen. It was full, unguarded, gentle, and spoke of the deepest satisfaction. If Isabelle had not been in love before that moment she was now.

'Sit beside me,' Anne-Marie said, patting the bed.

Isabelle crawled over on all fours. Anne-Marie put an arm around her waist and kissed her full on the lips. Her tongue pushed into her sister's mouth and the young girl was astonished by the feeling. She laid her hand on Anne-Marie's breast and pressed.

'Do you want to try again?' Anne-Marie asked, when they separated.

Isabelle was embarrassed once more and her sister had to take the girl's hand to her sex.

'A girl is so beautiful when she caresses herself,' Anne-Marie said. 'There is nothing to be ashamed of.'

Isabelle started moving her hand, using her fingers as Anne-Marie had. At first she felt uncomfortable, then the feelings came, the feelings that made her dizzy. Anne-Marie seemed to sense this and turned the girl to face her. She held Isabelle with her eyes and Isabelle's feelings strengthened. Her belly filled with the unfamiliar sensations of deep arousal and she began to gasp.

'Steadily, my darling,' Anne-Marie warned when Isabelle's fingers moved faster and faster. Isabelle slowed and the arousal became less sharp but fuller. She continued for a long time and the sensations in her belly spread to her breasts then down the insides of her thighs.

She might have climaxed but Anne-Marie took her hand and pulled it from her sex.

'There is no hurry,' she said.

Isabelle was disappointed but the sensations had been so good that she hugged her sister. 'I didn't know it could be like that.'

'It can be better.'

'Will you show me?'

'In good time.'

They held each other for a while then Anne-Marie

disengaged herself and sat on the edge of the bed. 'It is time for you to sleep.' She took the nightdress that lay on the floor and helped Isabelle into it. When the girl was tucked up in bed, Anne-Marie leant over and kissed her.

'I will come for you tomorrow night,' she said, 'if you want me too.'

Isabelle nodded.

'You mustn't touch yourself though, not unless I'm here.'

'Why not?'

'I want to be with you the first time. Will you swear?'

Isabelle frowned. 'Not even the way that I used to touch myself?' she asked.

'Not even that. I will know if you do. A girl is different after she has climaxed, boys see it too, though they don't know what they see. They simply start wanting you. In Paris next year, after I have let you climax, they will follow you like motherless lambs, but for now I want you to swear that you will not play with yourself.'

Isabelle swore. Anne-Marie kissed her cheek and left, taking the candle with her. It was hard for Isabelle to sleep with all that she had heard and seen. Strong feelings still lingered in her belly and it was hard to keep her promise and not touch herself.

The next day, Isabelle hardly saw Anne-Marie. She was in the habit of going to the villa every day and she went that day too. Isabelle found it difficult to concentrate on her studies and by afternoon she had abandoned them. There was a strange feeling between her legs, a sense that her sex was somehow open, as if something that had always covered it were gone. The feeling was not something that she could explain to herself, but it focused her attention on the places that Anne-Marie had explored and left her no peace.

That night she deliberately slept naked so that her sister would find her that way. She dreamt of Paris, as she often dreamt of Paris, but this time it was different. She saw herself in the garden on the Boulevard St Etienne with Anne-Marie and the older man. He was handsome in a dark way, not smiling but strong. He touched Anne-Marie's breasts and made her groan then he turned and looked at Isabelle. Anne-Marie beckoned and Isabelle went to them. Her sister took hold of her dress at the bust, pulling downwards. The dress came away and Isabelle was completely naked. The man touched her stomach and the arousal was powerful.

In this way, she was already excited when Anne-Marie woke her. Once she was fully awake Isabelle related the dream and asked about the man. Anne-Marie was reluctant to begin with but eventually, after Isabelle had reminded her of her promise to tell everything, she told the story. She had been introduced to the man, Abelard, the previous year at the theatre but he had many women and would only see Anne-Marie occasionally. That first spring he was charming and he treated her as a grown woman though she was barely more than a child. He seduced her with little presents and meals in secluded corners of restaurants where lovers met. Even though her cousins warned her of Abelard's reputation, Anne-Marie allowed him to take her the first time that he lifted her skirts. His love-making was tender those first few times, but strong. With him it was always strong. During the most recent visit to Paris, Abelard made quite different demands on her. Anne-Marie met them, partly because she feared that he would forget her if she didn't, and partly because they excited her.

Isabelle lay on her front as she listened to her sister. She had a pillow between her legs which raised her behind and pressed into her sex. Anne-Marie said that she should imagine that she had a man's sex and that the pillow was a girl. She said that only when she could understand how a man felt and what a man wanted could she truly give herself. And only when she could truly give herself would she be a woman. Isabelle rocked her pelvis slowly as Anne-Marie told her story and the wetness flowed from her into the pillow. There was the scent and heat of female desire in that room, but in her mind, Isabelle lived the story through the man's eyes.

'Abelard would write me little notes when he wanted to see me, and he would say what it was that he wanted or what it was that he intended to do. He was always very blunt, very detailed. The notes alone excited me. I won't tell you all of the things that we did, not tonight, only the things that . . . the things that don't make me blush.'

Isabelle smiled. She could hardly believe that her sister was capable of blushing and wished to see it.

'The afternoon that you saw us in the garden we had deliberately met there so that we would be seen. You were not the intended audience though. That was to be Lucien. Abelard wanted to take me while the boy watched. If you had looked above your head, you would have seen Lucien at the window on the stairs.'

Isabelle gave a little gasp as she heard this. 'How could you be so cruel?' she asked, shocked.

Anne-Marie paused, looking a little abashed. 'It was for Abelard. He cast such a spell over me, he –' She could not explain. 'Shall I stop?'

Isabelle shook her head. She half understood, at least the lower half of her body understood, for she was very excited. In her mind, as she took Abelard's part, she sensed the excitement of compelling a woman to betray a man who loved her.

'When Abelard saw that you were in the garden he abandoned the idea,' Anne-Marie continued. 'He took me to the restaurant off the Avenue Foche instead. He knew that was where I went with the boy. To our surprise, well to mine at least, the boy followed us. Abelard took me to the bar first and we drank absinthe. He touched me all the while and though I didn't look, I knew that Lucien would be watching us through the street window, just as you once did. After we had finished drinking, Abelard called for the manager and asked for a room. The manager recognised me of course, but said nothing. It is easy to imagine what he thought.

On the stairs Abelard put his hand under my skirt and

touched my thighs. The manager was behind us. I don't know how much he saw but he was sweating when he unlocked the door and handed Abelard the key. We had hardly undressed when we heard the door to the adjoining room opening and then slamming shut. Abelard was convinced that it was the boy. I felt it too. I thought that he would burst in at any moment, I even imagined that he would have a knife or a pistol and that we would be killed. He didn't burst in but he must have listened. The walls were so thin you could hear someone sigh on the other side. Abelard took me with great passion, he issued instructions as to how I should lie or kneel and told me in a loud, clear voice how much he was enjoying my mouth or my cul. Lucien must have heard everything. It was cruel and it was despicable and it excited me. When I climaxed, and Abelard ensured that I climaxed many times more than I had ever climaxed with Lucien, I made such a noise that I thought the manager would return and expel us. I couldn't help it. As soon as Abelard had done with me he pulled on his clothes and went, leaving the door to the room wide open. I was still breathing heavily and still naked when Lucien came to the door. He stood there and looked at me. His face was entirely white as if someone had died. He said nothing and after a few, very long minutes he went. A few days later I heard that he was leaving Paris. It was said that a woman had broken his heart.'

Anne-Marie paused and looked at her sister. Isabelle was clearly spellbound by the story and Anne-Marie continued. 'One day, just before Lucien was due to leave, he came to the house and asked me to go to the private rooms with him. He was very cool as he spoke, as if I were a stranger. After what I had done, I couldn't refuse him. I fetched my hat and gloves and we walked quickly through the streets in silence. I didn't even try to apologise, what could I have said? When we had taken the room he pulled money from his pocket and dropped it on the table near the bed. He asked me if it was enough and said that he wanted all my services. On impulse I took the crumpled notes and counted them. It wouldn't have been enough to buy a girl in one of the worst districts and he knew that. I slipped the notes into the table drawer and said that it would cover anything that he wanted. He watched as I took my clothes off and washed at the little sink in the way that girls who have sex for money do. He had me pose for him, standing at first, then lying on the bed. He liked telling me what to do. He had me hold myself open –'

Anne-Marie paused and looked at her sister. 'I shouldn't be telling you all of this,' she said.

'You promised,' Isabelle breathed.

Anne-Marie could not fail to see her sister's arousal nor the slight but continuous movements of her pelvis. 'Is the pillow me?' she asked.

Isabelle smiled. 'It is what you said I should do.'

Anne-Marie laughed and continued her story. 'Lucien didn't trouble to undress, he just pulled his cock from the front of his breeches and knelt between my legs. There were no caresses, he just spat on his hand and made me wet that way. He used his sex as if it were a sword and he wanted to disembowel me. I had never seen such cold anger on any face before. He pinned my hands to the headboard and just went into me, relentlessly, without any tenderness. He had me turn over and took me from behind while I was lying down. He talked then, calling me names, calling me every bad thing. He wanted to know exactly what I'd done with Abelard, how many times, and he jeered at me when I told him, spitting the words into my ear. I began to get excited and he taunted me about that, saying that whores who took pleasure with their clients were worse than animals. I won't tell you everything that he said, but all the time that I climaxed he whispered insults and obscenities in my ears. When he was ready, he stood and turned me on to my back. He shed his seed on my face and in my hair, holding me from the bed by the back of my neck and shouting that I must not move nor close my mouth nor eyes.'

Isabelle's own eyes had grown wider and wider as the story was told and at the end she gasped. 'Did you see him again?' she asked.

Anne-Marie shook her head.

'Do you think that you will?'

'He will have forgotten me by now.'

Isabelle shook her head. She knew that he would never forget. She had seen through his eyes in that sordid room and she knew what it had meant to him. She took her sister's hand and squeezed it. 'You were very, very bad,' she said, 'but so brave!'

Anne-Marie laughed. 'And you, my brave man,' she said, 'is the girl soaked with your emissions?'

Isabelle blushed.

'Show me,' demanded Anne-Marie.

Isabelle took the pillow from between her legs and held it out. Where it had rested against her sex, the linen was saturated.

'Then that is enough for tonight. Tomorrow we will do something else. Meet me at the stables at three o'clock. Be prepared to ride.' With these words and a light kiss to each of Isabelle's cheeks she slipped from the bed and disappeared.

The following afternoon Isabelle met her sister at the stables. Anne-Marie would explain nothing, simply telling Isabelle to follow her as she mounted her white gelding. It was a struggle for the younger girl to keep up as they made their way down the dusty tracks and eventually came to the villa. They allowed the horses to drink from a stream and tied them in the shade of a broad cedar tree.

'Are we allowed to?' asked Isabelle, as Anne-Marie led them into the villa through an open door at the side of the building.

'Monsieur Alain lets me come whenever I want to. He probably isn't here.'

They walked down a long corridor lined with marble busts standing on classical pillars. A serving girl came out of one of the rooms carrying a tray and curtsied when she saw the girls.

'Is the master at home, Antoinette?' Anne-Marie asked.

'He went out this morning, mademoiselle,' replied the girl. 'We don't expect him back until nightfall.'

Anne-Marie smiled at Isabelle. 'Then we have the whole afternoon and evening to ourselves.'

Since they had no respects to pay and since the villa was very warm they went out into the gardens. The sun was no longer at its most fierce and there was a cooling breeze. Anne-Marie took Isabelle through the parterre and into a secluded nook formed of carefully clipped box hedges. A rose trellis gave some shade and there was a small pond with a tiny, gurgling fountain. Anne-Marie sat on the stone surround to the pond and, raising her dress to her knees, dangled her feet into the water. Isabelle sat on the other side of the pond and did the same. She felt like a peasant girl as she moved her legs back and forth, scattering the water lilies. Their mother would have been shocked.

'Do you like it?' asked Anne-Marie. 'It's one of my favourite corners.'

'It's beautiful.'

'Did you have any more dreams?'

Isabelle shook her head. They were silent for a few moments as they listened to the afternoon, to the cicadas, to the light breeze, to the fountain.

'Are we going to be bad again?' Isabelle asked.

'Of course.' Anne-Marie had the face of an angel as she said this.

'Here?' Isabelle asked a little apprehensively.

'No one can see us.'

The spot was well hidden, but certain of the windows in the villa overlooked it and besides this there were gardeners; Isabelle had seen a number of men with wheelbarrows and hoes as they rode in.

'Take off your dress,' Anne-Marie told her.

Isabelle laughed. 'No.'

Anne-Marie kicked some water into the air, and a few drops fell on to her sister soaking into the cream coloured silk. 'Take it off.'

'If you take yours off.'

Anne-Marie stood up and walked around the pond. She knelt behind her sister, opening her legs so that they went around Isabelle's slender waist and held her. She turned the girl's face to her own and stroked her lips with the tip of a finger.

'Today is going to be special,' Anne-Marie said, 'but you have to do as I tell you.'

The embrace, the closeness, melted Isabelle. She would have agreed to anything at that moment. When Anne-Marie rose and touched her lightly beneath the arms, Isabelle stood and allowed herself to be undressed. There was a small grassed area beneath the rose trellis and Isabelle knelt there when she was told to. As the breeze moved through the rose leaves, light and shadow played across her naked skin. Anne-Marie looked at her for a moment then crouched and reached into the pond. Her hand emerged dripping and, as she shook it, water droplets span through the air, glistening. Clasped in her fingers was a lily flower, not fully open but more than a bud. She carried this to Isabelle and knelt before her. They looked into each other's eyes.

'Open your legs, and put your hands behind your back,' Anne-Marie said softly.

Isabelle edged her knees apart and folded her hands together in the small of her back.

Anne-Marie trailed the flower across Isabelle's skin and its coolness made her gasp. She drew the stiff, waxy petals of the flower around her sister's nipples so that they stood erect, and then moved downwards. At Isabelle's navel, Anne-Marie turned the flower around and pressed the bulbous, sepalled base into the shallow opening. Because it was still moist and because Anne-Marie twisted it, the flower was held in place by suction when she removed her hand. They looked down simultaneously at the strange growth, the petals so very white against the smooth skin.

'Pretty,' said Isabelle.

'Yes.'

Anne-Marie leant forward and took Isabelle's lips with her own. The kiss was delicate, a girl's kiss. Anne-Marie's tongue was a nervous caller as it repeatedly pressed at the junction of her sister's lips. When those lips opened it darted inside for a moment only to withdraw as quickly.

Isabelle pushed the tip of her own tongue outwards, catching at her sister's as if trying to draw this shy visitor in, to offer reassurance, to embolden by acquiescence.

Isabelle tried to push into Anne-Marie's mouth but was not allowed to – the teeth closed against her. Only when Isabelle opened her mouth and lay her tongue quietly aside did the visitor return, searching along her parted lips before entering quickly, like a thief. As soon as Isabelle tried to make any movement, the tongue withdrew and she was forced to wait passively again. In this way Anne-Marie took possession of the other girl's mouth, the kiss becoming stronger and stronger as Isabelle gave her mouth more and more freely. It excited her to be treated in this way, to have her hands behind her back and to give her mouth without any say in what was done. When Anne-Marie withdrew, Isabelle remained with her eyes closed and her mouth softly offered.

Anne-Marie plucked the flower from Isabelle's navel and drew it across her breasts again. 'Where else could I put this?' Anne-Marie asked as she stimulated the fully dilated, so very sensitive, coral tips of those sweet breasts.

Isabelle knew what Anne-Marie wanted to do. 'My cul,' she whispered.

Anne-Marie kept at her breasts for a while and kissed her repeatedly. The kisses were not delicate now. She went to Isabelle's mouth as if it was a jar of honey and she was scooping out the contents with great slow licks of her tongue. When she had her fill of this she told Isabelle to lean back and support herself on her elbows. This raised her pelvis and made her sex split open. Anne-Marie teased the skin of Isabelle's tautly stretched belly and circled the inflamed pink of her opening. When she slipped the base of the flower inside, Isabelle sighed. When Anne-Marie used her tongue on the flesh around the flower she groaned. When the excitement mounted to a fever pitch, Anne-Marie withdrew and told Isabelle to get dressed again. The girl did this without complaint, pulling the silk dress over her head and adjusting the high waist so that it fitted smoothly to her bust. The flower still nestled inside her, moving against her sensitive membranes insistently, so that it felt as if her sister were still touching her. Once Isabelle had finished dressing, Anne-Marie took a tiny pair of scissors from her pocket and asked Isabelle to raise her arms. She did so, but when Anne-Marie started to open the seam of the dress, at the join that ran from arm to waist, Isabelle protested.

'It is nothing,' her sister said. 'A needle and thread will repair it in an hour.' She opened the whole of the seam and now she could reach into the dress and touch Isabelle as she wished; both sex and behind were in easy reach. Anne-Marie opened the seam on the other side as well so that Isabelle could be touched from either the left or the right.

'Monsieur Abelard made me adjust some of my dresses so that he could reach inside them like this,' Anne-Marie said, stroking her sister's belly. 'He could undo the little hooks and eyes that secured the openings whenever he wished. He liked to torment me at the opera or in an open carriage as we drove along the streets. Once he made me climax while one of his friends watched in a restaurant.' Anne-Marie smiled when she saw that the thought of this excited her sister.

They walked through the gardens. Anne-Marie lay her arm around her sister's waist, inside the dress so that her fingers could reach the lily flower and ensure that it stayed in place.

'It was Monsieur Abelard who told me that you wanted me,' Anne-Marie said as they walked. 'He saw it in your face in the garden when he touched me.'

Isabelle remembered Abelard's expression. He had the kind of eyes that seemed to listen to another's thoughts rather than see. They seemed to follow the girls as they walked on. From time to time Anne-Marie would take the flower that nestled in Isabelle's sex and twist it, or pull it upwards, nudging against the little bud of pleasure until Isabelle felt faint with desire. They could see men in the distance tending to the gardens, and Anne-Marie steered her sister that way, teasing her that her first climax would

be in front of those rough men. Isabelle followed
Anne-Marie's lead meekly, but was grateful when they
turned into the villa instead.

Inside, as they walked down the long corridors,
Anne-Marie kept up the stimulation of her sister.
Eventually, Isabelle could no longer walk and collapsed
against a wall. Anne-Marie let her rest for a moment as she
hovered over the precipice of orgasm. Her hips were
moving strongly and she might have triggered her own
release if Anne-Marie hadn't told her to be still. As the
arousal faded and Isabelle was able to walk again,
Anne-Marie slipped her hand inside the dress and cupped
one of the cheeks of her sisters behind. The fingers touched
the flower from underneath but also the opening of the
unfilled passage, the passage that Anne-Marie had
neglected so far. The tip of her middle finger pressed
against the ring of muscle and circled until it gained a
shallow but definite entry. Thus, Isabelle was led to the
bedroom. Every step she took made those firm cheeks rub
one against the other. And those things that pushed into
her, the flower and the finger, edged her closer to her long
delayed crisis.

The room that Anne-Marie had chosen was large, with
high, open windows that looked across that part of the
gardens where they had just walked. A bed beneath an
awning of carefully draped gauze stood against one wall
and facing it was a long, low couch in the Ottoman style.
One wall of the room was formed of a wooden screen.
Intricate moorish patterns of the sort Isabelle had seen in
books had been carved into and through the light coloured
timber so that it formed a kind of fretwork. There were
other eastern artefacts, and the floor had been tiled in
white and black ceramic so that the whole had an exotic,
Arabian flavour.

Anne-Marie took Isabelle to one of the windows and
released her hold. There was a steady breeze into the room
which threaded its way through the opened seams of
Isabelle's dress, cooling her heated sex. This cooling was
only momentary though, for Anne-Marie moved behind

her sister and slipped both arms into the dress. After encircling Isabelle's waist for a moment and squeezing, the hands began their work again. They stood together in the full blaze of the sunlight, looking out into the gardens. All the time that they did, Anne-Marie's fingers moved and Isabelle groaned.

'Do you see the pond?' murmured Anne-Marie.

Isabelle found it impossible to focus, such was her closeness to pleasure's critical point. Anne-Marie pinched her hard, using thumb and forefinger on the soft flesh of her inner thigh. The girl squirmed and moaned.

'Look!' whispered Anne-Marie, 'I want you to see.'

Isabelle looked. From their vantage point, the little pond that they had sat beside was clearly visible, as was the place where she had knelt and where Anne-Marie had inserted the flower.

'When we were there none of these windows were open,' Anne-Marie said. 'Who do you think opened them?'

Isabelle didn't want to think about this question, she didn't care if anyone had seen them then, or if anyone saw her now. The fingers at her sex and the feelings that they stirred were too insistent. Anne-Marie left the question hanging as her lips grazed along the slope of Isabelle's neck to nibble at the lobe of the delicate childlike ear. When her fingers withdrew from Isabelle's sex they left a terrible sensation of wanting deep in the girl's belly.

'Can I trust you to touch yourself?' Anne-Marie asked. 'Can I trust you not to go too far and to stop when I say?'

Isabelle murmured that she could and her sister told her to do it. Isabelle reached inside the dress but it was awkward, the seam hadn't been opened far enough for her to touch herself easily. Anne-Marie took her arm and pulled it clear, then used her other hand to raise the dress to Isabelle's waist. Now Isabelle did think of who might see her framed in the open window. But when Anne-Marie placed Isabelle's hand over her sex, and she touched herself, the feelings were strong. Anne-Marie made Isabelle hold up the dress by herself, and sat on the low, broad window sill. From here she looked up at her sister as waves of excitement shook her body. Twice, Anne-Marie had to intervene, lightly pushing aside Isabelle's hand when the crisis point was too near. The girl allowed this with hardly a murmur of protest but the trembling of her lips and the shaking of her legs betrayed the cost of this compliance. When Anne-Marie pushed aside her hand for the third time Isabelle started to shake convulsively and sank to her knees in a near faint.

It was only then that Anne-Marie realised that she had asked too much and she quickly took the young girl in her arms. She held Isabelle steadily, whispering endearments and begging for forgiveness until the girl's breathing returned to normal and the shaking subsided. When all was well, Anne-Marie stood and removed Isabelle's dress completely, then lifted the girl in her arms and took her to the bed. Isabelle smiled to be carried in this way, like an exhausted child.

'You are making yourself heavy,' teased Anne-Marie as she struggled with her burden. When she reached the bed she dropped her charge in the middle of it with a sigh of relief.

The white gauze of the awning floated in the breeze above Isabelle as she lay there, naked, smiling. Her legs had been thrown open as Anne-Marie had let her fall and Isabelle made no move to close them. With her dark hair and wide brown eyes she must have looked like a houri awaiting her master in the seraglio. She gripped her toes in the sheet of fine golden damask for the pleasure of feeling its softness and let her head fall back with a satisfied sigh. Anne-Marie would have known well her sister's satisfaction in being seen like this. She had lain waiting for her own lovers in a similar way, waiting and wanting to see her beauty reflected in their eyes.

Anne-Marie undressed while Isabelle watched, then climbed on to the bed. The simple touch of her hand to the young girl's breasts was enough to arouse her again.

'Tell me more about Abelard,' Isabelle demanded, thinking of his darkly handsome features and his way of seeing into a person.

213

'There are others,' her sister replied.

'No, I want to know about Abelard.'

'A story?'

'Yes. The most wicked thing that you did.'

Anne-Marie thought for a while, then told the story of the day she had been summoned to a small hotel in the 9th Arrondissement. Isabelle lay with her head in her sister's lap as she listened and, from time to time, Anne-Marie would touch her, enough to keep her aroused but not so much as to excite her beyond her tolerance.

One afternoon in early June a note had arrived for Anne-Marie at the Boulevard St Etienne. It was unsigned but she recognised Abelard's hand as soon as she saw it. It told her the name and address of a hotel that she was to go to and said that there would be another note for her at the reception. It was a hot day and she had taken a carriage through the busy streets. At the hotel, the desk clerk had looked at her a little oddly when she gave her name, but said nothing as he handed her the key to a room on the top floor and a small envelope. The room was surprisingly grand, probably the best in the hotel and had a balcony from which she could see Notre Dame and the river.

Anne-Marie sat on a chair facing this view and opened the envelope. The note said that she was to remove her clothes and place them in the laundry basket in the hall. When she had done this she was to wait on the bed on all fours with her behind facing the door and a blindfold over her eyes. The blindfold was in the chest beside the bed. She was not to speak or ask any questions when the door opened but she was to be sure that she was ready for a man, that is, she was to be wet between the legs. Anne-Marie did as the note bid. The laundry basket was several paces down the hall from her door and, since she was naked, her heart was racing as she placed her clothes into it. Once back in the room, she knew that she was virtually a prisoner. In such hotels, clothes left out in this way were quickly taken for cleaning. She found the blindfold and slipped it over her eyes. She did not hurry but there was no telling when Abelard would choose to come and she wanted to be found exactly as the note instructed. She knelt and played with herself until she was wet and breathing heavily. There was no need to use any daydreams, the mere fact of preparing herself for her lover excited her. Then she waited. She remembered their last meeting at his apartments in the Place de Lyons. As they had lain in his bed, as he had moved inside her, he had asked if she would consent to have other men of his choosing take her. She had refused. Such a possibility had never occurred to before and she was still young enough to be shocked. He was cool with her for the remainder of the afternoon and though he made love to her a number of times he did not allow her to climax . In the evening he had taken her to a restaurant near the river where they met a friend of his, a Monsieur Dellyse.

Abelard had discussed Anne-Marie's refusal with his friend, making her blush. Dellyse had cool, grey, disrespectful eyes that wandered across Anne-Marie's skin, across her lips and neck and bust, as if she weren't entirely present, as if only her body was there. Abelard showed his friend the openings at the sides of Anne-Marie's dress and asked her to undo the hooks that secured them. Her first thought was to flee the restaurant, but then she would never see Abelard again. With shaking fingers she complied and Abelard slipped his hand inside the dress. He told her to open her legs and then touched her belly and sex. After her denials of the afternoon Anne-Marie quickly became aroused. Dellyse watched her, unmoved, as the pleasure mounted. When the climax came Abelard made her look at his friend. His cool eyes didn't flicker as her own melted and she felt her pleasure tainted by his disdain. Afterwards she cried and Abelard had thrown his hands in the air, as if to say, 'what can be done with such a girl?' Even so, he had taken her head on to his shoulder and comforted her.

For the remainder of the evening he had been his most charming and by the end she had recovered her good spirits. When he took her to his carriage though, he had told her, quietly but forcefully, that she would indeed sleep with others of his choosing and that she had better get used to the idea. She said nothing as he kissed her good night.

As Anne-Marie waited in the hotel room in the 9th Arrondissement with her behind in the air and her eyes blindfolded she realised that it would be impossible for her to tell when the door opened if the man who entered was her lover or a complete stranger. The thought that it might be a stranger chilled her and she tried to dismiss it from her mind. Abelard had never done anything with her that she had not first agreed to. Certain of his demands had been difficult to accede to but he had always used persuasion. She waited for a long while, thinking of these things, touching herself from time to time as her arousal faded, keeping herself ready. At one point she heard footsteps outside and her heart fluttered, until she realised, from the light tread, that it was only a maid. There was a scraping sound of objects being dragged across the floor and she guessed that the laundry basket had been taken away and replaced with an empty one. Now she truly was a prisoner as she waited in her cell of blindfolded darkness.

After half an hour or so, she heard the heavy tread of a man's feet in the corridor outside and the door opened. There was silence for a while and Anne-Marie guessed that she was being looked at. She felt herself flush as the imagined eyes scanned her body; then there was the sound of clothes being removed, of a chair being pulled closer to the bed and a case being opened. The first touch was the touch of a crop being drawn along her back, from her neck to the base of her spine. Hands pushed into the small of her back so that her behind was fully presented. She felt the bed give as someone rested a foot on the mattress and then she was struck with four quick blows, each one falling above the other. She cried out but kept her position and waited, trembling, expecting more until the foot was removed from the bed and she sensed the figure moving away. A few tears squeezed from her eyes and soaked into the blindfold. Her hands lay quite still at her sides and she felt unable to move them to rub away this irritation. It bothered her as much as the burning of her behind. After a few moments she heard the window to the balcony being opened. From the absence of footfalls she guessed that Abelard, if Abelard it was, for he had not spoken, was barefoot now and probably naked. Street sounds came into the room and she wondered if he was looking out at Notre Dame or looking at her.

She wanted to see his sex. She wanted to know if it had made him hard to use the crop. Abelard had only used it once before and it had aroused him enormously, more so than any number of tender caresses that she offered with her mouth or hands. He had taken her with such force afterwards that she had felt like a toy in his hands as he had bent her this way and that. Her climaxes had been like no others, as if torn from her very soul. She wanted him like that again.

The man returned to her side and she felt his hand on her behind. His thumb trailed down the divide which was slick with perspiration. At the tighter opening, it tested her willingness to give herself there, pushing until she opened. The fingers touched the welts left by the crop and the thumb pushed in. For whatever reason, Anne-Marie suddenly felt that the man doing this to her was not Abelard, she sensed another presence and began to struggle, reaching for the blindfold.

'Absolutely still!' a voice hissed, and to her immense relief it was the voice of Abelard. She became quiet again, giving herself to the pleasure of being opened. The thumb didn't leave her until she was stretched wide and ready to receive a man. Then the crop was taken up again and used once. Anne-Marie's behind closed tight as the blow was struck and the thumb returned to open her again. This was repeated another three times and she finally understood that she was to remain open while the crop fell. With sweat pouring from her body and her behind blazing, she managed to give her torturer what he desired. Though she gave a deep, guttural groan when the crop landed for the final time, the opened ring of muscle no more than quivered. Anne-Marie described the excitement of being touched when she couldn't see, by hands that had no constraints on what they might choose to do. The girl looked into Anne-Marie's face with rapt attention, desire and envy as the story unfolded. She was greedy for her sister's hand at her sex and closed her thighs convulsively when touched.

After the beating, Anne-Marie was left alone again, her behind still high in the air, her legs shaking. She heard the chair being moved and the sound of a cigar being trimmed before it was lit. A moment later the scent of Cuban tobacco filled the room. Abelard had once tried to teach her how to smoke. She had said that she liked the smell, but the taste was far less pleasant and she had curled her lips in such disgust that he had laughed and given up.

Breaking into this train of thought, Abelard told her to touch herself but to keep her behind open as she did so. The first touch of her fingers nearly provoked a climax and she forced herself to keep away from her most sensitive parts. She went slowly, wanting him to be inside her when she came. A man's sex was presented to her lips. It was as hard and smooth as the tip of the crop that stroked her as she sucked. The cigar smoke enveloped her. A hand touched her fingers as she played with herself, pushing her further towards her climax. Thumb and finger pinched the bruises on her behind making her groan. She was slapped several times on the sensitive part of her thighs, at the very top. She concentrated on keeping her mouth soft and her tongue working in the tiny opening of the sex that filled her. The slaps sent little shocks through her and felt like sharp, unfinished climaxes. She was writhing and moaning and had forgotten herself completely until the man pulled away and went behind her. He pushed her hand away and went into her sex slowly. Her whole body flooded with arousal as if a liquid were being poured into the opening and rushing from there to her veins. Even the very slowest movements of the man made her cry out with excitement. From time to time he would press his thumb to the well of her behind, reminding her to stay open, slowing as he did so. After a while he stopped completely and moved her instead with a hand on her hips. When his hand stopped she continued. She fucked him with slow strong strokes and groaned all the while. He took her head and lifted it, turning her to face the window side of the room. She moved faster and faster and began to climax. As she did so the blindfold was removed and she was shocked to see Abelard sitting in the chair beside the bed, fully clothed and watching her as he smoked his cigar. She froze like a frightened animal and his eyes narrowed with displeasure. Only when she started to move again did he smile.

He watched as she impaled herself on the stranger's flesh and offered encouragement, telling her to use her whole body. Soon all inhibition disappeared and the orgasms took her in a long, slow procession. She continued until she was sated and her body was slack and spent. Abelard bent over then and took her head from the other man, kissing her deeply and thanking her for giving him such pleasure. He asked if she would ever refuse one of his friends again and she murmured a 'no'. When he ran his finger across her lips she took it into her mouth and started to suck.

'I think she wants more,' Abelard said to the man behind her, and he began to move. Anne-Marie hadn't even looked at the stranger's face but as soon as the man began to move her pleasure began again. He thrust hard and upwards, into the back wall of her sex as if trying to break through into her behind. His thumb went to that opening so that he could touch his sex through the thin membrane that separated the two passages. Anne-Marie was dissolving in the gaze of her lover as the other man took her. His eyes seemed to find their way into her as surely as the other man did. She reached out her hand to him and he took it, raising it to his lips as the convulsions took her one last time and as the man behind her grunted out his own climax.

Afterwards, as Anne-Marie lay exhausted on her belly, her sweat soaking the sheets of the bed, the two men sat near the window and discussed her. They each commented on her body, especially on the smoothness of her skin and the richness of her breasts. The stranger congratulated his friend on such a find, saying that to possess a well bred girl of such beauty and such willingness was a coup. Abelard agreed that the girl was exceptional, pointing out that her breasts would become even fuller as she matured and that her sexuality could only deepen. One flaw according to the stranger was that though her lips were marvellously soft and she clearly liked to suck a man, her mouth didn't fully accommodate his sex in the way that he wished and declared that she needed more practice. Abelard replied that he gave her as much instruction as he had time for but that perhaps he could use some help in that department. The two men laughed in the bawdiest of ways and Anne-Marie coloured as they looked at her. They talked like this, as if Anne-Marie wasn't present, the way certain men like to talk of women when they are alone. Abelard declared his intention of using her behind and the other man said that he too wanted that pleasure. They both agreed that she should be beaten again but disagreed on which instrument should be used. The stranger took a short heavy belt from the case and declared that used on the inside of the thighs it was more effective than the crop and left no bruises. Abelard protested that it was the bruising that would remind her of the afternoon. He pointed out that Anne-Marie had a number of young lovers who would learn a great deal from discovering her body marked by the crop. So the discussion went on, with an amicable bickering that seemed a pleasure in itself for the two men.

On the matter of the beating, they consulted Anne-Marie as to which would most suit her. The stranger sat on the bed and, taking her hand in his, he asked in the mildest and most considerate manner whether she would prefer the crop or the belt. As outrageous as the question was, she replied with the same civility that she had never felt the belt. He offered to demonstrate it, with the assurance that the crop was a mere irritation in comparison. She declined his offer with a shudder and he teased her, asking how she could take part in an informed discussion when she was unacquainted with the facts. It

220

transpired that he was a lawyer and well versed in both fact and fiction. Abelard intervened and declared that they would toss a coin. Thus it came to be that Anne-Marie would receive the belt.

When they were ready, the two men took her again, together this time. Abelard pulled leather cuffs from the case and secured Anne-Marie's wrists to the headboard of the bed. He stripped and knelt between her legs stroking the thighs that were soon to be beaten. She looked at him tenderly, opening her legs further when he asked her to. The lawyer looked on as Abelard knelt across Anne-Marie's ankles so that she could not close her legs. The men were in no hurry; they wanted to savour her fear, her consent and her arousal, for Anne-Marie was very aroused to be treated in this way. It aroused her to be tied, it aroused her to have her legs spread wide by her lover while another man watched. It aroused her to see her lover's sex stir as the belt was laid between her legs so that she could feel it's weight and know that inside the double layer of leather was a strip of lead. It aroused her when the strap struck and her lover grew strainingly erect.

As the whipping proceeded so she began to howl, unable to hold in the sound and not caring if she was heard in the street or at Notre Dame itself. When the lawyer paused from time to time, Abelard touched her thighs and her sex and Anne-Marie bucked as much as she had when the strap was falling. Abelard took her twice, first using her sex and then her behind. He drew the deepest pleasures from her belly before retreating unspent so that the whipping could continue. When tears were streaming down her face Abelard went to her mouth and took her there. He had told her many times of the intense pleasure that could be had from enjoying a woman's mouth when she was weeping. He did climax then, driving into her mouth with a cruel urgency and filling her with satisfaction as his cry exploded from deep within. Then he gave her to the lawyer who wanted only her behind and spent a long time inside her. She was sore by the time he was finished but they gave her no respite. Abelard took her again immediately. She had never seen him so feverish in his desire or felt his sex so fiercely hard.

By the end she was exhausted and limp, like a doll, and they could do with her as they chose. They untied her and took her to the balcony, having her kneel there so they could use her mouth. They had her play with herself until she climaxed in full view of the hotel across the way. They took her while she was standing and lying, and her excitement kept re-igniting itself. Abelard brought a chair to the window so that he could sit and Anne-Marie used her behind to make him climax one more time, working up and down on his sex with the last of her strength. At the end, after they had had their fill, the men washed and prepared to go.

'But I have no clothes!' Anne-Marie protested weakly.

'Will you spend the evening with me, mademoiselle?' the lawyer replied with the smile of a devil, as if this were an answer.

She glanced at Abelard who looked away, leaving her to make her own decision. Given this freedom and looking at the lawyer's smile, she said that she would.

'Then you will need no clothes,' he told her, 'I shall send a servant for you at six.' With that the two men left.

'Two men!' Isabelle gasped, when the story was finished.

'Two demons,' Anne-Marie replied, with a smile.

'Did you tell me everything?' Isabelle had seen her sister falter from time to time as she spoke, she had seen Anne-Marie's eyes narrow as she recast the story or glossed over certain events.

'Of course not. You are too little!'

Isabelle frowned playfully, rocking her legs from side to side as she lay with her head in her sister's lap.

'Tell me what you didn't tell me before.'

'No! You have heard far more than you should already.'

When Isabelle tried to speak again, Anne-Marie leant forward and put her lips over the girl's mouth. She silenced her with her tongue and Isabelle reached up and laid her hand on her sister's face drawing her downwards, kissing back strongly.

'Are you wet too?' Isabelle asked, when Anne-Marie broke away and touched her hand to Isabelle's soaking sex.
'Yes.'

Isabelle smiled. 'Is it me? Or is it telling the story?'

'Both.' Anne-Marie knelt up. She swung her legs astride her sister's head and opened her lips with two fingers. 'See?'

Isabelle saw the wetness and had an urge to kiss but her sister told her to keep still. She leant across the length of Isabelle's prostrate body and took the girl's slender ankles in her hand. Pulling back, Anne-Marie brought Isabelle's feet above her head so that her behind was raised from the bed a little and her sex was stretched and bulging between taut thighs. Then she took an ankle in each hand and drew them apart so that the whole length of Isabelle's behind could be seen. Pushing down on the widespread ankles, pushing them to the bed beside the girl's shoulders raised Isabelle's sex high enough for Anne-Marie to reach it easily with her mouth. Isabelle groaned as the tongue entered her. She reached up and touched her sister's breasts as they swung above her own. She kneaded them and pushed them against her belly as the tongue worked in and out, up and down, probing and opening, licking and flicking at the bud of pleasure, pushing fully into the opening to her belly. From time to time Anne-Marie would pause in this pleasure and, keeping Isabelle's ankles firmly pinned to the bed she would kiss her mouth or suck her toes until the girl squirmed and begged to be released. But Isabelle was not released until Anne-Marie had her quaking with desire. Even then she was freed only to kneel astride Anne-Marie's thigh as she sat against the headboard so as to stimulate herself by working her pelvis.

Anne-Marie took Isabelle's breasts and squeezed hard, digging her fingers into the soft flesh so that Isabelle threw back her head and groaned in desperation. Yet however hard Anne-Marie worked her, the girl made no move to escape. Isabelle's sex continued to drench the smooth thigh trapped between her legs, and her lips opened to kiss and suck the warm skin as her pelvis ground out its greedy rhythm. It felt to Isabelle that she was sliding down a long, dark tunnel, a tunnel of pleasure, fear and excitement and that there was no escape until the end.

The end came when Anne-Marie told Isabelle to stand facing the screen wall and stimulated the girl while her legs were spread wide and she was bent forward, her fingers looped through the fretted wood for support. Anne-Marie used her whole hand to rub Isabelle's mound in a soft steady motion, occasionally sharpening the excitement with little pinches to the bud of pleasure. She took each of Isabelle's breasts in her free hand alternately, and drew the nipples across the polished wood, or pushed them into the openings of the screen. And all of the time these things were done, Isabelle entreated her sister for delivery from the fire that consumed her belly.

When the release finally came, when her body felt as if it were no longer her own but a shaking, screaming brawl of uncontrolled excitement, strange thoughts entered her mind. She imagined that there was someone behind the screen and that her fingers were touched and her nipples pinched. She imagined that she felt another's breath on her face and heard a man whisper to her, words that her ears could not quite capture. She sank to her knees, overwhelmed by what her sister had done and tears rolled down her cheeks. Anne-Marie lifted her after a time and helped her back to the bed.

For the remainder of the afternoon, Anne-Marie treated her sister with great kindness, for she was very emotional and tears came regularly without any apparent reason. She took Isabelle to orgasm several times more, using her tongue between the girl's legs, making these climaxes easy, if not as strong as the first ones. Later that evening, after they had returned home, Isabelle looked in the bedroom mirror to see if she had changed. It seemed to her that she had, that her eyes were somehow steadier, fuller and more knowing. She wondered if the boys would want her now and if they could be as exciting as her sister.

22

The Equations of Desire

Isabelle remembered that summer as she sat in Alain's study. At least, she remembered certain incidents; the kiss in the wood, the visits in the night. She remembered that after the first visit to the villa with her sister there had been others, no less exciting. She remembered realising that Anne-Marie was having an affair with Alain and remembered her feelings of jealousy. Then there was the announcement that Anne-Marie was going away, and the great disappointment that it brought to her and the upset it brought to her mother. A few months later, Isabelle was taken to Arronville and introduced to Monsieur Chabard. It seemed then that her fate was sealed, that she would pay the price for Anne-Marie's profligacy in a dull provincial marriage. She would be the good, dutiful daughter and it seemed that nothing would turn aside the currents that swept her to this gloomy end until Robert appeared. And now, quite suddenly, she was a creature of the villa, as Anne-Marie had once been.

She opened her eyes and saw that Alain was still seated in the chair opposite her. He smiled.

'Are you going to tell me what happened?' he asked after a moment.

She shook her head slowly. 'Will you have me banished from the estate?' Isabelle asked.

Alain pursed his lips. 'I would never banish you.' His eyes were tender as he said this and she looked at him in surprise.

A thought that had been lying dormant in her mind for a long time suddenly came to the surface. It was a thought that she had never admitted to full consciousness because of its madness. But as she looked at him now, in a moment when his severity had slipped away, when his cool disdain had melted, it seemed inescapably true. Alain loved her. It was not like the love that she bore for Robert but it was a kind of love. The realisation fell through her, breaking a hundred misconceptions in a disorientating rush.

'You have always been so cold,' she said in her confusion.

He frowned as if he were unable to follow her train of thought. 'To you?'

'Yes.'

'I have always been courteous.'

'In the library you were cruel.'

'Denying you?'

'Yes.'

Again he shrugged. 'It will be for your greater pleasure as well as mine when you surrender to others.'

She shook her head as if it would help her to order her thoughts. 'I never understood why Anne-Marie went with you before.'

'Do you understand now?'

'Perhaps.'

He nodded. 'Tell me.'

'You knew who she was. You understood.'

He thought about this. 'And she understood me. She understood that I had to possess her completely.'

'And me? Do you want to possess me?' she breathed.

'Perhaps.'

'But why? Why completely? You can take me whenever you choose.'

It was a while before he answered.

'If a man desires a woman and is held in her spell, he must secure her. If the spell that she casts is strong, the man must secure her completely. Her obedience is the only way of balancing the equation.'

Isabelle nodded. She knew that with Robert she felt the

226

constant need to assure him of her willingness to meet his desires. She understood the strength of those desires and since she had stirred them, even if by doing no more than exist, she accepted that she must satisfy them.

'Do you desire me?' she asked, softly.

He looked at her steadily, his eyes betraying nothing.

'I didn't understand before, I thought . . .' she murmured, not knowing what she had thought.

Before she could say another word, he rose abruptly and told her to dress. As she did so he wrote out a note and, when she was ready, he handed it to her. The note was addressed to Absolem and she was dispatched immediately to deliver it. As she opened the door he called to her. 'Come back to me afterwards. I will expect you to tell me everything.'

Isabelle closed the door and walked very slowly to the stables, her head spinning. When she handed the note to Absolem, he glanced at it briefly and called for Benjamin. The son's eyes burnt her as his father read out the note.

'She is to be whipped severely. The crop on her behind and her thighs, the dog whip on her breasts and belly. Let the boy do it.'

Absolem laughed when he saw the blood drain from Isabelle's face.

Benjamin tied her to the beam in the harness room with her legs spread wide. When she smiled at the boy he looked at her with insolence and desire but he did not smile in return. There was a harshness in him that she would not have imagined from her previous meeting and she wondered if she had somehow hurt him. Benjamin started with the crop, laying on more strokes than Isabelle could count. She was shaking, tear-stained and hoarse with screaming by the time he was finished. He took hold of her hair and pulled her head back so that he could look into her eyes as he undid his breeches. Then he coolly took her anus, giving her no pleasure but taking his own in full measure. This done, he took up the dog whip and stood before her. His sex protruded from his breeches and gleamed with a mixture of mucous and semen.

227

'Is this still what you want?' he asked.

'Finish it!' she groaned.

He struck her one blow, laying it across the tops of her thighs and mound. She twisted against her bonds pitifully.

'I've dreamt of this,' he told her, and she realised that even if she begged, he would not stop.

He used the dog whip across the whole of the front of her body. Only her face was left untouched. Her breasts bore the brunt of his attentions as he returned to them repeatedly. It seemed to give him great satisfaction to see her eyes open wide in disbelief each time he interrupted the lashing of her abdomen or the tops of her thighs to begin again on this most vulnerable area. He took her again in her behind before cutting her down. Then he obliged her to use her mouth to bring on his second climax. Afterwards, he thanked her ironically and left her to weep. One of the stable boys came to her later and took her outside to a trough so that she could wash the sweat and semen from her face and breasts. The boy watched as Isabelle squatted and splashed water between her legs and into the divide of her buttocks. He touched his groin several times, nervously as if he had an itch and, despite her distress, she smiled.

Isabelle was still shaking when she knocked at the door to Alain's study. He called for her to enter and when she did so, she found him working at his desk. Without a word she undressed and sat in the same chair that she'd occupied earlier.

'Shall I begin?' she asked.

He nodded and she told the story of the summer that her sister had seduced her.

When she became excited she caressed herself. Her palm lay on the belly that was criss-crossed with the red stripes of her beating. Her fingers pushed aside lips swollen with arousal to touch the shining blister of her clitoris. She held back nothing, answering his questions as fully as she could, climaxing several times while he watched. At the end he thanked her and kissed her hand.

'It wasn't the beating,' she said, as she made ready to

leave. 'I told you because I wanted to. I wanted you to know everything.'

That evening Isabelle didn't see Robert and dined alone in what had become her bedroom. As evening turned to night she stepped out into the courtyard to take a walk through the cool, scented air. Nearing the baths, she was startled to see a figure leaning against the stonework that supported the cupola. It was Benjamin. He looked abashed and apologised for surprising her.

'I was watching you,' he said.

She looked towards the bedroom. The many candles lit it like a stage and she could clearly see the remains of her meal on the little table near the open doors.

'I often watch you,' he said. 'Do you mind?'

She shook her head.

'I'm glad that you came out. I wanted to make sure that you were alright,' he told her.

'After you were so cruel to me, this afternoon?' she asked.

He nodded and moved closer to her, resting his hand on her belly. Her dress was of the thinnest silk and he could feel the ridges where the whip had raised her flesh. 'Does it still hurt?' he asked.

'Of course.'

'Do you forgive me?'

She leant forward and kissed him on the cheek. 'Is that enough forgiveness?' she asked.

His hand slipped downwards and cupped her sex. 'I wanted to know how it would feel to be as cruel as my father.'

'Did you enjoy it?'

'Yes.'

The hand at her sex started to move.

'Now you want more?'

'Yes.'

'So soon?'

He smiled and nodded.

She remembered what Alain had said about helping the

boy to become a man and knelt down in front of him. He walked behind her, undoing his breeches. She raised her dress to her waist and leant forward so that she was on all fours. He took her behind, not cruelly this time, but steadily, allowing her to touch herself as her pleasure built. After she'd climaxed, he wanted to see her breasts, to see the marks that he'd made. She stripped completely and he stroked all of her bruised flesh as she sucked him.

23

The Screen

In the afternoon of the next day, Helene came to Isabelle as she sat reading in the courtyard by the library. Alain wanted her again. Before they set off to meet him, Helene asked Isabelle to raise her arms above her head. Isabelle did so and Helene produced a pair of small scissors which she used to open the two seams at the side of Isabelle's dress. As they walked down the long corridors, Helene slipped her hand inside the dress and touched Isabelle, cupping her behind and searching for her anus, just as Anne-Marie had once done. Helene, finding her target, was not content with only a shallow entry as Anne-Marie had been. Her finger wormed its way inside until it was buried to the hilt. From time to time, Helene would bring Isabelle to a halt so that she could kiss her lips and, kneeling, also her sex, so that when they finally reached the room where Alain was waiting, Isabelle was fully aroused.

As soon as they entered the large, light bedroom with its moorish floor and fretted screen wall, Isabelle recognised it as the one that Anne-Marie had taken her to. Alain was sitting on the broad, low window sill and Helene led Isabelle to him, positioning her so that she could look out on to the little pond and the rose arbour.

'Is this the right window?' Alain asked.

Isabelle nodded.

Helene released her and Alain had Isabelle raise her dress and touch herself. When she became too excited, Alain pushed her hand away. This continued until she was gasping and her legs were weak, then he rose and carried her to the bed. He sat at the end and watched as Helene stripped Isabelle and began to touch her. He told her some stories that Isabelle hadn't heard before. He told of how he'd seduced Anne-Marie when she was the same age as Isabelle had been when she'd first come to this room. He described the time that he'd first used the crop on Anne-Marie and how he'd once given her to Absolem, a man that she detested, every day for a week to test her faithfulness. He told Isabelle how he'd introduced Anne-Marie to his friend Abelard so that her sexual education could be rounded out in the capital. Helene teased Isabelle all the time that the stories were told, using her hands and lips to both arouse and deny, as Anne-Marie had done before.

When Isabelle was quaking, when it seemed the lightest touch to her breast would trigger a climax, Alain took her hand and led her behind the bed. In the centre of the wall was a kelim woven with patterns of interlocking gold diamonds. Alain drew this aside to reveal a small door. He opened it and indicated that Isabelle should enter the dark corridor that was revealed.

Once Isabelle entered the corridor, the door was closed behind her and she found herself in darkness. It was a while before her eyes adjusted, then she could make out a slight glow of light to her left. Since Alain had given her no instructions to the contrary, she edged her way along the narrow corridor until she reached a corner. Turning this she found herself behind the screen wall. Through the ornate fretwork she could see all that happened in the room she had just left. In the light that passed through the many openings in the screen she saw a table and chairs, so that any voyeur might be comfortable as he viewed the bedroom. At that moment Alain had Helene lying on her side with one leg high in the air and was plundering her sex with his hand. Isabelle remembered all that Anne-Marie had done to her younger self on that same bed and realised that Alain had watched it all, had in fact arranged it all, including the scenario by the pond which he could have seen from the window. She remembered the fingers that had touched her breasts as she had climaxed, the voice she had half heard and thought she'd imagined, and realised that those fingers and that voice had been real. Had she discovered these things even a single day earlier she would have had a sense of betrayal, a feeling that her childish trust in her sister had been violated. After all that had happened there was simply the surprise that she hadn't already guessed the truth; that, and a feeling of the all-inclusiveness of Alain's desire for her. It was as if he had always existed and that nothing of her life had escaped him, from her birth to the very moment that she stood behind the screen. As she watched, Alain bade Helene stand and led her to the screen. He had her stand facing it and told her to bend forward so that she supported herself with her fingers looped through the fretwork. He stimulated her from behind and Isabelle watched the girl's face as the pleasure mounted. Unable to contain her own desire, Isabelle touched herself. As Helene began to cry out so did Isabelle and she took the other girls fingers in her mouth as the crisis ensued.

24

The Mexican Room

Isabelle sat on a chair in Alain's bedroom facing a full length mirror. Maria was fussing with Isabelle's hair, a clutch of pins held in her teeth. The maid had used gold braid to plait a dozen strands or more. Now she was twisting and coiling the strands so that they formed a harmonious whole, neatly compacted against Isabelle's scalp. Maria had already spent almost two hours painting an intricate series of interlinking geometric patterns on to Isabelle's naked body. She had laboured with the dark pigment and a small brush until every part of her charge was ornamented in this way. Isabelle had been forced to lie down, to stand, to raise her arms, part her legs, lift her breasts, hold her hair clear of her neck, open the cheeks of her behind and generally endure the itchiness of the brush and the coarseness of the ground plant that formed the pigment. As the paint dried, so it lost much of its colour, becoming dark grey, matt and scratchy to the touch.

As Maria put the finishing touches to her hair, Isabelle looked through the glass doors that led to the Mexican room. This was not strictly a room but a sprawling, iron-framed conservatory that pushed out from the side of the villa into the surrounding gardens. She could see cacti growing from yellow sand and large, smooth boulders. It was the first time that she had been in Alain's bedroom and it was entirely ordinary apart from this view, this astonishing glimpse of another continent. She expected to see exotic birds and strange animals but nothing moved except for the occasional wisp of cloud visible through the glazed roof.

When Maria had finished Isabelle's hair she went to a wardrobe and took out a long, thin, rather battered cardboard box. It was the kind of box that might contain canes made for the schoolroom. The maid set it on the dressing table and opened it. Reaching her hand inside, Maria brought out nothing more dangerous than a handful of long, brightly coloured feathers. These she arranged in Isabelle's hair, pushing the shafts into the compacted plaits and carefully fixing each with pins. When she had finished, Isabelle turned to face the mirror and saw that they formed a sort of head dress. The feathers drooped at the ends, each finishing in what appeared to be an eye, dark blue and shimmering. The filaments were so soft that the eyes seemed to float above her as she moved her head. The effect, when seen with her painted body was to turn her into something unrecognisable; she looked savage yet beautiful, as she imagined a jaguar or a leopard to be, but more exotic still than those creatures.

Maria began to oil her skin. The dark, greyish pigment was long dry and the oil soaked into it, reviving its colour so that it became a brilliant indigo. The patterns seemed to swirl before her eyes as Isabelle looked at them. Maria had her stand so that she could oil her back and behind and the length of her legs. She took sandals from the dressing table and dropped them to the floor obliging Isabelle to step into them. They were made of a coarsely woven fibrous material and had cords that Maria wound around her ankles and the lower part of her calves to secure them. The final item was a gold mask, the metal beaten thin and burnished. It was fashioned after the image of a beautiful boy and, though it was perfect and un-scratched, it had the feeling of something ancient. Maria slipped it over her head and attached it with leather bands which she fed beneath the plaits so that they were invisible.

'I need to tie your hands, mademoiselle,' said Maria.

Isabelle put her hands behind her back and the maid lashed them together with the same material that had been

235

used to make the sandals. When this was done Maria walked over to the glazed, double doors and opened them. A blast of hot air swept into the bedroom. Isabelle stepped forward and was about to pass through the doors when Maria suddenly stopped her as if something had been forgotten.

'Excuse me, mademoiselle, there is one more thing.'

The maid dropped to her knees and reached for Isabelle's sex. She took the labia and pulled, stretching each lip repeatedly, with little regard for Isabelle's comfort, until they stood out conspicuously, pink against the darkly painted skin.

Satisfied, Maria stood and led Isabelle into the Mexican room. The heat that had swept into the bedroom now surrounded Isabelle, pressing like a giant hand against her throat, making it hard for her to breathe. From time to time she was forced to dip her head to avoid the cacti, those at least which branched and spread like trees. Most seemed to grow straight up in thick green columns or squatted as malevolent spheres, armed with great spines as sharp as needles. It was unnerving to walk among them naked and bound, and with her vision restricted by the mask. At one point she heard a series of cries coming from ahead of them. The voice was a woman's and added to the sharpness in the air.

Quite soon, Alain came into view. He was seated in a cane chair wearing the loose trousers, open white cotton shirt and felt hat of a plantation owner. Behind him, and dwarfing him, were the remnants of a stone building that Isabelle recognised as a pyramid, or at least part of a pyramid. The original structure must have been vast. What was presented here was a single corner, ragged where it would have joined the remainder of the building, but otherwise surprisingly well preserved. The sharp, square, inclined edge of the pyramid was clearly visible and the stones were crisply dressed to fit tightly, one to the other. At the front of the ruin were broad steps that led up the inclined face but which finished abruptly in a broken line at a height of about five metres. Later, Alain would tell her that this structure had nearly sunk the ship that carried it back from the New World. It was the reason for the Mexican room, the only addition made to the villa since the time of Alain's grandfather.

In front of the pyramid and next to the place where Alain was sitting, was a table made of the same stone. Sprawled on this was the naked figure of a woman. Although the figure faced away from her, Isabelle was sure that it was Anna, no other woman in the villa had such a body, firm and athletic, yet yielding, soft in its offering.

Alain appeared to be in a kind of reverie, and so quiet were the footfalls of the two women in the sand that he only noticed them when they were almost upon him. It must have been the sound of Maria's starched, black dress rustling that caught his attention. His eyes widened as he turned and looked at Isabelle. For the first time, she saw him take an unreserved interest in her, an interest untainted by irony. He rose from his chair and, when she halted, walked around her, taking in every detail, reaching out and touching her at intervals as if touching something extraordinary, something that might disappear like a mirage. When his eyes met hers though, they looked straight through her. Isabelle realised that it wasn't she herself that merited such attention, but only her surface: the surface of indigo and gold that had been applied by Maria, but which he had designed himself. She realised that it was his own dream that interested and aroused him; she was simply the carrier, the canvas on which the image had its representation.

'Turn around Anna,' he said in a hushed voice.

The woman on the stone table turned. She smiled at the vision.

'What do you see?' he asked.

'A spirit.'

'Yes. A spirit of the desert. Or a goddess.'

His hand touched the cords that bound Isabelle's wrists as he walked around her for the hundredth time. Beads of sweat were running down her back, converging in the depressions on either side of her spine and running on into

237

the valley of her gleaming, oiled behind. He ran the back of his hand upward, from her waist to her neck, and she shivered. His hand came away covered in a mixture of oil and perspiration but the pigment stayed pristine. Isabelle could feel his desire as a resonance in the dry, furnace air. She wanted him to take her when she was like this, invisible behind her mask. It would be like sex in the dark, the way it had sometimes been with Anne-Marie. Isabelle was disposed to pleasure at that moment. It was the heat and the place, and it was Anna gazing at her with dark, gleaming eyes. It was also the man behind her with all of his power, and it was the promise she had given to him, the promise of herself.

At that moment Anna shifted her position slightly and for the first time Isabelle could see between the girl's legs. Her sex was inflamed and the lips were fuller than usual, but it was not this which caught Isabelle's attention. Standing from Anna's left thigh, the back of which was pressed to the surface of the table, was a cluster of cactus spines. They stood vertically from the swell of flesh which curved inwards to meet her sex. The spines were at least six inches long and as thin as needles. Isabelle looked at the girl's face but saw nothing there to betray any discomfort; instead she saw a perverse satisfaction and pride.

'Remove her mask, Maria,' Alain said abruptly.

It took a few moments for the maid to accomplish this. When she had, Isabelle looked no less exotic. The geometric patterns covered and transformed her face as surely as they covered and transformed her body.

Alain went over to Anna. He must have seen Isabelle tense as she glimpsed the spines. Now he ran his hands over the top of them, brushing them so they vibrated. Anna started to close her legs reflexively, but checked herself, stretching them wider instead and offering herself fully.

'Use your mouth on her sex,' he told Isabelle.

Isabelle knelt before the girl and pressed her lips to the heat of that inflamed place. Anna tasted of the sea and Isabelle sucked deep. Above her head, she knew that Alain was manipulating the spines. She could hear Anna's groans and feel the spasms that passed through her body. Whether it was pain or pleasure she did not know.

'More spines,' Alain said to Maria and the maid hurried away.

Isabelle continued to work her tongue and Anna lifted her belly, rotating it slowly. Since Isabelle's hands were still tied, she could not steady the girl, only follow her as she moved. From time to time she would suck in the flesh around Anna's little bud and pull it into her mouth, nipping and licking, until Anna bucked. When Maria returned, she handed the spines to Alain who went to stand at the other end of the table, out of Isabelle's field of view. Whatever he did there had a strong effect. Soon, Anna was writhing around, and Alain told Isabelle to pause for a moment, so she sat back on her heels. Looking up, she saw Anna supporting herself on her elbows and reaching to kiss Alain who stood above her. As she kissed him, he pushed one of the spines into the flesh of her breast, piercing her just below the nipple. For as long as she kissed him, he maintained the pressure on the spine. Isabelle watched with a fascinated horror. This spine was not the only one that impaled her. Two small forests grew from the areas around her nipples.

When the girl's lips withdrew from her master, so he released the spine. The girl's face was flushed and sweating with excitement. She glanced at Isabelle as if to persuade Alain to have the kneeling girl begin again at her sex. He said nothing. Instead, he took another spine and laid it on the down slope of Anna's breast, pressing hard enough to indent the skin but not enough to break it. Anna looked from the spine to Isabelle. Her expression was a compound of desire and greed, mixed with a little madness. As Isabelle watched, the girl reached for Alain with her lips again and he pushed the spine home. Anna groaned and rolled her shoulders voluptuously, kissing for a long time as he twisted the spine in his fingers.

Twice more Isabelle watched this procedure and then Alain told her to use her tongue again. Anna moaned from the moment that Isabelle's lips touched her and she continued to moan until, many climaxes later, Alain told Isabelle to stop. This time, when Isabelle sat back she saw that Anna's body was a complete arch. Her head hung down from her shoulders as she supported herself on her elbows, and her breasts and belly were uppermost, pushed out. Alain smiled at Isabelle.

'She has told you of Don Luis?'

Isabelle nodded.

'It was one of his games. I play it to please her. A great advantage is that the spines leave no scars so the procedure can be repeated over and over again.'

Anna raised her head and gave each of them an unusually shy smile, thanking them in a quiet voice.

Alain took the mask from the chair where Maria had laid it. He looked at it carefully, perhaps seeing his reflection in the polished surface; he then carried it to Isabelle. He slipped it over her face and attached it himself this time.

'The bag, Maria,' he said when he was finished. This evidently meant something to the maid because she immediately turned and hurried back to the bedroom. He offered his hand to Anna, who rose shakily and seated herself on one of the chairs. For the first time, Isabelle could see that there were a number of iron rings embedded in the surface of the table, which might be used to secure a person. With Anna there had clearly been no need. As Isabelle looked at the girl, a rivulet of sweat ran from her breast, slid across her belly and pooled between her thighs. Isabelle wanted to lick her again and she wanted to suck on those pierced breasts. She wanted to taste the salt and excitement. She wanted to know what else had happened in the desert in Mexico, the real desert. The sight of the spines brought crueller thoughts to the surface, impulses that centred on the dun-coloured nipples, spared by Alain as yet. Isabelle forced herself to look away, fearful of her own cruelty.

When Maria returned she was carrying a small, red, leather bag scuffed with use.

'Take her into the pyramid and get her ready,' Alain told the maid. 'Leave the bag, I will need it later.'

Maria set the bag down on the stone table while Isabelle looked at Alain mutely.

'A small surgical procedure,' he explained in response to the unspoken question.

Before Isabelle could ask more, Maria took her arm and led her to the overbearing, alien structure with its impossibly large blocks of stone and its savage reliefs. At the side of the building, invisible from the table, was an iron door. Maria paused when they reached it and produced a key from her pocket. Isabelle felt herself pulling away from the maid against her will. Alain's words had provoked in her a cold terror, and she was suddenly shaking. When the door was opened and the shadowed interior gaped before them, Maria tried to lead the bound girl inside, but Isabelle couldn't move; when Maria tugged at her arm, Isabelle dug in her heels.

Finally, Alain came over to them. 'Don't disappoint me in this, Isabelle,' he said.

'What will you do?' she asked in a trembling voice.

'Nothing that you cannot bear,' he replied. 'I expect your submission in this, as in all things, without consultation or negotiation. Robert has already agreed it. Shall I put him to the inconvenience of coming here? Or would you rather leave?'

Isabelle bowed her head and, after a moment's further hesitation, walked slowly into the pyramid. Maria was already inside and lit an oil lamp as Isabelle entered. The space was small, no more than a few metres square. The walls, floor and ceiling were covered with tiles that gleamed in the light of the lamp. The same grotesque motifs that she had seen carved on the stones outside were repeated on their surfaces.

In the middle of the room was a leather couch, glaringly European and out of place in this setting. Beside the couch was a glass cabinet filled with jars and bowls and neatly arranged surgical instruments. Maria stepped behind Isabelle as the girl gazed about herself in horror. The bleak, sterile surfaces were designed for easy cleaning, for the efficient removal of body fluids, for the eradication of evidence perhaps, evidence of the most intimate crimes. Fingers picked at the cords that bound Isabelle's hands as she tortured herself with images of the worst kind.

'Sit on the couch please, mademoiselle,' the maid said coolly.

Isabelle did as she was bid, lying back when Maria pressed on her shoulders. The surface of the couch was slick against her back and smelt new, as if it had never been used before.

Maria was taking a series of objects from the inside of the cabinet and setting them out on an enamelled metal tray. There were sounds; sounds of metal, sounds of glass, gurglings, murmurs from the maid. In her anxiety, all that Isabelle felt able to move were her eyes, and she cared not to look. Even so, her ears unerringly identified those many small sounds. The metal sounds were the sharpening of a knife. The gurgling came from alcohol being decanted, and the scent was overpowering. The murmurs were sounds of pleasure; the maid was anticipating her actions, enjoying them already.

Isabelle's knuckle whitened on the edges of the couch as she tried to keep herself still, keep herself from fleeing. She was aware of Alain pacing back and forth before the opened iron door, like a guard. Occasionally he would glance into the room – or cell – and briefly examine her naked, offered body.

For a moment the maid came to stand before her, looking down at her sex. In Maria's hand was a glass dish and in the dish a white paste that she worked vigorously with a fine, steel spatula. She then returned to the cabinet and there were new sounds and smells.

'Why don't you tie me?' groaned Isabelle.

The maid appeared at her shoulder, still working on the paste, although it was thicker now and tinged with brown.

'There is no need, mademoiselle. The procedure is nothing. No worse than having your ears pierced.'

'Pierced?' asked Isabelle.

Maria seemed to realise that she had said more than she should and turned away from the naked girl. That is the way that Alain found them a few minutes later when he entered the room. His bulk made the space seem impossibly crowded and claustrophobic.

'Is it ready?' he asked, glancing at the paste.

The maid nodded.

'Has she been cleaned?'

'Not yet, monsieur.'

Alain took up one of the dishes. 'Alcohol,' he said, confirming what Isabelle had already guessed. He took a ball of fresh lint from the metal tray and soaked it in the clear liquid. 'It will sting.'

He pushed open her thighs and ran the lint around the whole area of her sex. When the liquid touched the pinkness of her nether lips it did indeed sting, and she tensed as if she had been slapped.

'It is said to dispel bad humours that might be carried in the air,' he told her. 'We want no infection.'

His insistent application of the alcohol brought a stream of tears from Isabelle's eyes. When he was satisfied that the area was clean he stepped back and allowed Marie to apply the paste.

'An extract of the leaves of the cocoa tree,' he told her.

There was more alcohol in the paste, Isabelle could feel it evaporating as the girl smeared it carefully on the lips about her clitoris. Then a cold numbness seeped into her flesh, radiating in a slow wave from the coated area.

Alain stroked her legs thoughtfully as they waited for the anaesthetic to take full effect. Maria busied herself with the task of removing a series of needles from a small leather pouch, laying them out on the table of Isabelle's belly. That belly was tense and still as Isabelle regarded the shining steel implements with a frozen horror.

Alain examined several of the needles for size and sharpness, laying them experimentally against the lips that were to be pierced. Finally he chose one of the larger ones and handed it to Maria. She dropped it into a bowl of alcohol and methodically removed the others from

243

Isabelle's belly. Alain made Isabelle edge down the couch until her behind was poised on the very edge and her feet were pressed to the sides of her hips.

Then, when all was ready, Maria came to stand between Isabelle's widespread thighs. At a nod from Alain, she pulled at the lips of Isabelle's sex, as she had done in the bedroom, but this time she concentrated on the area around the clitoris, stretching out the membranes as far as they would go. Isabelle, unable to help herself, began to wriggle.

'If you don't keep absolutely still this will injure you,' Maria told her.

Isabelle looked down to see the needle approaching her sex and an apologetic but determined look on Maria's face. Isabelle froze in horror as Maria lay the needle horizontally on her belly directly in line with that part of her lips that overlay her clitoris. She could hardly believe her eyes as Maria drove the spine through her flesh in a single clean motion. There was no pain, only a numb tearing sensation, but still Isabelle screamed. She screamed for her body which was longer as God had made it.

Alain smiled. 'Such drama,' he murmured, 'and over such a tiny thing. Later you will have cause to scream.'

Isabelle gazed at him in a state close to shock. He stroked her face gently as Maria tidied away the various instruments and jars.

'Leave the needle in place for now,' Alain said, turning to the maid. 'And bring her outside when you are ready.'

When Isabelle was calmer, and this took some time, Maria took her once more into the openness of the Mexican room.

'On the altar I think, Isabelle,' said Alain.

She hadn't thought of it as an altar before and hesitated before approaching. Alain took her arm and guided her forward. She felt his large hands on her waist and suddenly she was lifted as if she were a child and carried through the air. He deposited her lightly on the table and stepped back. Her sex was level with his eyes now. He would see clearly that she was wet and he would know that what he had done to her had excited as much as it had terrified. He told her to open her legs wide and she edged her feet sideways. When the nether lips split apart, a tremor of excitement passed through her body. She opened herself until the tendons of her thighs were visible as hard rods running from knee to sex. The cheeks of her behind tightened and also parted. Her second opening was revealed and the circling vortex of indigo drew the eye.

Alain told Maria to open the red bag and lay out its contents. A number of the items that Maria arranged neatly on the uneven stone surface between Isabelle's feet were familiar to her; there were silk ties, cuffs, a number of leather straps, a small whip and some of the smooth, black rods that she had seen in the chest in Robert's bedroom. As familiar as they were, she could not look at these items without a tightening of her throat and a butterfly tingling in her belly. Besides these things there were a number of glass jars, some containing liquids, others creams. In a small wooden box, the lid lying beside it, gleamed a collection of gold rings.

Isabelle felt a hand on her ankle at that moment and looked down. Alain was stroking her foot as he gazed at the various objects, perhaps deciding which he would use.

'Secure her legs, Maria,' he said.

The woman took two of the leather cuffs and buckled them around Isabelle's ankles. The cuffs had metal eyes and Maria slipped silk ties through each, knotting them. The ties were rather short and Isabelle was obliged to open her legs still further so that she could be secured.

Alain picked up one of the jars and removed its glass stopper. From it came an unfamiliar, chemical smell. He passed the jar to Maria.

'Rub it into her breasts and between her legs,' he said.

The smell grew stronger as Maria dipped her fingers into the jar. She started at Isabelle's breasts, rubbing in the cream with circular motions of her hand. At first there was a sensation of heat and then cold as the cream began to work. Her nipples became very erect as Alain watched. It felt as if someone were blowing on them and pulling on them at the same time. It was very arousing. A tingling spread from these sensitive places to her surrounding skin, to her neck and to her stomach. There was an irritation too, and a desire to scratch herself.

Maria's hands went to Isabelle's sex. She worked across the whole area of the smooth hairless mound and inside too, across and under the thin membranes, carefully avoiding the needle. Here the effect was much stronger: a simultaneous burning and cooling; a feeling that a thousand tiny tongues were licking her, rough and rasping; a sensation of air rushing over the membranes. Her belly flooded with excitement and she took a series of deep breaths.

Alain came to stand before her. 'Bend right over,' he said.

She bent from the waist, her head hanging vertically so that her hair lay on the stone between her legs. In this position her behind was the highest point of her body and the parted cheeks could be seen, even from the front, where Alain now stood. He ran a hand up the outside of one thigh to the hips that flared from the narrowness of her waist like an exotic, darkly patterned flower. Her bound hands rested in the small of her back, the fingers clasping and unclasping as the cream worked its magic.

Alain picked up one of the black rods. It was of a kind that was narrower in the middle than at the ends. He dipped it into the cream and passed it to Maria telling her to push it into Isabelle's behind. When the maid had it pressed to the whorl of tightly closed muscle above Isabelle's sex, Alain lifted Isabelle's chin until she looked directly at him. Against the gold of the mask, the darkness of her eyes was especially fine.

'Open yourself,' he told her.

Her eyes slid away.

'Open,' he repeated, 'and look at me.'

He clearly wanted to see her reaction as the rod penetrated her and the cream affected those sensitive tissues. It was not easy for Isabelle to comply. She remained stubbornly tight despite her best efforts to relax.

'I can't,' she groaned.

'Play with her sex, Maria.'

The woman's thumb pushed into the wide, wet opening and her fingers rubbed along the inside of Isabelle's nether lips. Alain watched as the girl's eyes sparked with arousal. Maria worked around the little opening to her urethra, not touching it directly, not over-stimulating it, but drawing feelings from deep in Isabelle's belly to that place and teasing her with them. All the time that she did this the rod was pressed to her anus, nudging and demanding entry, demanding that Isabelle should want it. Finally Isabelle gave a deep groan of pleasure and opened. The rod slipped in as if finding its true home. Maria pumped back and forth until the passage was easy and the rod slipped in silkily, as it should in a girl's behind. Alain watched all of this in Isabelle's eyes, seeing every part of the drama unfold. Then, satisfied, he told her to stand. The rod was visible between her legs, protruding obscenely. It was held in place by muscles feeble with desire but it was still secure because of the tapered middle. It burnt her, cooled her and stirred her as Robert's sex had in the library.

Alain stepped back and admired this thing that he had created, part woman, part dream, then turned to Anna. 'I must ask for the pleasure of your mouth,' he said.

Anna, composed now, smiled. 'It is yours,' she murmured.

Alain seated himself in one of the cane chairs and Anna rose from hers to kneel in the hot sand before him. He parted his legs and she edged forward so as to undo his trousers. His sex was already hard when it emerged and Isabelle could not help but stare. It was unusually thick, at least as thick as her wrist although no longer than normal. Anna's lips were fully stretched as she took it into her mouth, and her cheeks distended as if she was trying to swallow an apple whole.

'Use the needle,' Alain told Maria, 'You know what to do.'

Isabelle gasped in surprise. 'No,' she said, though the word was muffled by the mask.

The needle had missed her clitoris by the tiniest fraction, as Maria knew that it would, and when she had released the pulled-out lips they shrank back, pressing the shaft of the needle tight against that nexus of sensitive nerves. Now that the anaesthetic effect of the paste was wearing off, the needle hurt but also stirred. Maria took the end and slowly turned the instrument that impaled Isabelle so intimately. The friction on the bud was so subtle, so tantalising, so surprising in the pleasure that it gave, that Isabelle pushed out her belly to feel more. It was by this means that Isabelle was brought to the edge of climax. Alain watched Isabelle intently as Anna used her lips and fingers on his sex. From time to time he would give instructions. He would have Maria apply more cream to the girl, to her breasts so that the heat was increased, to the inside of her thighs, to the join between sex and anus. He would have Maria twist or pump the rod in Isabelle's behind until she was gasping. When she was too close to a climax he had Maria pull the needle outwards so there was no pressure on her bud, only a burning where it pierced her. In this way he prolonged and heightened the process until Isabelle begged for release, begged to be allowed to climax. When she was frantic with need he told Maria to step back and they watched Isabelle as she twisted in her bonds. Sweat poured from her body and her groans were delicious in their despair.

'You have my permission to climax,' he told her. 'You have only to move, to dance for us, if you want that pleasure.'

Isabelle found that when she did move she could stimulate herself. As the muscles of her thighs contracted and relaxed so they forced the needle back and forth across her bud. If she twisted in a slow, primitive sort of dance the stimulation was strong. She watched Alain as she did this and saw his arousal. She danced for him like a slave girl for a sultan. She raised and lowered her pelvis, opening her legs, stretching out her sex, and all the time the needle moved against her. Wetness ran from her sex on to her thighs. The rod in her behind slipped in and out, riding on the taper, falling slowly as she opened the ring of muscle, rising as she tightened and squeezed it back in. There was great pleasure in seeing Alain's eyes narrowing as they swept across her, a sense of her power, a satisfaction that she could move him to feelings other than anger, could make him gasp as she ground her pelvis faster and began to groan in the depths of her need. He delayed his own climax several times, pushing Anna's lips away, so that he could continue to watch Isabelle. Anna's eyes, as they feasted on the vision of gold and indigo, were black with desire, and Isabelle performed for her too. Alain toyed with the spines that pierced Anna's breasts, firing Isabelle's crueller impulses. When he pushed the kneeling girl's head to his sex for the final time he began to pluck the spines from Anna's breasts, slowly. Each time that he did, she moaned.

Isabelle's climax was strong, as strong as anything she had ever felt with Robert. As she writhed in a final paroxysm, so Alain climaxed and Anna drank his seed.

Afterwards, all was still, except for the breathing of Alain and Isabelle which synchronised as they regarded each other. She saw nothing monstrous in his features now, not as she once had.

'Untie her, Maria,' he said, as soon as he was able to speak.

The maid complied, picking at the ties around Isabelle's feet until they fell away, then bade her turn around so that she could free her hands. Since he said nothing about the rod in her behind or the needle at her sex neither woman touched them.

'Lie down,' he said to Isabelle. 'Rest for a moment.'

Carefully, so as not to injure herself she settled to her knees on the stone surface and lowered her body with a sigh. She was exhausted in such a heat and sprawled on her back, yawning, stretching out her legs which were heavy with the exercise.

'Go to her Anna, hold her, treat her as a sister.'

Isabelle smiled to hear this, remembering her confessions in the study. Alain knew all of her desires.

Maria cleared the table, packing the various items into the red bag. Anna looked on as the maid fussed, smiling to see her friend. As the girl climbed on to the table, Isabelle took her hand and squeezed it. Anna responded with a light kiss to her shoulder.

'Her mask?' she asked, looking over her shoulder at Alain.

'Remove it if you wish.'

This was not so easy since Anna didn't know how it was fastened. She pulled Isabelle's hair by mistake two or three times and they giggled, Anna to see Isabelle jump and Isabelle to hear the girl's overly profuse apologies. When the mask was free, Anna handed it to Maria and then lay her head on Isabelle's breasts. They cradled each other and rocked back and forth in a barely perceptible motion like lovers reunited after a long absence.

'Fetch water and a sponge please, Maria.'

When the maid returned with a large copper bowl, Isabelle was lying on her back with her eyes closed and Anna was stroking her gently. Her hand ran slowly from Isabelle's neck downwards across her breasts and belly, seeking out all the sensitive places but not to arouse, only to soothe and bestow affection. When the hand returned to her neck, Isabelle took it and pressed her lips to it. Anna allowed this and then slipped her fingers into Isabelle's mouth so that she could suck. Maria watched this for a moment, envious perhaps, and then went over to Alain. She sponged his face and washed his sex.

As Maria finished, so Alain rose and went to stand over the two girls. Anna was lying on her side with her back to him as he approached. Her behind was very full when seen in this position. He took her ankle and pushed the leg upwards so that the taut, shining cheeks opened and her sexual parts could be seen. He was hard again and he pushed into her sex. She groaned and looked over her shoulder but his eyes were not on her, they had themselves fixed on Isabelle. Anna reached her hand down her back, arching to grasp his sex and make a tight ring about the shaft with her fingers. He groaned and looked at the girl.

Perhaps it was this tightness that made him think of her anus, as he withdrew, and pushed at her narrower opening. She held her cheeks apart with the hand that had grasped him so that it was easier for his entry. Even so, his thickness made her gasp and he had to halt when he was no more than half embedded. Isabelle, realising the difficulty, used her hand to lift the girl's leg high. Perhaps the sense of being opened in this way helped Anna to open her behind. Certainly Alain was finally able to push in until his belly rested on her cheeks. Isabelle sucked at Anna's breasts, nipping the brown tips with a sharp, quick motion that made Anna groan. Soon, Alain was able to move freely and settled into a steady motion. Anna closed her eyes and withdrew into herself. Every muscle in her body went slack. Only her throat seemed to work and she emitted a great, low moan. Isabelle let the girl's leg down and lay on her back. She was very aroused and began touching herself as Alain watched. She pinched up her nipples and ran her hand across her belly.

'Let me see you,' he said.

Isabelle opened her legs wide and pulled them up to her chest. Nothing was hidden then. As he looked at the rod in her behind, she clenched with the sudden thought that he might take her there and he saw it jerk. She saw how that aroused him and she began to clench and unclench, exciting herself in that way. He moved back and forth more quickly and Anna's moans became groans. Her neck contracted and her head arched back. Alain took hold of her hair using it to pull her on to his sex. Isabelle touched the rod in her behind and looked into his eyes. It was an invitation. She used the other hand at her sex, taking the needle in two fingers, one either side of the lips and pulling upwards. She pulled until it hurt and then pulled further until her bud was exposed. She didn't touch it, but the pulling made her feelings very strong and her mouth opened wide.

'Climax,' he told her in a choked voice, 'I want to see you break open with the pleasure.'

She used the needle to caress herself. She took the rod

251

in her hand and began to twist it. Alain was pounding into Anna ruthlessly now. Isabelle's legs opened unnaturally wide and her knees came to rest on the table beside her breasts. She quivered from head to toe. Great juddering waves of excitement coursed through her. Her eyes didn't leave his until the climax took her by storm and she burnt and broke and wept and screamed. His own climax began as he watched her and he tore into Anna's behind in a frenzy.

Before Isabelle was allowed to rise from the table, Alain told Maria to remove the needle. Isabelle winced as it slipped from her. Alain went through the little wooden box that she'd seen earlier and chose one of the gold rings for her. It was small, too small even to fit over Isabelle's little finger, but when Maria slipped it through the punctured labia it felt like one of the heavy iron rings she had been tied to. The maid closed the ring with her fingers and it lay gleaming at Isabelle's sex like a golden pearl in an oyster.

'It is only temporary. We will find you something else when the wounds are healed.'

Isabelle examined it proudly, laying her fingers on the skin of her stomach and pulling so that it moved. It felt as if she were being held at that sensitive place, as if two fingers were lightly pinching her.

'It will help you to remember what you are,' Alain said, 'and it will be useful for tying you.'

He held out his hand and she took it. As she rose from the table the ring pushed against her bud and there was a stab of pleasure. He saw her eyes widen and knew it.

'Go to Robert,' he told her, 'he will want you when you are like this.'

Robert did indeed want Isabelle when he saw what Alain and Maria had made of her. He took her into the gardens, having her walk in front of him so that he could admire her transformation. The headdress of feathers made her seem taller and emphasised the length and slenderness of her legs and waist. Against the greenness of the foliage she seemed even more like a beast of the imagination, dangerous and seductive. The gold circlet at her sex

252

fascinated him and he had her stop a number of times so that he could toy with it and excite her that way. He took her to the lake and made love to her there, on the green banks and among the plants that grew at the water's edge. She crouched like a leopard in the shallow water among the reeds while he sodomised her. The salve in her bowels took his breath away as he entered her, making him use her roughly.

Afterwards, as they lay on the green velvet of the gently sloping bank, he told her that they would be leaving for London the next day; news of a ship had arrived that very afternoon. His words were casual, delivered as she lay on her belly and his hand delved, once more, into the space between her legs. When he was ready, he took her again, but for once, her mind wasn't with him. All that she could think of, was that her farewells hadn't been said, and that her clothes hadn't been packed.

25

Leaving Severcy

The exhausted, sore, stiff, but excited Isabelle spent the remainder of her time at Severcy in bed, in the room by the baths. The villa was a chaos of hurrying servants, desperately preparing for the sudden departure. As she recovered, Isabelle listened to impatient cries and oaths, to Alain issuing his instructions, to Robert reprimanding, encouraging and organising. It was a pleasure to be excused this and a pleasure to receive the visits from Robert and Alain. When they asked her, and they asked her often, she would pull back the sheets of the bed to reveal the circlet of gold between her legs.

Her mother visited her on the morning of the departure to say goodbye. When Isabelle pleaded a slight indisposition due to a fall from her horse, her mother was sympathetic, but it was doubtful that she was deceived. She would have known that she was being lied to, but also that the lie was for her sake. They talked about London and about seeing Anne-Marie again. Madame Belloque had brought some of Isabelle's clothes, and left these for her as they made their tearful farewells.

As it happened, those clothes were not allowed to Isabelle. Alain decided that she should take nothing of her old life to London. When all was ready, when four carriages were packed and provisioned and standing in the driveway, Isabelle, too stiff to walk, was carried naked to the leading one by Benjamin. He kissed her tenderly as he placed her inside, saying that he would never forget her, that she was his first love. She heard Robert telling Anna to hurry or they would leave without her, then Alain swung into the carriage and shouted to the driver. The horses strained and the cavalcade pulled away. There was a sadness in Isabelle's eyes as she craned her head to catch a last glimpse of the villa.

'You love Severcy as much as I do, don't you?' said Alain.

She nodded.

NEW BOOKS

Coming up from Nexus and Black Lace

Nexus

The Mistress of Sternwood Grange by Arabella Knight
April 1998   Price £4.99   ISBN: 0 352 33241 7

Amanda Silk suspects that she is being cheated out of her late aunt's legacy. Determined to discover the true value of Sternwood Grange, she enters its private world disguised as a maid. The stern regime is oppressively strict and Amanda comes to appreciate the sharp pleasures and sweet torments of punishment. Menial tasks are soon replaced by more delicious duties – drawing Amanda deep into the dark delights of dominance and discipline.

Annie and the Countess by Evelyn Culber
April 1998   Price £4.99   ISBN: 0 352 33242 5

Annie enjoys her dominant role at the Academy, nurturing nascent submissives among her charges and punishing genuine miscreants, until she meets the Countess, who teaches her how to submit herself. The Countess proves to have unparalleled skills in the subtle arts of sensual pain and takes Annie on as an acolyte. Will Annie succeed in her ambition to become this beautiful voluptuary's favourite companion?

There are three Nexus titles published in May

The Correction of an Essex Maid by Yolanda Celbridge
May 1998   Price £4.99   ISBN: 0 352 33255 7

Rescued from degradation, naive young orphan Sophia joins the House of Rodings, a training school dedicated to the worship and correction of the naked female rear. She meets a cast of submissive and dominant females, all adoring or envious of Sophia's voluptuous bottom. Becoming mistress of the school's flagellant society, she thrives in the complex ranks, rules, and punishments of the House's hierarchy. By the author of the popular *Governess* and *Maldona* series, also available from Nexus.

NEXUS NEW BOOKS

To be published in June

DRAWN TO DISCIPLINE
Tara Black
£5.99

Student Judith Wilson lands a job at the Nemesis Archive, an institution dedicated to the documentation of errant female desire, under the imperious Samantha James. Unable to accept correction at the hands of the Director, she is forced to resign. But one manuscript in particular has awoken her guilty fascination with corporal punishment, and leads her to its author and her obscure Rigorist Order in Brittany. The discipline practised there brings Judith's assertive sexuality into a class of its own, and she returns to the Archive to bring her wayward former co-workers to heel.

ISBN 0 352 33626 9

SLAVE REVELATIONS
Jennifer Jane Pope
£5.99

The third book in Jennifer Jane Pope's *Slave* series continues the story of the bizarre pony-carting institution hidden from prying eyes on a remote Scottish island. Those who seek to investigate befall some curious fates: Tommy is now Tammy and Alex is – well, still not at all happy with pony girl slavery. And who or what has given the pony-girls their genetically re-engineered pain thresholds?

ISBN 0 352 33627 7

PLEASURE ISLAND
Aran Ashe
£5.99

The beautiful Anya, betrothed to the prince of Lidir, has set sail for his kingdom. On the way, her ship is beset by pirates. Captured and put into chains, Anya is subjected to a harsh shipboard regime of punishment and cruel pleasures at the hands of the captain and his crew. When landfall is made on a mysterious island populated by dark-eyed amazons, Anya plots her escape, unaware of the fate that awaits anyone who dares to venture ashore. A Nexus Classic.

ISBN 0 352 33628 5

To be published in July

PENNY PIECES
Penny Birch
£5.99

Penny Pieces is a collection of Penny Birch's tales of corporal punishment, public humiliation and perverted pleasures from nettling to knicker-wetting. But this time Penny lets her characters do the talking. Here she brings you *their* stories: there's Naomi, for instance, the all-girl wrestler; or Paulette, the pretty make-up artist who's angling for a spanking. Not least, of course, there's Penny herself. Whether finding novel uses for a climbing harness, stuck in a pillory, or sploshing around in mud, Penny's still the cheekiest minx of them all.

ISBN 0 352 33631 5

SEX TOY
Aishling Morgan
£5.99

Set in an alternate world of gothic eroticism, *Sex Toy* follows the fortunes of the city state of Suza, led by the flagellant but fair Lord Comus and his Ladyship, the beautiful Tian-Sha. When a slaver, Savarin, appears in their midst, Comus and his ursine retainer, Arsag, force him to flee, leaving behind the collection of bizarre beasts he had captured. Their integration into Suzan life creates new and exciting possibilities for such a pleasure-loving society. But Suza has not heard the last of the slaver, and its inhabitants soon find that Savarin's kiss is more punishing than they had thought.

ISBN 0 352 33634 X

LETTERS TO CHLOE
Stefan Gerrard
£5.99

The letters were found in a locked briefcase in a London mansion. Shocking and explicit, they are all addressed to the same mysterious woman: Chloe. It is clear that the relationship between the writer and Chloe is no ordinary one. The letters describe a liaison governed by power; a liaison which transforms an innocent young woman into a powerful sexual enigma. Each letter pushes Chloe a little nearer to the limits of sexual role-play, testing her obedience, her willingness to explore ever more extreme taboos until, as events reach their climax, the question must be asked: who is really in control? A Nexus Classic.

ISBN 0 352 33632

If you would like more information about Nexus titles, please visit our website at www.nexus-books.co.uk, or send a stamped addressed envelope to:

Nexus, Thames Wharf Studios,
Rainville Road, London W6 9HA

BLACK LACE NEW BOOKS

To be published in June

STRICTLY CONFIDENTIAL
Alison Tyler
£5.99

Carolyn Winters is a smooth-talking disc jockey at a hip LA radio station. Although known for her sexy banter over the airwaves, she leads a reclusive life. Carolyn grows dependent on living vicariously through her flirtatious roommate Dahlia, eavesdropping and then covertly watching as her roommate's sexual behaviour becomes more and more bizarre. But Carolyn's life is thrown into chaos when Dahlia is murdered, and she must overcome her fears – and possibly admit to her own voyeuristic pleasures – in order to bring the killer to justice.

ISBN 0 352 33624 2

SUMMER FEVER
Alison Ricci
£5.99

Lara McIntyre has lusted after artist Jake Fitzgerald for almost two decades. As a warm, dazzling summer unfolds, she makes a journey back to the student house where they first met, determined to satisfy her physical craving somehow. And then, ensconced in the old beach house once more, she discovers her true sexual self. Playing with costume, cosmetics, blatant exhibitionism and the inspiration of a younger lover, the hot frenzied season builds to a peak – but not without complications.

ISBN 0 352 33625 0

CONTINUUM
Portia Da Costa
£5.99

When Joanna Darrell agrees to take a break from an office job that has begun to bore her, she takes her first step into a new continuum of strange experiences. She is introduced to people whose way of life revolves around the giving and receiving of enjoyable punishment, and she becomes intrigued enough to experiment. Drawn in by a chain of coincidences, like Alice in a decadent wonderland, she enters a parallel world of perversity and unusual pleasure. A Black Lace Special Reprint.

ISBN 0 352 33620 8

To be published in July

SYMPHONY X
Jasmine Stone
£5.99

Katie is a viola player running away from her cheating husband and humdrum life. The tour of Symphony Xevertes not only takes her to Europe but also to the realm of deep sexual satisfaction. She is joined by a dominatrix diva and a bass singer whose voice is so low he's known as the Human Vibrator. After distractions like these, how will Katie be able to maintain her wild life and allow herself to fall in love again?

ISBN 0 352 33629 3

OPENING ACTS
Suki Cunningham
£5.99

When London actress Holly Parker arrives in a remote Cornish village to begin rehearsing a new play, everyone there – from her landlord to her theatre director – seems to have an earthier attitude towards sex. Brought to a state of constant sexual arousal and confusion, Holly seeks guidance in the form of local therapist, Joshua Delaney. He is the one man who can't touch her – but he is the only one she truly desires. Will she be able to use her new-found sense of sexual adventure to seduce him?

ISBN 0 352 33630 7

THE SEVEN-YEAR LIST
Zoe le Verdier
£5.99

Julia is an ambitious young photographer. In two week's time she is due to marry her trustworthy but dull fiancé. Then an invitation to a college reunion arrives. Julia remembers that seven years ago herself and her classmates made a list of their goals and ambitions. Old rivalries, jealousies and flirtations are picked up where they were left off and sexual tensions run high. Soon Julia finds herself caught between two men but neither of them are her fiancé. How will she explain herself to her friends? And what decisions will she make? A Black Lace Special Reprint.

ISBN 0 352 33254 9

NEXUS BACKLIST

This information is correct at time of printing. For up-to-date information, please visit our website at www.nexus-books.co.uk

All books are priced at £5.99 unless another price is given.

Nexus books with a contemporary setting

ACCIDENTS WILL HAPPEN	Lucy Golden ISBN 0 352 33596 3	☐
ANGEL	Lindsay Gordon ISBN 0 352 33590 4	☐
THE BLACK MASQUE	Lisette Ashton ISBN 0 352 33372 3	☐
THE BLACK WIDOW	Lisette Ashton ISBN 0 352 33338 3	☐
THE BOND	Lindsay Gordon ISBN 0 352 33480 0	☐
BROUGHT TO HEEL	Arabella Knight ISBN 0 352 33508 4	☐
DANCE OF SUBMISSION	Lisette Ashton ISBN 0 352 33450 9	☐
DARK DELIGHTS	Maria del Rey ISBN 0 352 33276 X	☐
DARK DESIRES	Maria del Rey ISBN 0 352 33072 4	☐
DISCIPLES OF SHAME	Stephanie Calvin ISBN 0 352 33343 X	☐
DISCIPLINE OF THE PRIVATE HOUSE	Esme Ombreux ISBN 0 352 33459 2	☐
DISCIPLINED SKIN	Wendy Swanscombe ISBN 0 352 33541 6	☐
DISPLAYS OF EXPERIENCE	Lucy Golden ISBN 0 352 33505 X	☐

Nexus books with Ancient and Fantasy settings

THE WARRIOR QUEEN	Kendal Grahame ISBN 0 352 33294 8	☐

Edwardian, Victorian and older erotica

BEATRICE	Anonymous ISBN 0 352 31326 9	☐
CONFESSION OF AN ENGLISH SLAVE	Yolanda Celbridge ISBN 0 352 33433 9	☐
DEVON CREAM	Aishling Morgan ISBN 0 352 33488 6	☐
THE GOVERNESS AT ST AGATHA'S	Yolanda Celbridge ISBN 0 352 32986 6	☐
PURITY	Aishling Morgan ISBN 0 352 33510 6	☐
THE TRAINING OF AN ENGLISH GENTLEMAN	Yolanda Celbridge ISBN 0 352 33348 0	☐

Samplers and collections

NEW EROTICA 4	Various ISBN 0 352 33290 5	☐
NEW EROTICA 5	Various ISBN 0 352 33540 8	☐
EROTICON 1	Various ISBN 0 352 33593 9	☐
EROTICON 2	Various ISBN 0 352 33594 7	☐
EROTICON 3	Various ISBN 0 352 33597 1	☐

Nexus Classics
A new imprint dedicated to putting the finest works of erotic fiction back in print.

AGONY AUNT	G.C. Scott ISBN 0 352 33353 7	☐
BOUND TO SERVE	Amanda Ware ISBN 0 352 33457 6	☐
BOUND TO SUBMIT	Amanda Ware ISBN 0 352 33451 7	☐
CANDY IN CAPTIVITY	Arabella Knight ISBN 0 352 33495 9	☐

- - - - - - ✂ -

Please send me the books I have ticked above.

Name ....

Address ....

....

....

.... Post code ....

Send to: Cash Sales, Nexus Books, Thames Wharf Studios, Rainville Road, London W6 9HA

US customers: for prices and details of how to order books for delivery by mail, call 1-800-805-1083.

Please enclose a cheque or postal order, made payable to **Nexus Books Ltd**, to the value of the books you have ordered plus postage and packing costs as follows:

UK and BFPO – £1.00 for the first book, 50p for each subsequent book.

Overseas (including Republic of Ireland) – £2.00 for the first book, £1.00 for each subsequent book.

If you would prefer to pay by VISA, ACCESS/MASTER-CARD, AMEX, DINERS CLUB, AMEX or SWITCH, please write your card number and expiry date here:

....

Please allow up to 28 days for delivery.

Signature ....

- - - - - - ✂ -